Still Broken

Still Broken

Understanding the U.S. Health Care System

STEPHEN M. DAVIDSON

Stanford Business Books
An Imprint of Stanford University Press
Stanford, California

Stanford University Press
Stanford, California

Special discounts for bulk quantities of Stanford Business Books
are available to corporations, professional associations, and other
organizations. For details and discount information, contact the special
sales department of Stanford University Press. Tel: (650) 736-1782,
Fax: (650) 736-1784

Printed in the United States of America
on acid-free, archival-quality paper

Library of Congress Cataloging-in-Publication Data
Davidson, Stephen M.
  Still broken : understanding the U.S. health care system / Stephen M.
Davidson.
    p. cm.
  Includes bibliographical references and index.
  ISBN 978-0-8047-6196-3 (cloth : alk. paper)
  1. Health care reform—United States. 2. Medical policy—United
States. I. Title. [DNLM: 1. Health Care Reform—United States.
2. Health Expenditures—United States. 3. Health Services
Accessibility—economics—United States. 4. Health Services Needs
and Demand—economics—United States. 5. Quality Assurance,
Health Care—economics—United States. WA 540 AA1 D253s 2010]
  RA395.A3D385 2010
   362.1'0425—dc22

                                                    2009049992

Typeset by Classic Typography in 10.5/12 Bembo

To the memory of Nachman Davidson and Odin W. Anderson,
the two men who introduced me to the mysteries of the health care system

    and

For Noah, Aaron, Tess, Hannah, and Eli, in the hope that
the health care system of the future will serve them well

Some look at things that are and ask, Why?
I dream of things that never were, and ask why not?
—George Bernard Shaw,
quoted by Robert F. Kennedy

I still have faith in the American people to do the
right thing.
—Theodore Sorensen
Counselor: A Life at the Edge of History

Contents

List of Tables and Figures

Tables

Figure

Preface

FOR YEARS, OBSERVERS have described the U.S. health care system as broken. Yet, as I write, it appears that—against the odds—the Congress may actually pass reform legislation. With a century of failed attempts behind us, that would be a remarkable accomplishment for President Barack Obama and his congressional allies.

This book is for people who want to understand why the health care system is so important for us, how it really works, what caused the problems that have persisted for decades (and will continue under a new law), how we can solve them, and why we have failed to surmount these problems in the past. It will describe six elements that are critical to a successful reform plan and how various compromises with those elements can affect what a new law will produce. It will also help the reader understand what to expect from the government's new policy and what will need to wait for another time.

The bill that is most likely to pass will make progress toward achieving some reform goals. It will require that almost everyone have insurance, create an insurance market for those without employer-based coverage, establish minimum standards for coverage, and subsidize those who cannot afford available policies. Yet it will leave much undone. For example,

- Millions of Americans still will not have coverage, even though every other developed country covers all its citizens for less than we spend. Despite the new law's subsidies, insurance will still cost too much for many people to afford, most of whom will not qualify for Medicaid.

- Even with insurance, many will have to pay so much out of pocket that they will delay care until they are so sick that the services they need then will keep them in debt for years. At least one bill in the Congress will require insurers to pay only 65 percent of the cost, leaving a whopping 35 percent for the patient and creating a new generation of *under*insured Americans.

- Covering more people will increase total spending unless the incentives for providers that have propelled excess utilization, and therefore unnecessary spending, also change. Because the likely new law keeps the same provider incentives in place, we can expect to continue to spend more on health care than other countries—by a wide margin.

- Similarly, the new law will do little to stimulate changes in the delivery of services to increase the quality and safety of care, or to reverse the deterioration of the delivery system caused by decades of failure to solve truly key problems.

In sum, millions of Americans will still have access problems and, as a nation, we will still pay too much and get too little from a system that will continue to get worse—because it will not have incentives for people to make it better.

While this book is not intended as a critique of the new legislation, it will help readers understand the new law and draw their own conclusions. This book will also assist policymakers. For them, the final four chapters of the book will be particularly important. On the basis of the data and analysis that come before it, Chapter 8 details six elements that any plan must include to truly solve the system's problems. Chapter 9 reminds us how we reached this legislative point in time by offering a brief history of reform, starting with Theodore Roosevelt's Progressive Party platform of 1912. Chapter 10 sets out components of a political strategy to enact the six reform elements from Chapter 8 and identifies obstacles that stymied previous administrations and will need to be overcome by any administration—present or future—that wants to pass reforms. Finally, since any substantial proposal requires compromises to become law, Chapter 11 assesses the probable effects that various possible compromises would have on those six elements. Policymakers will need to pay particular attention to these concessions when efforts to perfect the new policies begin.

The writing of this book began in late 2007, and continued into 2009, during the most active and promising reform episode since passage of Medicare in 1965. Having labored hard for so many months to enact these changes, however, it is likely that neither the Congress nor the president will want to return to these issues soon. Even if this is all we will get for now, this book will help the reader to assess how far we have come and how much remains to be done. And the next time these matters come to the fore—whether in the coming months or years—this book will help policy analysts and public officials to take us even closer to our ultimate objective: a health care system worthy of the world's oldest, most prosperous democracy.

Stephen M. Davidson
Boston
November 2009

Acknowledgments

EVEN THOUGH MUCH of the research I have done on the health care system over the years has had implications for public policy, I have generally resisted the temptation to take a position on controversial policy questions. The reason is that I wanted my research to be taken on its own merits. Did I address an important question? Were the data relevant and the samples representative? Was the analysis appropriate? Were the conclusions supported by the study design and the data? I was afraid that if I took a stand on a difficult policy question, those who had different views would tend to dismiss the research. In fact, I had seen that happen with friends in other fields who became identified with a particular policy position and whose research came to be viewed, rightly or wrongly, as an extension of their views on those issues.

This book represents a departure from that stance. To write it, I broke my informal rule for two main reasons: first, the challenges to the health care system have reached what I believe to be a critical point, and the need for substantial reform is urgent. When I started in the field, I recall my professor, Odin Anderson, remarking that the medical care field was one of the most stable sectors in the American economy. Although major scientific and clinical breakthroughs had occurred over the years and been incorporated into standard care, the way medicine was organized and practiced had not changed much in many decades. The past forty years stand in dramatic contrast to that picture of relatively gentle evolution. Following the passage of Medicare and Medicaid in the mid-1960s, we have tried—and often rejected—a dizzying array of new ways of organizing and paying for care. We tried to expand the concept of managed care (an old idea that previously had affected only a few), we tried to stimulate price competition among insurers and providers, and we changed the incentives hospitals face by paying them on the basis of their patients' characteristics (using Diagnosis Related Groups, DRGs) instead of on the charges for the individual services they delivered. In the end, none of these experiments produced more accessible, more reliable, or more efficient care or slowed the trajectory that has brought us to our present unsatisfactory state.

Second, after more than thirty-five years in the field, I believe I have something to say that can add to the debate. In making this contribution, I have tried to adhere to the same standards I set for myself in earlier work intended primarily for other scholars. And given the nature of the situation, which I believe is likely to get worse unless we take it on, it is hard to justify holding back.

Having taken the plunge, I learned once again the great extent to which scholarly work can benefit from the contributions of others. In that regard, I was fortunate to have several research assistants at Boston University who helped with various aspects of the undertaking. They include Hayley Cotter, Caroline Hotchkiss, Nichole Szembrot, Ed Szkutak, and Jonathan Urbach. In addition, I am grateful for the generosity of several colleagues and friends for reading some or all of the book and giving valuable feedback that helped me to strengthen it. They include Ron Andersen, Gene Bardach, Michael Davidson, Robert Davidson, Allen Maxwell, Tom Rice, Robert Wolf, and two anonymous reviewers engaged by the Press. In addition, I benefited from a wonderful conversation with Jim Morone, as we shared a taxi from Chicago's Hyde Park to O'Hare Airport and then a meal while we waited for our delayed planes to arrive so they could take us to our respective destinations. He also graciously shared the copyedited version of the final chapter of the book he and David Blumenthal had recently completed about the role of the presidency in health care reform. And I would be remiss if I failed to acknowledge that I have learned much about so many things over the years from my long-time Boston University colleagues Alan Cohen, Fred Foulkes, Ken Hatten, Janelle Heineke, Jim Post, Joe Restuccia, and Michael Shwartz. Parts of several chapters started as conversations with one or more of them or drew on work we did together, and others benefited from their comments following seminar presentations.

I am grateful, too, for the enthusiasm and support of Margo Beth Crouppen at Stanford University Press, who liked the idea for the book when she first heard it and never wavered in her support for the project. Her encouragement was constant, expressed with good humor, and very much appreciated. David Horne, the copyeditor, helped improve the book's readability.

Finally, once again, I am happy to be able to acknowledge my debt to my wife, Harriet, who contributed in so many ways, large and small, to the completion of this project—as she has to so many others, scholarly and otherwise, for more years than either of us likes to count. Undoubtedly, she is as pleased as I am that the project has ended.

Part One

Problems with the U.S. Health Care System

Chapter 1

The Promise and Disappointment
of U.S. Medical Care

FOLLOWING PUBLICATION of the influential Flexner Report on medical education in 1910,[1] the United States built on a foundation of science a health care system that, by the end of the 20th century, was the envy of the world. A visible symbol of that accomplishment is the astonishing number of health-related Nobel Prizes won by American physicians and other scientists. Since 1950, of the 133 prize winners in medicine and physiology, well over half have been either Americans or scientists who trained or worked in the United States.[2]

Indeed, modern medicine is one of the unnamed wonders of the contemporary world. But it is more than a collection of impressive intellectual achievements. It has made a huge difference in the lives of many ordinary people in the United States and throughout the world. New treatments developed over the past one hundred years cure previously fatal acute illnesses. Even when the impact has not been to improve mortality rates, patients often recover much more quickly and with much less disruption of their daily lives and reduction of household income than in earlier times. Moreover, many chronic conditions that once were tantamount to a death sentence can now be managed effectively so that people who have them can carry on relatively normal lives.

It is no exaggeration to say that new drugs, new medical devices, and new surgical procedures have changed the face of illness to the point that we no longer need to fear many diseases that once evoked only the grimmest of images for the future. Following are some examples.

From the time of the Black Death, which is estimated to have killed one-third of the population of 14th-century Europe, until the advent of antibiotics, there was no good antidote to the effects of deadly microbes. Before the development of antibiotics, infections were major killers. "[U]ntil 1936, pneumonia was the No. 1 cause of death in the United States, and amputation was sometimes the only cure for infected wounds."[3] Penicillin, one of the first antibiotic drugs, discovered in 1928 by Sir Alexander Fleming, kills harmful bacteria that cause illness and infection in humans. In the early 1940s, two researchers discovered how to make it in powdered form and helped mass produce it in time to curtail the risk of infection leading to amputation of damaged limbs or even death on the front lines of World War II.[4] After the war, penicillin and other antibiotics were used widely to fight infection in the civilian population, dramatically reducing the harmful effects of many infectious diseases and contributing to the upward kink in life expectancy in America in the latter half of the 20th century.[5]

With people living longer, partly as a result of "wonder drugs" such as penicillin, illnesses associated with age have become increasingly important, leading to other new treatments. Among the most common—and most frightening—conditions that primarily afflict older Americans are cardiovascular events, including heart attacks (myocardial infarction) and strokes, both of which usually result from hardened or blocked arteries. Blood pressure measures how clear and flexible arteries are and is a direct assessment of their ability to handle the pressures of blood flow. Higher blood pressure indicates that a patient is having trouble maintaining adequate blood flow through arteries that probably are constricted. For that reason, doctors want to measure blood pressure frequently in patients at higher risk (say, above age fifty) and to lower it with medications in order to reduce the risk of heart attack.

Take Janet, a fifty-five-year-old female with high blood pressure unknowingly at risk of a heart attack. She experienced extreme fatigue and indigestion and, later, nausea and vomiting, and she felt faint. Janet went to the emergency room of a nearby hospital, and though she was almost sent home for not displaying a classic sign of a heart attack (chest pain), the attending physician decided to run more tests. An old technology, the electrocardiogram, showed no acute abnormalities, but the ER doctor's suspicions were raised when a serum troponin blood test suggested that Janet had microscopic amounts of heart muscle damage.

Partly because of the potential for false positive results from the blood test, a cardiologist was called in to make a more definitive diagnosis. Following an examination, the cardiologist suggested immediate catheterization. This technique involves inserting a thin plastic tube (catheter) into an artery or vein in an arm or leg and advancing it into the chambers of the heart or into the coronary arteries. In Janet's case, it revealed an important blocked artery that the cardiologist was able to treat by angioplasty, a procedure in which a balloon is used to open a blockage in a coronary artery narrowed by atherosclerosis. He placed a small hole in Janet's femoral artery (near her groin) where, after dye was injected to document the blockage, a thin wire was passed through the blockage. Then, a small balloon was passed over the wire into the blockage and inflated to open the artery. Next, a separate catheter was deployed, leaving behind a spring-loaded stent in the part of the artery that had been expanded by the balloon. The metal struts of the stent significantly reduce the chance that the now-dilated artery will close again.

After her procedure, Janet was placed on aspirin and clopidogrel, an oral antiplatelet agent used in the treatment of coronary artery disease, both of which help to prevent her arteries from becoming blocked again by "sticky" blood platelets. Her physician told her that she had chronically high blood pressure, hypertension, which likely led to her fatigue and feeling faint as well as to the risk of a heart attack. He prescribed a statin drug to lower her cholesterol, another risk factor associated with constricted arteries, and an Angiotensin-Converting-Enzyme (ACE) inhibitor to stabilize the internal environment of her arteries.

Higher-resolution imaging, better drugs, minimally invasive catheterization procedures, and advanced devices are all facets of the modern practice of medicine that benefited Janet. Her condition was caught relatively early and as a result, she recovered fairly quickly from her procedures and resumed her normal life sooner than she would have even a generation ago. It is no exaggeration to say that her life was saved by what not so long ago was the cutting edge of medical research and clinical progress.

Janet's story tells of a modern medical success. For another example, consider the story of Bill, a patient who was held by medical care at the brink of life for months, though ultimately he succumbed to his disease.

Following CT scans and biopsies, Bill was diagnosed with metastatic kidney cancer. After standard drug treatment and chemotherapy, Bill underwent a radical nephrectomy to remove his right kidney and right adrenal gland, along with four lymph nodes infected by cancerous cell growths. The pain after surgery was hard to control, and heavy narcotics were necessary to keep it at bay. For some time, the surgery and medication gave Bill a life that resembled the years before he was diagnosed.

Unfortunately, Bill's cancer resurfaced and was spreading to other organs. Liver surgery was necessary only months after his nephrectomy. The surgery was deemed successful, but Bill's doctors told him that his cancer had metastasized too much, and surgery was no longer a viable option. He was given six months. Bill's family was devastated, though solace was found in the fact that the newest drugs, procedures, and therapies had all been used to help extend Bill's life for almost three years. Although for many cancer patients, full remission is a happy ending to their bouts with cancer, for Bill and his family, it was enough that his life was extended beyond what many could have dreamed possible just a generation ago.

The Importance of Primary Care

The value of modern medicine is not demonstrated only by dramatic tales of surgery and specialty care, which occur many times every day with patients like Bill and Janet. Ordinary primary care also provides enormous, measurable benefits to the people who are able to access it. Barbara Starfield, a distinguished physician-researcher at Johns Hopkins University Medical School, has taught us a lot about primary care. As she defines it, it is the gateway to the wonders of modern medicine. Indeed, in its ideal form, it embodies much of what we want our medical care system to be.

First among primary care's four defining characteristics is *first-contact care*. It is the entry point into the larger system of care, which "implies accessibility to and use of services for each new problem or new episode of a problem for which people seek health care."[6] A well-functioning primary care practice must not only be accessible but also *seem* accessible to patients who want to use it. The way we can know how well a medical care system is doing on that score is by measuring how services are actually used.

Longitudinality, which implies the presence of a single "regular source of care and its use over time," is the second component of primary care.[7] The third characteristic, *comprehensiveness,* means that practitioners and facilities must be able to provide or arrange for all types of needed services, even those not available efficiently on site. Finally, the fourth element is *coordination or integration,* by which Starfield means some form of continuity connecting one episode with another. It can be provided directly by specific primary care physicians and other clinicians, or through the use of accessible medical records, or both. While primary care in this conceptualization would, almost by definition, ensure that people would be able to get their health care needs taken care of to the extent that science and the art of medical practice make that possible, the reality is somewhat less positive—at least in the United States. We will learn much more about that in the next three chapters.

The Disappointment of Medical Care in the United States

So although in theory the explosion of private and public-sector health insurance in the 1960s brought access to the benefits of American medicine to almost everyone, it turns out that many people in the United States do not have easy or regular access to primary care in Starfield's terms—even when they are able to visit a physician in an examining room. In fact, the situation has become so bad in some places and for some groups that now, early in the 21st century, we are in real danger of destroying the impressive achievements that help to define the American medical care system.

Among the key objectives of this book are identifying some of the obstacles to achieving real primary care and then planning ways to overcome them.

Consider this: an uninsured thirty-eight-year-old Texas woman with insulin-dependent diabetes "mixed occasional doctor visits with clumsy efforts to self-manage [her condition] . . . , getting sicker all the while." Because $120 physician visits were usually beyond her reach, she visited her doctor only occasionally, her health deteriorated, and this married mother of four was forced to give up her job. (Neither her job nor her husband's job as a truck driver provided them with insurance.) One result was that she was "rushed almost monthly" to a hospital emergency room, eventually totaling weeks in intensive care and causing the hospital to provide almost $200,000 of uncompensated care. The hospital "solved" its financial problem by offering her regular, outpatient care at no charge—so that it would not need to absorb the much higher costs associated with emergency and inpatient care. As a result, the woman's diabetes is now managed effectively, and the hospital cut "nearly in half" its bad debt related to her care. The *New York Times* quoted one close observer of the health care system who called the hospital "visionary" for taking this action, but who also likened it to "sticking fingers in the dikes" while noting that finding ways to avoid the uninsured is the more common approach taken by community hospitals.[8] Hospitals that do provide uncompensated care to uninsured people pass on as much of that cost as they can to those who do pay, contributing to the rise in insurance rates that, in turn, causes some employers or their employees to drop insurance.

In this one example, we find evidence of most of the critical issues afflicting the health care system: although scientific advances make it possible for patients with any number of chronic conditions, including diabetes, to manage their health and carry on most normal activities, the growing numbers of people with those illnesses need care regularly to keep their conditions under control. Yet many of them have no insurance to pay for that care, and because they tend to get less care than they need, the quality of their interactions with the medical care system declines and so do their benefits. For them, it is almost as if the scientific breakthroughs never occurred.

However, it is not just that people do not get the routine care they need. Because hospitals and other providers of care are unpaid for some of what they do, they increasingly lack the funds to maintain their facilities, equipment, and skills or to invest in the innovations for which American medicine is justly renowned. In addition, they often perform under great pressure, generated not just by the clinical implications of treating serious illness but also by inadequate systems for managing care and insufficient or outmoded resources of various kinds. These too often combine to produce rushed interactions with patients and inadequate attention to detail. As a result, many professionals and health care organizations do not perform up to their potential, avoidable errors occur, and instead of being helped, patients sometimes are made worse off by the care they receive.

The Importance of Health Insurance

The bottom line is that failure to solve these interrelated problems perpetuates the vicious cycle. Central to the solution is the simple statement that everyone needs to have comprehensive health insurance. There are three key reasons: first is the obvious one that it provides financial access to the care they need and thus removes what is arguably the main barrier to access to that care. Second, universal health insurance coverage means that the individuals and institutions responsible for their care—whether doctors, nurses, hospitals, or others—will be paid for every patient they treat. As a result, they will have the funds they need not only to provide good service to individual patients but also to upgrade their resources continually. And third, the combination means that per capita expenditures will be lower than if we continue to tolerate high—and growing—rates of uninsurance.

People without insurance get sicker because they don't get the care they need. Many eventually require emergency services and hospitalization, which might have been avoided if they took care of their condition earlier. And much of the care they get goes uncompensated, causing hospitals to raise their rates, insurers to raise premiums, employers and employees to drop coverage, and medical institutions to decline service.

The tendency for many Americans who can recite health-care-related problems they have experienced personally or that they know about from others is to want to correct each error and ensure that that particular problem does not occur again. That is our tradition—to tackle problems, one at a time, taking small steps, moving forward incrementally until the sum of an extended period of steady progress is large enough to be noticed and measured.

As I will show in the pages that follow, however, that approach is no longer adequate to the scale of the problems we face. A more dramatic strategy is needed to accomplish the goal of saving the medical care system so that we can rely on it to take care of us when we need it.

Because it is no longer enough to approach the problems one by one, we need not only to understand their causes but also to have a good idea of what we would like the reformed system to look like at the end of the improvement process. I will get to the causes in due course, but we can begin to define a well-functioning system here.

Following reform, the most beneficial condition for the society, not to mention individual Americans, would be for everyone to have access to the care they need to keep them healthy, return them to health when necessary, and help them manage their chronic conditions. In addition, Barbara Starfield's conceptualization of primary care would become a reality for everyone. Sufficient services would be available so that everyone can actually avail themselves of the ones they need. And these services should be of reliably good quality. The reformed system should avoid any features that discourage people from seeking appropriate care from the most appropriate, usually least expensive, source at the most appropriate time. At the same time, it should avoid other characteristics that encourage providers to reject some patients or that discourage them from providing the care they believe their patients really need. Finally, patients should get services they need but not ones they don't need, and providers should be efficient in delivering those services so that we don't waste money. We should want all these conditions to be in place not only because individuals would benefit, but for two other reasons as well: one is that a healthy populace is good for the society and the economy, and the other is that without the stability and predictability these achievements imply, the service delivery subsystem will deteriorate; indeed, its erosion has already begun, and it is becoming increasingly unreliable, as I will show in Chapter 4.

To achieve this end state, the following are needed:

- Everyone must have comprehensive health insurance. There are two main reasons. First, because health care is so important both for individuals and for the society, everyone should have financial access to those benefits. There is no good justification for any other outcome. And this is the case even though actual use of services is determined by more than the ability to pay for care. (Other factors include the local availability of services; transportation; baby-sitting; other non-financial barriers to utilization; and beliefs about the value of health care, among others. More about them in Chapter 5.)

  Second, universal coverage is the single most important step needed to arrest the deterioration of the health care delivery subsystem. Among other reasons, a stable program of universal coverage will permit providers to count on a reliable source of income no matter where they locate. Therefore they will be able to open offices in any area that has potential patients (because residents will have a means of payment) but that does not have enough providers to meet their needs now (in part, because in the current system, payment is too uncertain or too low).

- Everyone should be able to sign up with a personal primary care physician and to use care when it is needed.

- The reformed system should eliminate doubt as to whether a needed service will be covered. Providers should know that if they exercise their best clinical judgment in serving their patients, they will be reasonably compensated for their work. Retroactive denials of payment, which encourage providers to withhold even needed care from patients of some payers, must end.

- Costs—from insurance premiums, patient cost-sharing arrangements, and utilization—must be kept under control. There are two important reasons: first, out-of-pocket costs they cannot afford tend to discourage individuals from seeking the care they need. And second, total expenditures that climb too high force cutbacks in the services that are covered and make insurance too expensive for many to afford.

- System-generated obstacles to good-quality, safe care must be eliminated,[9] and opportunities to improve quality by building teams and coordinated care and by taking advantage of information technology must be maximized.

Although the vision reflected in these five points is a representation of my own values, I believe most Americans would support it. And, anticipating the recommendations to come later, those who have other views should be asked to defend them, as I will defend these in the chapters that follow.

The evidence is clear, both from stories like the one about the Texas woman with diabetes and from careful aggregate research, yet we have been ignoring the obvious: the U.S. health care system is broken—it is producing a multitude of outcomes we do not want. Instead of dealing with the problems we face—and about which there is very visible evidence—we tend to act like the frog who enjoyed being in the water on the stove as it got progressively warmer until, as it approached the boiling point, it was too late for him to get out. Will we respond in time to signs about the worsening state of the U.S. health care system? Several Institute of Medicine reports over the past ten years have called attention to the alarming trend revealed by study after study that demonstrated the erosion of safe, high-quality care. At the same time, many middle-class Americans have been losing their access to medical care because so many firms have either dropped health insurance coverage for their workers or made it more expensive than their employees can afford. A by-product of these trends is that many provider organizations that might be inclined to invest in improving quality have less income with which to do so.

Again, however, few to date have drawn the clear conclusion from the accumulating evidence: tinkering with it, as we are accustomed to doing and many still advocate, cannot fix the broken system. Here is a case in point: for forty years, scholars have written that information technology (IT) can help doctors improve quality, avoid errors, increase efficiency and productivity, and, in the process, transform the health care system for the better. Despite enormous interest in these innovations, however, disappointingly few physicians use electronic health records, which many believe are the central element of the potential IT revolution.[10] IT simply has not diffused throughout the health care system. A key reason for this fact—although there are others as well—is that incentives in our current system actually make it rational for most medical practices, especially the relatively small ones that provide care for most of the population, to *not* purchase IT.

IT systems are expensive, both to buy and for ongoing technical support; they result in lower productivity for cash-strapped practices at least for many months; and since existing IT products vary a lot in their capabilities, it is not always clear which ones can add value to a practice. But perhaps even more important is the fact that, regardless of the expense, whatever benefits IT does produce accrue to others. First among these are the insurers, which would benefit from lower costs, fewer errors, less duplication of services, and less paper. For the medical practice that must find the cash to pay for IT, moreover, even if it solidifies its reputation for quality and innovation, IT does not result in additional practice revenues from attracting either more patients or higher fees. If anything, it reduces income by eliminating no-longer-needed, often duplicate, services. And finally, incremental adjustments, such as giving tax breaks to medical practices that adopt IT systems, may lower acquisition costs but will not change the basic conditions for those practices. So is it any wonder that IT has not spread more widely through the system!

What to Expect in This Book

Now is the time to come to the aid of the failing American health care system. We need both to think creatively, "outside the box," about the health system *as a whole*[11]—not just its components, as we usually do—and to have the determination to see the change process through to completion. The goal is not simply to improve access to care for individuals. It is nothing less than to save the health care delivery system itself.

In this book, I present key elements for reform of the health care system (Chapter 8) and include the outline of a political strategy that can bring it to fruition (Chapters 10 and 11). The first step is to recognize that the current system does not *and cannot* do the job. A system of private insurance based on employment will always leave many people uninsured, and the number of uninsured will grow as the cost of covering them rises faster than the economy as a whole. Moreover, as a number of authors have written, the "business case" for quality is often missing.[12] That is, given current conditions, the hospitals and physician practices that must make the large financial investments required to enhance safety and quality might not even be able to cover their costs. Because all they and others can do is tinker at the edges, the quality problems, too, persist.

Finally, it is worth noting that many books have appeared already about reforming the health care system. The number is large and growing. Why do we need another one? How is this one different?

First, the sad fact is that although the problems have confronted the U.S. health care system for decades, we have not yet solved them. Some of the books and articles still to come might just hit on the missing idea needed finally to get the job done. In this context, it is okay even if some books overlap in their data, descriptions, or proposals because they will help build consensus in the public. Further, each will present its argument in a distinctive manner. Readers unpersuaded by one formulation may find another's reasoning or perspective compelling, and the combination may provide additional insights and perspectives.

Each book is written from the point of view of specific individuals. These include, among others, physicians concerned about freeing up practitioners to take good care of patients as they were trained to do;[13] physician-managers who want new financial incentives that will allow them and others to create effective health care organizations that not only will provide good care but also will succeed in a competitive market;[14] academics—economists, sociologists, political scientists—who provide insights informed by their disciplines;[15] and reporters who tell heart-rending stories about ways in which the insurance system, the delivery system, or both have failed to serve good people in need of care.[16]

The point of view I will take is of the public interest. I am not a physician, a manager, or a journalist. My academic field is the health care system, how it operates and what it produces, and my concern is with the system as a whole and how well it serves the public now and in the future.

In addition, this book does several other things that most do not. One is it that, after detailing the problems, it examines their underlying causes in more comprehensive detail than is typical.

Also, while the book includes the familiar indicators of persistent problems (high rates of spending, large numbers of uninsured, problems with quality of care, among others), it adds an understanding of the dynamic forces—some, economic; some, clinical; still others, sociological—that have produced those and other problems. My recommendations flow from the composite analysis.

Having said that, however, I am mindful of the warning of Victor Fuchs, who wondered about the relative inability of his fellow health economists to influence the outcome of policy debates.[17] Economics has well-developed theories about the functioning of markets in general, which some apply to the health care system,[18] and health economists have conducted thousands of empirical studies over the years, which have added to our knowledge about ways in which health insurance and the health care system actually function.

Because of their many contributions, therefore, I was somewhat surprised to read of his concern. Indeed, from my perspective, health economists appear to have dominated much of the conversation about health policy issues over the past thirty years. One reason, of course, is the prominence of the expenditure and cost dimensions of system problems in the national discussion. Another may result from the perception that their theory, especially of markets, appears to non-economists to be so strong that it has become part of the conventional wisdom. Indeed, some of its appeal for Americans may be that it fits so easily with the stereotypical picture of the quintessential American man as rugged individualist. As a result, the process of extolling the market's virtues has tended to negate or undermine alternative policy choices, making it harder to adopt other proposals. Moreover, because their research tends to be quantitative, they express their results in numbers, which gives an air of precision that may not always be fully deserved.

In pursuing the question of why economists have not been more influential on policy matters, Fuchs discovered disagreements among economists that appeared at first glance to be about factual matters but on further consideration were found actually to mask different value preferences. It turns out that economists are as influenced by values as the rest of us, especially when they are uncertain about the impact or magnitude of empirical effects. When they agreed on the evidence, he found greater consensus among health economists about policy choices. The importance of this observation follows from the recognition that public policy incorporates assumptions, not just about the effects of various conditions or factors on desired or undesired outcomes but also about what is important in society—that is, values. And, despite the availability of so many empirical studies, much remains uncertain about the probable effects of many policy choices.

Nonetheless, if we can agree on the need for action, the fact is that consensus on the underlying facts will help to focus the discussion regarding what actions to take even though, alas, they will be based in part on values. One of my goals, therefore, is to present evidence about which there is widespread agreement in the hope of both strengthening the resolve for action and narrowing the range of reasonable policy alternatives. In taking this approach, I am building not only on Fuchs's insights, but also on advice attributed to the late Senator Daniel Patrick Moynihan, a sociologist as well as a distinguished public servant, to the effect that "Everyone is entitled to his own opinion, but not to his own set of facts." Providing the facts and insisting they not be ignored, I believe, can help to promote consensus on key elements, thus reducing the areas of controversy.

Finally, one of the three main sections in this book will be about the political dimension of reform. Other books tend to focus on defining problems, and many include sections on what they think the nature of the reforms should be. Few, if any, who propose reforms also discuss the politics of the matter, even though a number of political scientists have contributed important health policy studies. Yet it is a dimension that we ignore at our peril, given that all of the proposals—even those that would want to free up the market—require public policy decisions which in our system of government need the agreement of the Congress and the president. Moreover, one does not need to be a professional student of American government to know that a variety of groups benefit financially from the current system and will resist changes that will threaten those benefits. And those groups tend to have the resources to make themselves heard by decision makers. They are the proverbial "special interests." Somehow, their expected resistance must be overcome in service of the greater interest of the public and the society. Toward the end of the book, therefore, I will consider what will be needed to accomplish that daunting task.

My approach, which is intended to be both comprehensive and analytic, attempts to build on the lessons gained from past reform efforts with the goal of helping to make reform a reality. My hope is that others will build and implement an effective strategy based on the insights I will provide.

Chapter 2

How Much We Spend

FOR MORE THAN thirty-five years, commentators have complained that we spend too much on health care in the United States. Beginning in the late 1960s, when expenditures for the new Medicare and Medicaid programs began to exceed the original projections, alarm bells have been raised about the size of the health care sector. In a memorable article published in 1975, Howard Hiatt, then dean of the Harvard School of Public Health, argued that we needed to "protect the medical commons," a metaphor for the idea that the resources available for medical care are finite.[1] As a result, he said, we needed to find ways to limit the demands for health care funds.

Hiatt took off from a 1968 article in *Science*[2] in which Garrett Hardin, a biologist, wrote about a class of problems for which no technical solution was possible. Examples, he said, include the avoidance of nuclear war and "the population problem." While in some cases science-based knowledge might help select a particular strategy, the necessary first step was a commitment to actually achieve a solution. And that required a "change in human values or ideas of morality." To illustrate what he meant, Hardin described a commons on which area herdsmen graze their cattle.[3] Each one, seeking "to maximize his gain," periodically adds cattle to his herd. And that is okay because each additional cow has little impact on the whole—that is, until "the day of reckoning" when the capacity of the commons is reached and "the inherent logic of the commons . . . generates tragedy." The problem is that the commons is a finite piece of land, and eventually it becomes too small to support the next cow. To avoid disaster requires that each person put aside his effort to achieve a short-term personal gain in favor of actions that benefit the collectivity.

Applying the same logic to the growing expenditures on health care, Hiatt wrote that the "total resources available for medical care can be viewed as analogous to the grazing area on Hardin's commons. . . . Surely, nobody would quarrel with the proposition that there is a limit to the resources any society can devote to medical care, and few would question the suggestion that we are approaching such a limit."[4] Yet even as we approached that limit, he wrote, we still had unfinished business that needed attention—not only in the health-care sector (including, even then, large numbers of Americans without insurance or access to care), but that society had other demands for its resources, as well, and these too were growing. So a way needed to be found to limit health care spending.

Despite the warnings of Hiatt and others, however, in the more than thirty years since his famous article, the amount of spending on health care has continued to grow—and we still have not found a way to contain it. Was Hiatt wrong? *Are* the resources for medical care really finite, or, alternatively, is there no limit to what we can spend on health care? In fact, some do argue that, although we may choose *not* to do so, we really *can* afford to spend a lot more on health care.[5] Who is right? Can we relax, or now, so many years later, do we need to be even more concerned? And even if we can afford to spend more, are there other reasons to limit spending? Let's start by looking at the spending data.

Trends in Health Care Spending—in Dollars

In 2006, we spent much more on health than in 1970.[6] National health expenditures (NHE) grew from about $75 billion in 1970 to $2.1 trillion in 2006 in actual or nominal dollars, a whopping increase of more than 2,700 percent (Table 2.1). Clearly, that is a lot. How do we know whether it is too much?

Is there some objective criterion that allows us to compare actual spending to an ideal amount? As the controversy referred to earlier suggests, it should be apparent that no such figure exists. So the best we can do is try to put health care spending in context by comparing it to other figures. In that way, perhaps we can come to a judgment about whether we should be satisfied or concerned.

Maybe expenditures grew just because the population grew. After all, we would expect to spend more in the aggregate simply because more people live in the United States now than in 1970—even if they used services at the same rates and even if prices did not increase. In fact, however, annual per capita expenditures grew, too, from $356 to $7,026 (Table 2.1). This gain is less than the aggregate growth in nominal dollars, but it is still so large that the numbers are hard to interpret. To put these big numbers in terms we can all relate to more easily, $7,000 per capita means that the total for the average family of four in 2006 was more than $28,000, a very large amount,

TABLE 2.1

National health expenditures (NHE) and health services and
supplies expenditures (HSS), selected calendar years, 1970–2006

Spending Category	1970	1980	1990	2000	2006	Percentage of Change 1970–2006
NHE, billions	$74.9	$253.4	$714.0	$1,353.6	$2,105.5	2,711%
NHE, per capita	$356	$1,100	$2,813	$4,790	$7,026	1,874%
Real NHE, billions[a]	$272	$469	$875	$1,354	$1.806	564%
NHE as percentage of GDP	7.2%	9.1%	12.3%	13.8%	16.0%	—
Program administration and the net cost of private health insurance, billions	$2.8	$12.2	$39.2	$81.8	$145.4	5,093%

[a] Deflated using the implicit price deflator for GDP (2000 = 100.0).

SOURCE: National Center for Health Statistics, *Health, United States, 2008, with Chartbook,* Hyattsville, MD, 2009, http://www.cdc.gov/nchs/data/hus/hus08.pdf; accessed June 17, 2009. Calculation of real NHE taken from Aaron Catlin, Cathy Cowan, Micah Hartman, Stephen Heffler, and the National Health Expenditure Accounts Team, "National Health Spending in 2006: A Year of Change for Prescription Drugs," *Health Affairs* 27(1) (January-February 2008): 14–29.

especially when we realize that some people incurred no expense because they used no services at all.

Another possibility is that, although the actual dollars we spend on health care now are much larger than in 1970, when inflation—the extent to which a dollar buys today what it bought thirty-six years ago—is taken into account, the growth is more modest. And indeed, the spending increase *is* smaller when a deflator is applied that takes into account changes in the cost of living (Table 2.1). So we see that, using the year 2000 as the base year, the numbers grew from $272 billion to $1.8 trillion, a thirty-six-year increase of 564 percent instead of 2,711 percent growth when NHE are presented in nominal dollars.

Another perspective is to take into account the size of the economy as a whole. Since it, too, grew during this period, maybe we are still spending on health the same share of the gross domestic product (GDP)—the sum of all the goods and services produced in the country—as in 1970. In other words, although we spend a lot more now than before, maybe health care's share of the total economy has not changed.

It turns out again, however, that even as a percentage of GDP, NHE grew. In fact, in percentage terms, it more than doubled from 7.2 percent in 1970 to 16.0 percent in 2006, even though the lion's share of the real increase in per capita income was devoted to non-health-care items.[7] Indeed, a report by the Congressional Budget Office warns that "[i]n the absence of an unprecedented change in the long-term trend, health care spending will continue to grow as a share of GDP over the coming decades," reaching 25 percent in about 2025.[8]

To sum up the argument so far, the United States spent a lot more money on health care in 2006 than in 1970—whether we consider nominal dollars in the aggregate, inflation-adjusted spending, per capita spending, or the share of GDP. By all these measures, health care expenditures have grown dramatically.

But we still have not settled the question of whether the amount is too much. In fact, because there is no objective criterion against which to compare the spending, how can we ever know? Some people, including Harvard economist Michael Chernew and his colleagues, think we can "afford" to spend an even larger proportion of GDP on health care.[9] We may choose not to do that, but they think we could do it if we wanted to. So in the absence of a clear answer, why not just recognize that whatever the level of spending is, it reflects what people are able and willing to spend on health care? Why not simply acknowledge that this level of spending represents what we value in what is still the world's richest economy?

Part of the answer is that, as Hiatt recognized, we have "unfinished business" related both to health care and to other sectors that require investment—education and physical infrastructure, to mention just two. Whether the total available funds are finite or not, money spent on health care is not available for other purposes.

Another element is that this level of spending, as well as the rate of increase each year, occurs in the system as it currently exists. So maybe the discontent being expressed so widely is less about the amount of spending on health and more about what we get for it—and, by implication, about how much more value we could be getting if the system were somewhat different. We will return to this issue in the next two chapters, but for now, let's digress briefly from the evidence of problems facing the system to consider some introductory comments about health insurance and the role it plays in our problems.

The Role of Health Insurance

One reason for higher rates of spending on health care is that although it is the patient who uses services, much of the cost is paid for by third parties (usually a private insurer or a government program such as Medicare or Medicaid) that typically are not responsible for the delivery of care itself. (In this formulation, the first party is the patient and the second is the doctor, hospital, or other provider of care. The third party is the payer.)

What is health insurance, and why is it so expensive? To begin, most insurance is designed to protect people from the financial consequences of expensive, relatively rare, usually random events that few can plan for in advance. A classic example is insurance to protect against the possibility that fire may destroy your home. The probability that it will happen is small and, in a given population with known characteristics, it can be calculated. So, on the basis of data collected over a number of years, an insurer can figure out what proportion of, say, one hundred thousand houses it insures will burn down and what it will cost to replace them. Neither the insurer nor any individual knows which particular houses will burn, however. Although typical homeowners will not know whether their own homes will be destroyed, they *will* know that replacing them will be more expensive than they can afford. So they will take out insurance and pay a manageable monthly premium that will permit the insurer both to cover its losses for those fires that do occur and to provide enough for a reasonable profit. In exchange for the premium, the insurer agrees to pay an amount determined by terms of the policy (for example, the cost of building a similar house) in the unlikely event that the customer's house does burn. Some argue that people with insurance are likely to be less careful than they otherwise would be since they know they will be compensated if their house burns. (In the extreme case, some may even be tempted to burn down the house deliberately in order to collect the money.) The term for this phenomenon is "moral hazard." It captures the possibility that an event is more likely to occur simply because the customer has insurance. I will discuss it in more detail further on.

Health insurance started out similarly, but has evolved into something different. It began by protecting people against the small but known probability that they would need to go to a hospital emergency room urgently, be hospitalized for a serious illness, or need surgery. At the time health insurance began to develop in this country, hospitalization and surgical operations were expensive and occurred relatively infrequently with a probability that could be calculated. As time passed, however, people began to go to an emergency room or be admitted to a hospital bed not because they needed the distinctive services offered there but in order to get the insurer to pay for the services they did need. Not only that, but it began to be recognized that some hospitalizations and surgeries could be prevented and avoided altogether if people got inexpensive, office-based physician care early. But because physician visits and the tests they ordered cost money, too, some of the people who could have benefited from them decided not to use them because the services were not covered and they would have needed to pay the entire cost out of pocket. Many of those people eventually did need more expensive care in the hospital, which was covered by insurance. Both these reasons led to a push to expand the list of services covered by health insurance.

As policies became more inclusive in what they covered, people did indeed begin to use those services more—that was the idea, after all. What is less clear is the extent to which those were services they should have used but had neglected previously because of the cost, or ones they did not really need but used anyway because now most of the cost was paid by the insurer. Regardless, however, the price of the insurance went up because the money insurers spent on services increased, and the carriers needed more premium income to pay those bills. Considering the potential benefit on their health, it is a good idea for people to get preventive services and to seek care for acute conditions early in an episode of illness. But then those events, which are not particularly expensive, are no longer rare or random and thus are not classic insurable events. Yet if the services are beneficial, it is a matter of concern that, as we saw in Chapter 1, the out-of-pocket cost of care keeps many people, especially those with limited discretionary income, from using them.

Health insurance contributes to higher rates of spending in two ways. Because coverage reduces the out-of-pocket cost to users of services, it makes care less expensive for them and therefore easier for them to use. That does not mean they use services frivolously, but in a marginal case in which a person is not sure whether to go to a doctor or not, having insurance may tip the balance in favor of utilization. That tendency is reinforced by the second way insurance contributes to spending. It increases the probability that the doctor or other provider of care will be paid. Not only are they usually willing to furnish care, therefore, but knowing that the patient has insurance may encourage physicians and other clinicians to provide particular services even when the likely benefit is uncertain. Providers may complain that the amount of the insurer's check is too low, but they do get paid and, as a result, do not need to pester a patient struggling to make ends meet to come up with the fee.

This situation contrasts with that in many developing countries where people tend to avoid health care for as long as they can because they have no insurance and providers want payment at the time of service. A particularly dramatic example concerned a fifty-year-old woman from a rural area in China who, for several years, had an undiagnosed tumor in her womb. Even though her belly was growing, she sought no medical care because she had no insurance and little money. Eventually, she collapsed and was taken involuntarily to a hospital where the tumor was surgically removed and her life was saved. Although some of the costs were waived, she was left with a medical bill equal to about $723. To pay it, she borrowed money from a brother, two sisters, and several distant relatives. Because she earned only about $120 a year growing corn and raising geese, she feared she might never be able to pay them back.[10]

Having insurance, whether publicly or privately provided, allows people to get the care they need and to avoid such dire situations. For that reason, people with insurance can be expected to use more services than people without it, and as a result, insurers' costs increase. So to pay their bills and keep their profits at an acceptable level, private insurance companies try to keep down their health care spending in two principal ways. One is they segment the market, trying to sell their policies to large groups, especially those with large numbers of young and healthy folks who are unlikely to need many services. To the extent they succeed, the insurers will collect more premium revenue, but—because so many policyholders are young and healthy—will pay out less as fees to the providers of services.

The other way they compensate for the tendency of insurance to increase utilization is by introducing and enforcing rules that make it more difficult to use or provide services that are covered. They discourage would-be patients from using services by requiring them to pay an additional amount (in the form of deductibles, co-payments, or coinsurance) at the point of service.[11] They may require the patient or physician to obtain approval prior to using certain services—even fairly common prescription drugs. Some also conduct reviews of medical treatments already provided and withhold payment for those deemed to have been unnecessary. While the apparently benign goal is to curb waste (defined as the cost of unneeded care), all of these measures take the practice of medicine out of the doctors' hands to some degree. Whether or not the presumed goal of ending medical decisions leading to waste is achieved, the delivery of services can be slowed or potentially compromised to better fit economic ends. And, although I referred here to private insurers, public-sector programs use similar methods to control utilization.

In carrying out these market segmentation and utilization-reducing tactics, private insurers incur substantial costs of marketing and rate-setting on the one hand and utilization control on the other. Given this scenario, it would not be surprising if the cost of insurance itself has increased. And, indeed, it has (Table 2.1). In fact, although the net cost of private insurance and program administration—that is, their non-health-care related spending—is still just under 7 percent of national health expenditures, that figure has almost doubled since 1970 (from 3.7 percent). Moreover, it is considerably more than the administrative costs of third parties in other countries (more about that later) and even of our own Medicare program, the national health insurance plan for the elderly and disabled, which spends less than 2 percent of its revenues on administration.[12]

That some utilization is unnecessary is assumed on at least two grounds, one theoretical and the other empirical. Theory suggests the possibility that

having insurance may cause individuals to engage in riskier behavior knowing that insurance protects them against its financial consequences. This is
"moral hazard," introduced earlier, which, applied to health insurance, means
that because what is insured against is the cost of services used, people might
use more services than they need just because, with insurance, they are a
bargain. The Princeton health economist Uwe Reinhardt has been quoted
as saying "Moral hazard is overblown." He asks rhetorically, Do people really
"check into the hospital because it's free? Do people really like to go to the
doctor?"[13]

Nonetheless, the theory of moral hazard applied to health insurance is
certainly plausible, and it appears to be supported by evidence of wide variations in utilization of certain services among small geographic areas (such as
counties in a state) that are not explained by differences in the incidence of
disease. John Wennberg, the physician-researcher who first called attention
to this phenomenon of small-area variations in utilization, attributes much
of the difference he has observed—in study after study—to differences in the
distribution of medical personnel and facilities. In other words, an area with
a higher ratio of surgeons to the population is likely to experience higher
rates of surgery. But that occurs only when people have the means to pay for
those services. In other words, insurance.[14] In fact, other studies also show
that people who are insured have higher utilization rates than people without insurance, and people who have policies with fewer restrictions tend to
use more services than those whose policies have more restrictions.[15] The
problem is that the very idea behind health insurance in the first place was to
lower the cost to patients so that needed services are financially accessible. So
what do the different utilization rates mean? In the absence of clinical data at
the individual level, observing that people with insurance use more services
than people without it means only that the two groups use services at different rates. At the aggregate level, it is certainly as plausible that at least some
of the difference in rates is accounted for by the fact that the *un*insured are
*under*using care as that those with insurance are *over*using it.

More than thirty years ago, the RAND Corporation conducted an experiment in which researchers randomly varied the amount of insurance people
had. The Health Insurance Experiment (HIE), as it was called, produced
many reports showing that people who faced *higher* out-of-pocket costs
(that is, had less generous coverage) tended to use fewer services than people
with *lower* out-of-pocket costs. We will talk more about this later. For now,
it is enough to say that cost-sharing works. It limits utilization and, therefore, expenditures just as it was intended to do by causing the insured patient
to shoulder some of the cost of the services he or she uses. The question is,
what care is being eliminated by those who must pay cost-sharing amounts?
Do the resulting patterns of care show that waste has been eliminated, or do

patients cut out useful services, too, simply because they must pay for them out of pocket?

Thirty years ago, the "HIE found that, on average, there were minimal or no adverse health consequences associated with higher cost sharing," but the authors of a recent paper—including the leader of the HIE itself—now call that conclusion into question. In 2008, they acknowledged that "relatively modest increases in cost sharing reduce utilization of important medications for managing chronic disease."[16] Other recent research suggests that higher cost-sharing also reduces the use of preventive and screening services. The authors believe that because "[f]ewer effective treatments for chronic disease were available in the 1970s, . . . the adverse consequences of cost sharing may be greater now than they were in the past. Second, over time diseases that were once untreatable or considered acute illnesses have become chronic in nature as technology has advanced, exacerbating the negative consequences associated with higher cost sharing."[17] Finally, they conclude that "it is reasonable to expect that higher cost sharing may lead to worse health and may increase health disparities."[18]

Whatever the effects, insurers incur substantial costs of marketing and rate-setting on the one hand and utilization control on the other to carry out these tactics. And engaging in these activities contributes to the high administrative costs of insurance in the United States, as noted earlier.

To sum up the argument to this point, we know that our health care expenditures are high and growing, and we understand that some of the growth is the inevitable result of the fact that we have insurance. But we still do not know whether we are spending too much or not. In the absence of an objective criterion to help us, we can look at the effects these increases are having on people. If we don't like what they do, that would be a good reason to conclude we have a problem that needs to be fixed.

Large Numbers of Uninsured

One effect of the high and growing cost of care is that health insurance has become unaffordable for many businesses and individuals who have had coverage in the recent past. But although the numbers may be growing, the United States has had large numbers of people with no health insurance coverage at all for many years—as well as many more individuals with inadequate coverage.

Among the non-elderly population, 17.9 percent had no health insurance in 2006, up from 16.1 percent in 1995.[19] Further, the proportion of the population with employment-based coverage declined by even more—by 2.6 percentage points in that period. In addition, since the decline in employer-based coverage was greater than the increase in public-sector coverage, it is clear that the public-sector safety net is not picking up the slack. Moreover, if we look back to 1977, we see how truly dramatic the erosion of health insurance has been. Since that year, the proportion of the non-elderly population without insurance almost doubled, from 9.5 percent to 17.9 percent.[20]

In defining the coverage-related aspect of health system problems, it helps to recognize that most uninsured Americans are either employed themselves or in the family of an employed head of household. In 2006, 89 percent of the 46.5 million non-elderly without insurance were in families headed by a worker.[21] Indeed, as Jonathan Cohn showed in heartbreaking detail, many people work two and three jobs to support their families—and still cannot buy insurance.[22] What else do we know about the uninsured who work?

Among uninsured employees, 54 percent worked in firms that do not even offer coverage. Another 19 percent worked for firms that did offer coverage, but they were not eligible for it. Reasons included that they had not completed the waiting period prior to eligibility (only about one-third of workers in firms with coverage were able to begin coverage without a waiting period),[23] they were considered contractors and not regular employees or were part-time or temporary employees and did not work enough hours to qualify, or they had a preexisting medical condition.[24] Of those offered insurance, 15 percent declined it, almost two-thirds of whom (64.4 percent) did so saying it was too expensive.[25]

These large numbers and trends might convince a policy wonk, on ethical grounds or in the name of equity, that the country's health system faces huge problems that need to be solved. But the numbers are so large and impersonal that many readers may have a hard time relating to them. Yet each number represents a person without insurance, many of whom get sick and are forced to make tough decisions about what they should do. The story in Chapter 1 about the Texas woman with diabetes but no insurance is one.

The situation is getting so bad that growing numbers of insured people have problems as well. Most Americans get their insurance through their employment. That was the case for the Orozcos from Nashville, Tennessee—Allen, Heather, and their three children. They had health insurance for their family through Allen's job with a mortgage company. The problem was that although his share of the premium cost him $800 each month—a struggle, but one they chose to endure—the coverage included a $1,500 per person deductible for each family member and it paid only 80 percent of most diagnostic tests and surgical procedures. These provisions caused the Orozcos serious difficulties. Though young, Allen had asthma and an inflammatory bowel condition called Crohn's disease, and his wife had a serious gall bladder condition. Her doctor recommended that she have surgery to remove her gall bladder, and Allen needed expensive medications, with the possibility of surgery looming in his path, too. Even with their insurance, the cost of their care was more than they could handle, and as a result, neither one could follow the doctors' recommendations.

Because Allen was the sole breadwinner while Heather was finishing school, they decided to do what they could to take care of his condition first. But the deductible for his prescription medications was so high that he "stretched them out" to make them last longer, even though by doing so he undermined their effectiveness and recognized he was playing "Russian roulette" with his life. In the meantime, Heather got no treatment for her gall bladder condition, which frequently woke her up in the night with severe nausea, depriving her of the sleep she needed to carry on her responsibilities, which included getting the children ready for school and being a student herself. More than once when her condition deteriorated to the point that she could no longer ignore it, she wound up in a hospital emergency room—at a cost to the insurer of five or six times the cost of regular appropriate care in her doctor's office.[26]

Unfortunately, the Orozcos' story is becoming all-too-typical.[27] These are people living the American dream—job, school, family—and it is all being threatened by inadequate health insurance. Health care spending has increased so much that the cost of insurance has led many firms to drop it for their employees. Others, like Allen Orozco's employer, cut it back so that they could retain at least some coverage. But those cutbacks include deductibles and coinsurance payments that are so high that, like those for the Orozcos, they keep families from getting the care the insurance is supposed to make accessible. And the Orozcos *have* insurance. Imagine what their story would be if—like forty-seven million other Americans—they had none at all!

The conclusion is that even though we have no explicit criteria to identify what the "right" level of spending should be, the long-term, apparently inexorable increase in health care spending clearly is putting both insurance coverage and health care itself beyond the grasp of more and more Americans. These trends are now reaching deeper into the middle class.[28] Indeed, given the growth in spending, even university professors and others in jobs with historically comprehensive insurance plans may no longer be able to count on having that same coverage in the years ahead. In fact, many of those policies, though still in place, have been eroding over the past ten years or more—so far, in relatively small ways. As we have already seen, they include rising premiums and cost-sharing, and prior-authorization requirements have been added for many services.

Why isn't health insurance simply a matter of individual responsibility? Yes, health care has benefits for individuals, but forced to choose, some—especially the young and healthy—determine other things are of more immediate importance for them and decide to forego insurance. Moreover, the evidence shows that employment-based health insurance has lowered wages.[29] Why shouldn't young, healthy people choose higher incomes over health insurance that would pay for services they probably won't use? Why should we care? This is an important question, and we will return to it later.

So far we have talked only about rising costs and their effects on the probability that people will have insurance coverage and that they will use health care services when they need them. These are matters of concern because, among other things, health care offers real benefits to individuals and, in the aggregate, to the society as a whole and its economy.

How Much We Spend on Health Care

At one level, the increases in spending mean simply that people bought more health care in 2006 than they did in 1970 and that prices went up, too. Employers and individuals buying health insurance are paying premiums that cover not only that higher spending on services but also the administrative costs and profits that we saw are almost twice as high as they were in 1970 (Table 2.1). It is not surprising, therefore, that growing numbers of employers are finding it too expensive to offer coverage to their employees, and that others are either reducing what they cover or passing on more of the cost to employees by increasing premiums and cost-sharing amounts.

To get an idea of the financial burden on employers and their workers represented by health insurance premiums, consider these figures for 2007. The Kaiser Family Foundation reports that the average annual premium was $12,183 per worker. Of that amount, the average worker's share was $3,304 and the employer's share was $8,879.[30] Given the fact that, on average, a firm needs to come up with almost $9,000 for each employee, it is not surprising that although 99 percent of large firms (200 or more workers) offered coverage, only 59 percent of small firms (3–199 workers) did so. Nor should we be shocked that, although almost all uninsured are employed, many have trouble paying $3,300 for their share of the average premium. Or that the situation is worse now for both groups, especially given the economic downturn of the past few years. Finally, the ratio of small firms to large firms is also important. Although virtually all large firms offered health insurance in 2007, they are such a small proportion of all U.S. firms that when their numbers were added to those of the small firms, the total number of companies offering insurance increased by only a single percentage point, from 59 percent to 60 percent.[31]

That the situation is deteriorating can be seen in the following facts: since 1999, the number of firms offering coverage dropped by 6 percentage points, the percentage of the population who had employment-based coverage dropped from 68 percent in 1999 to only 62 percent by 2006,[32] and the declining public-sector safety net left many more without any coverage. The proportion of those under age sixty-five with no health insurance at all increased from 15.9 percent to 17.9 percent between the two years.[33]

The bottom line is that higher health system spending is reducing the numbers of Americans who have health insurance and eroding the amount and comprehensiveness of the coverage that is available to them.[34] If the trend continues, the forty-year growth of health care spending may begin to taper off, especially for those individuals who lose health insurance coverage.

Table 2.2 presents trends in personal health care expenditures, that part of total national health expenditures that represents, in financial terms, the care actually used by individuals.[35] Although the overall picture of huge increases in spending is similar to that for total national health expenditures, in this table we focus on the sources of those funds.

Of particular interest is that per capita expenditures on health services themselves grew to $5,880 for every man, woman, and child in the United

TABLE 2.2

Personal health care expenditures, percent distribution, and per capita amounts, by source of funds: selected calendar years, 1970–2006

Spending Category	1970	1980	1990	2000	2006	Percentage of Change 1970–2006
Billions of Dollars						
Personal health care expenditures	$62.9	$214.8	$607.5	$1,139.6	$1,762.0	2,701%
Out-of-pocket payments	$24.9	$58.1	$136.1	$192.9	$256.5	930%
Private health insurance	$14.1	$61.2	$204.6	$403.1	$634.6	4,401%
Medicare	$7.3	$36.1	$106.6	$215.9	$381.0	5,119%
Medicaid	$5.0	$24.7	$69.7	$187.0	$285.7	5,614%
Percent Distribution						
Out-of-pocket payments	39.6%	27.1%	22.4%	16.9%	14.6%	—
Private health insurance	22.3%	28.5%	33.7%	35.4%	36.0%	—
Medicare	11.6%	16.8%	17.5%	18.9%	21.6%	—
Medicaid	8.0%	11.5%	11.5%	16.4%	16.2%	—
Per Capita Amount in Dollars						
Personal health care expenditures	$299	$932	$2,394	$4,033	$5,880	1,867%

SOURCE: Centers for Medicare and Medicaid Services, Office of the Actuary, National Health Statistics Group, *National Health Expenditure Data,* Table 6. Available at www.cms.hhs.gov/NationalHealthExpendData; accessed January 23, 2008.

States in 2006.[36] Private health insurance paid for 36 percent of the total; Medicare, the national program for the elderly and disabled, accounted for 21.6 percent; and Medicaid, the federal-state plan for the poor, accounted for 16.2 percent. At the point of service, individuals paid, on average, 14.6 percent of the total, or $856 directly out of their pockets in addition to their share of the insurance premiums. In 2006, the average cost for single and family coverage, including contributions by employee and employer, was $4,242 and $11,480, respectively.[37] Thus the total payments from individuals for premiums and cost-sharing was $5,098 in 2006. Given these big numbers, it is not surprising that single people, especially when they are young, decide not to buy health insurance.

Significantly, the table also shows that although health care expenditures grew dramatically over the thirty-six-year period, the average individual's out-of-pocket share of the total *dropped* from almost 40 percent to just under 15 percent. So while individuals had to come up with more money in 2006, health care represented a better value for that money than it had in 1970. And that is considering only the financial dimension. It is also worth more because, as we saw in Chapter 1, medicine offers more real help for people now than it did in the earlier period. Yet still, on average—in addition to the share of the insurance premiums charged by his or her employer—for the services actually used, the average individual needed to come up with almost $900 in cash in 2006 (more than $3,400 for the average family of four)—in addition to his or her share of the premium. When we recognize that many people spent nothing on care, it is still more apparent that the *average* out-of-pocket burden masks even larger cash outlays for many.

Further, the "financial burden of health care" is growing, since health care costs continue to increase at rates that are higher than general inflation.[38] The Kaiser Family Foundation "found that one in six adults who are privately insured—17.6 million adults—report having substantial problems paying their medical bills"—like the Orozcos in Nashville. "Added to the 22.9 million adults who were uninsured for the full year preceding the survey and another 17.6 million uninsured for part of the preceding year, a total of over 58 million adults in this country are at higher risk of incurring medical bills they may not be able to afford."[39]

As we saw, growing numbers of employers respond to these trends by dropping coverage altogether, and those that continue to offer it shift still more of the costs to workers as higher payments for premiums, deductibles, co-payments, and coinsurance.[40] Inevitably, a growing segment of the population can no longer afford to obtain insurance or even needed care. Thus the percentage of the population under age sixty-five with any health insurance, private or public, declined to "a post-1994 low of 82.1 percent." By

2006, the uninsured population was 46.5 million, an increase of 10 million since 1994.[41] To put the increase in perspective, it is as if the entire population of Michigan lost its insurance coverage.[42]

The combination of higher health care costs in general and the reduced numbers of people with any insurance coverage at all creates growing health-related financial burdens for large numbers of Americans. The Kaiser Family Foundation found that in 2003, 10 percent of non-elderly adults *with* private health insurance reported having medical debt.[43] Moreover, privately insured people with medical debt were increasingly likely to have skipped a recommended test or treatment, to have failed to fill a prescription, and to have postponed recommended care.

A more dramatic indicator of the impact of rising health care costs is the extent to which medical bills contribute to personal bankruptcy. A survey of 1,771 people who filed bankruptcy petitions in federal judicial districts in five states (California, Illinois, Pennsylvania, Tennessee, and Texas) was conducted to determine the extent to which medical bills were implicated as a reason for bankruptcy.[44] In the sample, "the average debtor was a forty-one-year-old woman with children and at least some college education." Most owned homes and were in the middle or working classes. "More than one-quarter cited illness or injury as a specific reason for bankruptcy; a similar number reported uncovered medical bills exceeding $1,000. Nearly half (46.2 percent) . . . met at least one of our criteria for 'major medical bankruptcy.' . . . A lapse in health insurance coverage during the two years before filing was a strong predictor of a medical cause of bankruptcy."[45] So the numbers of people with medical debt is growing, leading some, even among those with insurance, to file for bankruptcy.

How Our Spending Compares to That of Other Developed Countries

We have seen that high rates of spending mean that both coverage and care are too expensive for some people to handle, but even for those who do get services, the extra spending does not guarantee that those services are either safe or of acceptable quality. Before we take up that part of the story in the next chapter, we should complete the discussion of health care spending rates by comparing those in the United States to other countries. Although it is pretty clear by now that, largely because of the rising cost of both insurance and care, more and more Americans are joining the ranks of the uninsured, if U.S. spending is comparable to that of other countries, then maybe it is just a fact of modern life that we need to get used to.

We pride ourselves on having some of the best medical care in the world and, while that may be true, it is also true that many other countries—

including the United Kingdom, France, Sweden, Canada, and Japan, among others—also have well-trained medical practitioners and thoroughly modern facilities. So how does health care spending in the United States stack up against spending in other developed countries?

Table 2.3 presents health expenditure data for 2005 from the Organization for Economic Cooperation and Development (OECD) for seven developed countries, including the United States. From this comparison, we see that health care spending for those countries varies, but in a fairly narrow range of between 8.3 percent and 10.7 percent of their GDP. U.S. spending, at 15.3 percent, was 5 to 7 percentage points higher—a very large gap.

Similarly, per capita spending on health care in the other six countries, when adjusted for differences in the cost of living, ranges from $2,343 to $3,326, also a fairly narrow range of only about $1,000. U.S. spending, yet again, is in a class by itself at $6,401, almost twice as much as that of the next highest country, Canada. Moreover, the share of health care spending that individuals must pay out of their pockets at the point of service was $842 in the United States, more than $200 higher than the next most expensive country, Australia. The only measure on which the United States is not an outlyer at the upper end of the range is in the average annual growth rate for the ten years from 1995 through 2005. On that indicator, the United States

TABLE 2.3

Multinational comparisons of health systems data,
selected indicators for seven countries, 2005

	Australia	Canada	Germany	Netherlands	New Zealand	United Kingdom	United States
Percentage of GDP spent on health care	9.5%	9.8%	10.7%	9.2%	9.0%	8.3%	15.3%
Health care spending per capita	$3,128	$3,326	$3,287	$3,094	$2,343	$2,724	$6,401
Average annual growth rate of real health care spending per capita, 1995–2005	4.5%	3.2%	1.8%	3.3%	4.3%	4.2%	3.6%
Out-of-pocket health care spending per capita	$627	$482	$431	$250	$392	$0	$842

SOURCE: Taken from The Commonwealth Fund, *Descriptions of Health Care Systems: Australia, Canada, Germany, The Netherlands, New Zealand, The United Kingdom, and the United States.* Based on OECD Data 2007 (October 2007). Available at http://www.commonwealthfund.org/usr_doc/Country_Profiles_10-25-07.pdf; accessed June 17, 2009.

TABLE 2.4

Age-standardized death rates (per 100,000) among males and females
ages 0–74, from selected causes in seven countries, from the Organization
for Economic Cooperation and Development (OECD), 2002–2003

	Australia	Canada	Germany	Netherlands	New Zealand	United Kingdom	United States
Males ages 0–74							
Amenable causes	79.00	85.67	105.80	88.03	102.78	116.62	123.36
Ischemic heart disease (50%)*	28.25	4.44	36.96	27.23	41.70	46.28	47.78
Other causes	234.74	272.29	317.48	294.80	264.19	270.81	344.63
Total	341.99	392.40	460.24	410.07	408.67	433.71	515.76
Females ages 0–74							
Amenable causes	63.74	68.15	75.14	75.81	88.63	89.64	96.41
Ischemic heart disease (50%)*	8.90	10.78	11.41	9.00	4.46	15.44	19.48
Other causes	123.39	157.51	143.70	165.46	159.65	163.58	200.03
Total	196.04	236.44	230.24	250.27	262.73	268.66	315.92

*It was assumed that only 50 percent of deaths from ischemic heart disease were amenable to health care.

SOURCE: Data taken from Ellen Nolte and C. Martin McKee, "Measuring the Health of Nations: Updating an Earlier Analysis," *Health Affairs* 27(1) (January-February, 2008): 58–71.

ranks in the middle at about 3.6 percent.

Is this higher spending justified? Do Americans get more care? Do they get better care? How do we know?

Two British professors present data for the same seven OECD countries showing age-standardized death rates, including those "from amenable causes"—that is, conditions for which "timely and effective health care" should prevent mortality (Table 2.4). In every case presented, the U.S. death rates are the highest among the seven countries.[46]

Thus, among 100,000 males under age seventy-five, 123 deaths from amenable causes occurred in the United States, while in the United Kingdom the rate was 117 and in Germany, 106. The numbers were lower in Australia, Canada, the Netherlands, and New Zealand. Similar results were recorded for females, as well.

Moreover, as Anderson and his colleagues have written, "The higher level of U.S. health spending does not necessarily provide more resources or health care use. On several key indicators, the United States actually appears to provide fewer health care resources than many other OECD countries."[47]

TABLE 2.5

Supply and use of selected health care resources in Organization for
Economic Cooperation and Development (OECD) countries, 2003

	Australia	Canada	Germany	Netherlands	New Zealand	United Kingdom	United States	OECD median
MDs per 1,000	2.5	2.1	3.4	3.1	2.2	2.2	2.3	3.1
Nurses per 1,000	10.2	9.8	9.7	12.8	9.1	9.7	7.9	9.2
Acute care hospital beds per 1,000	3.6	3.2	6.6	3.2	n.a.	3.7	2.8	3.8

*2002.

SOURCE: Data taken from Gerard F. Anderson, Bianca K. Frogner, Roger A. Johns, and Uwe E. Reinhardt, "Health Care Spending and Use of Information Technology in OECD Countries," *Health Affairs* 25(3) (2006): 819–831.

These include physicians, nurses, and hospital beds per capita (Table 2.5). Further, although much new technology is developed and first used in the United States, "once the technology has diffused, it [the United States] appears to acquire technology at rates similar to those of other industrialized countries."[48] Examples include the number of computer tomography (CT) scanners per million people and magnetic resonance imaging (MRI) machines per capita. In both cases, a number of other countries had more of those machines per capita than were in use in the United States.[49] Yet U.S. spending is much higher.

Anderson and colleagues also point out at least one example in which the United States lags behind other industrialized countries, and that is the diffusion and use of health information technology (HIT). "[T]o the extent that HIT systems are cost-saving in the long run, the lack of an integrated, national IT system for health in the future could exacerbate the position of the United States relative to countries that are HIT leaders."[50] So although the United States spends a lot more than other countries by virtually every measure, it appears we do not get even as much value as many others do that spend less. Moreover, the evidence related to quality and safety, as well as to health outcomes, suggests that independent of comparisons with other countries, there is much room for improvement.

Conclusion

In this chapter we have seen that spending on health care is high and growing, taking an ever-larger share of GDP. And while many observers have called attention to these trends over the past thirty-five years or more, they show no signs of abating.

While these trends may not be sustainable, they are a matter for concern, given the potential for modern medicine to do so much good and the increasing numbers of Americans with no insurance coverage. Nonetheless, before concluding the situation calls for some type of corrective action, we should take a look at what we get for the money we spend. That is the topic of the next chapter.

Chapter 3

What We Get for What We Spend

CLEARLY, WE SPEND a lot on health care—by every measure—and the high rate of spending creates problems for many Americans as well as for American businesses and the health care system itself. In Chapter 2, we saw evidence that the level of spending contributes to high rates of uninsurance. In this chapter, we look at other effects, starting with the impact on measures of health.

Health Effects of Higher Spending

The health-related effects of health care spending offer both good news and bad news. Before we discuss spending's impact on the ability of people needing care to actually obtain it, it is important to provide a context that helps make clear why the issues are so important. That is the good news part of the equation. For the simple fact is that medical care does produce a lot of good for people, and besides the individual stories of dramatic cures that warm everyone's heart, much of it is visible in aggregate data even using the relatively crude measure of mortality rates.

David Cutler, a Harvard economist, puts it succinctly: "The evidence shows clearly that spending more has been good; we get a lot more out of the medical system than we put in."[1] Mortality rates have declined dramatically since the beginning of the last century. Until about 1940, he writes, the reductions resulted "almost entirely" from lower infant and child mortality. Medical care played a very small role in that achievement. Instead it was nutritional and public health interventions that improved the food people ate, on the one hand, and cleaned up the water supply and disposed of garbage and sewage more safely, on the other. In about 1950, the picture began to change, and since then, medical care has played a major role in continuing mortality-rate improvements.

Two examples are the reduction of mortality from cardiovascular disease among adults and continued reductions in infant mortality. The latter has resulted not from public health and nutrition interventions, as in earlier years, but from advances in the treatment of low-birth-weight babies. A third area is the improved health of the growing numbers of elderly, many of whom have one or more chronic conditions. After more than twenty years of surveys in which people have been asked about "their ability to perform basic activities such as bathing, eating, and walking, and social tasks such as shopping, managing money, and doing light housework . . . the results are clear: the elderly are much healthier than they were two decades ago."[2]

So we spend a lot of money on medical care in the United States, and that spending produces substantial value for us. It makes a difference to individuals with a variety of types of medical conditions as well as in aggregate mortality rates that have continued to fall. Moreover, as Cutler put it, "because so many people do not get care when they need it, we could spend more on those people with excellent results."[3] Other factors associated with our wealth—better food, better living conditions, even more exercise—have played a role; but medical care has contributed much to the improvements.

Yet not everyone shares in the benefits, and the high cost of health insurance, not to mention of medical care itself, is part of the problem. For example, a recent *New York Times* article reported that uninsured and Medicaid patients are more likely to get a late-stage cancer diagnosis than are patients with private insurance or Medicare. Presumably, a major reason is that they are less likely to seek services as soon after the appearance of symptoms as those with private insurance or Medicare coverage.[4] The probability of successful treatment diminishes as a result.

Moreover, the relationship between costs, insurance, and health is essentially circular. Health insurance facilitates use of services, which contributes to improved health. If health deteriorates, the need for services is greater and so is the need for funds or insurance to pay for them. Without those funds or insurance, people are less likely to get care when they need it, they are less likely to benefit from that care, and their health is still more likely to decline—unnecessarily—as a result. Since people with poorer health are also less likely to have coverage, they are less likely to get the care they need, and their health will tend to deteriorate still further. Why are people with poorer health less likely to have coverage? Because if they do not have employment-based coverage, insurance available in the individual or non-group market is too expensive, and even if they can afford it, they may be excluded by the presence of preexisting medical conditions.

We already saw that the financial burden associated with the use of services is growing.[5] But in addition, "those with medical debt are more than twice as likely to report being in only fair or poor health and they are almost twice as likely to have an ongoing or serious health problem compared to others with private coverage (38% vs. 21%)."[6] Moreover, people with fair or poor health—who by definition are highly likely to need care—are likely to experience a substantial decrease in their access to health care. Among the privately insured, even after adjusting for factors that might explain the differences, "those with medical debt were more than three times as likely to have skipped a recommended test or treatment because of its cost . . .; were more than twice as likely to have failed to fill a drug prescription due to cost . . .; and were four times more likely to postpone care due to cost."[7]

Thus, to sum up the effects of high and growing health care costs: "[H]igh financial burdens can lead to greater medical debt, problems paying medical bills, and bankruptcy. . . .[Further,] high financial burdens are often obstacles to medical care access, as many families (including privately insured families) with problems paying their medical bills delay or forgo needed medical care."[8] Finally, the aggregate "increase in families' financial burdens was driven entirely by people with private (employer-sponsored) insurance."[9] Yet lest anyone think that the nongroup market is a viable alternative source of coverage for workers whose employers drop health insurance, the same study found that "people covered by private policies purchased in the nongroup market were much more likely than those in any other insurance group to bear high financial burdens during 2001–2004."[10] The cost of coverage itself is high, partly because of the extent to which younger and healthier people, thinking they don't need it, exit the health insurance market as costs increase. So those still in that market *because* they are less healthy tend to need coverage more because they are more likely to use services and thus skew the risk pool toward higher spending. If they can afford it, they buy coverage even though it is expensive, tends to be less comprehensive, and includes more cost-sharing provisions, all of which add to their financial burden when they do use services. Recall the story of the Orozcos from Chapter 2.

So one effect of these increases in spending is to raise the cost of both coverage and care and, as a result, increase the numbers who try to make do without either.

Premiums increase more among small firms,[11] many of which cannot afford to offer coverage to their employees in the first place.[12] Moreover, for family coverage, the contribution to premiums was about $900 higher for workers in small firms than for those in large ones.[13] Most businesses are small, and many employees work for small businesses, frequently earning less than those in larger, more stable firms. Given what we already saw about the nongroup insurance market, therefore, it is an illusion to think that the coverage part of the problem can be solved by increasing private insurance—either among small businesses or for individuals in the nongroup market.

And as noted earlier, even when a firm offers health insurance, not all workers get covered. Some are not eligible, some have prior medical conditions, and others simply cannot afford their share of the premium.

Before leaving this section, we should recall that almost all large businesses do continue to provide health insurance for their employees.[14] They do it out of tradition; because they feel an ethical commitment to their employees; from a recognition that it helps create a more contented, loyal workforce; because it is required by a union contract; or because they need to continue to offer it in order to be able to hire and retain good employees in their industry. They may increase employees' share of the costs and impose features designed to reduce (unnecessary) utilization, but they tend to keep offering coverage.

Nonetheless, American firms that compete in the increasingly global economy are more and more at a disadvantage because the costs of health insurance—which are much higher in the United States than in other countries, as we saw in Chapter 2—are a burden that their international competitors do not share. Because the risk pool includes not just their own workers but everyone, the share of taxes those competitors pay to support a national system with universal coverage will be much lower than the private insurance purchased by American firms for their own workers (who even if they are not older and sicker will certainly be fewer in number, constituting a smaller, less stable risk pool, and therefore require higher premiums).

As we saw at the outset, medical care can make a major positive contribution to the lives of individuals and, through healthy people, to the society and the economy on which the society depends. Yet in spite of its demonstrated value, people who could benefit do not use it optimally, which adds to our list of problems.

The medical care itself is the source of another set of concerns. Many studies show that the quality of care in the United States is decidedly uneven and that large numbers of medical errors are made, some of which cause serious harm to patients and even death. We turn next to that aspect of the U.S. health care system.

Concerns About the Quality and Safety of Health Care

Until recently, most Americans believed that the U.S. health care system delivered high-quality care that was safe, some even calling it "the best health care system in the world."[15] Despite that assertion, however, there is much cause for concern about the state of safety and quality in the U.S. health care system. Indeed, the general perception has changed dramatically in the past ten years. Although a number of professionals had been raising alarms about quality for years, two landmark reports from the Institute of Medicine (IOM) began to focus wider attention on the topic. Public perception of the quality and safety of the health care system was altered with the release in 1999 of *To Err Is Human: Building a Safer Health System,*[16] which asserted that many thousands of people die in hospitals each year as a result of medical errors.

The Institute of Medicine based this conclusion on the results of two large studies of hospital admissions, one in New York (using 1984 data), and a second in Colorado and Utah (with 1992 data). These studies found that the proportion of hospital admissions experiencing an "adverse event" were 2.9 percent and 3.7 percent, respectively. By adverse event they meant an injury caused by medical management rather than the patient's underlying medical condition. Even more troubling, over half of the adverse events in both studies were attributable to errors (58 percent in New York and 53 percent in Colorado and Utah), which, by definition, are preventable.[17] An adverse event caused by a patient's allergy to a drug he had never used before is not an error in that sense. Amputating the wrong leg is.

By extrapolating the data from these two studies to the 33.6 million admissions to U.S. hospitals in 1997, the authors were able to estimate that, nationally, between 44,000 and 98,000 deaths of hospitalized patients that year were due to medical errors. These numbers attracted widespread attention in the press and elsewhere and put onto the front pages of America's newspapers the concern that until then had been expressed only by a handful of researchers in a few arcane medical journals. To put the numbers in perspective, even the low-end estimate of 44,000 preventable hospital deaths exceeds the annual number of deaths attributable to automobile accidents, breast cancer, and AIDS.[18]

A more recent report from the National Committee for Quality Assurance (NCQA), a private nonprofit organization focused on the improvement of health care standards of quality, shows that the situation continues to be a matter of great concern. It refers to "'quality gaps' [that] represent the continuing failure to consistently deliver care in accordance with well-established guidelines and exact a substantial toll in terms of both lives and economic costs. If the entire health care system performed at the level of the top accountable plans, between 37,600 and 81,000 deaths would be avoided per year and between $2.6 billion and $3.6 billion in unnecessary hospitalization expenses would be saved."[19]

It is now widely accepted that the quality of care in the United States is less than optimal, and calls to improve its reliability throughout the health care system have become common. Quality is a complex concept, however, that encompasses the extent to which appropriate services are used, the skill with which those services are provided, and their relation to certain clinical outcomes. Its many aspects can be indicated with a variety of measures,[20] but quantifying the extent to which it exists, with any degree of precision, is difficult.[21]

Donabedian demonstrated more than a generation ago[22] that, although the ultimate measure of quality health care is its impact on therapeutic outcomes (that is, the extent to which people benefit from services received), research on the topic cannot be *limited* to studies of the relationship of care to outcomes, for several reasons. One is that it is often difficult to obtain data on the outcomes of care because they tend to be missing from patient records. When an ill patient completes a course of treatment successfully, he does not typically call the doctor to say he has recovered, and the doctor does not usually enter a note to that effect in the patient's record. Similarly, even when the record contains multiple entries related to an episode of illness, when the patient does finally get better, again he does not typically provide that information for the doctor to enter into the record. As a result, to the extent that outcome evidence is available in medical records, it is likely to be skewed toward the negative. Second, even if the outcome data were available, it is difficult methodologically to establish a direct causal link between the care a particular patient received and his or her own future state of health. That is the case because the body has its own natural mechanisms to fight off illness, and many people get better even without visiting a doctor. As the distinguished physician and author Lewis Thomas once wrote, "most things get better by themselves; most things, in fact, are better in the morning."[23]

Since we cannot limit ourselves to research on outcomes, therefore, Donabedian argued that some inferences about quality of care could be drawn from data on the processes of care—that is, on the services used.[24] Even if randomized controlled clinical trials (the "gold standard" of medical research) have not "proven" their role in treating the disease, certain services may be considered by the consensus among experts to be appropriate for particular symptoms or diagnoses. In that event, it is considered good quality for people with those conditions to receive those services and lesser quality if they do not.

The need for some approximation of the role medical care plays in patient health is increasingly important, not least because we spend so much on it and reasonably want to know whether we are getting our money's worth. Despite their limitations, utilization data can be particularly useful in that context, and insurance claims are the most readily available source of evidence related to the fundamental services-used element of process. This is especially the case when there is widespread agreement among experts as to which services constitute appropriate care for patients in particular circumstances.

So despite its limitations, utilization data by itself can play a useful role in assessing the value of care in particular settings and in focusing efforts to improve quality in those settings. Claims data are also especially useful because they provide evidence of care received in the community—that is, outside of hospitals—where most medical care occurs; and they allow us to broaden the measures to include more than simply whether a patient died as a result of care received or not received.

Claims data can help us determine whether the priority should be to increase the extent to which people with chronic conditions visit a doctor or, having seen the doctor, to facilitate compliance with the physician's recommendations. Utilization data first uncover deficits and then can help us focus attention on discovering reasons for those deficits so that strategies can be developed to overcome them. By comparing the experiences of different groups of patients, we can answer questions such as the following: Are the quality results better for patients with managed care or indemnity coverage? For Medicare eligibles or younger patients? For patients who have had the condition for several years or those who are newly diagnosed?

Given this background, what can we say about the quality of care in the United States since publication of the Institute of Medicine reports?

NCQA's annual series called *The State of Health Care Quality* reports measures of quality—primarily process measures, for the reasons Donabedian identified—for HMOs and other health plans participating in its accreditation program. Its Health Plan Employer Data and Information Set (HEDIS) obtains and records the audited percentage of a plan's eligible patients who used a particular service and then reports the average percentage among all plans.

NCQA's 2006 report presents data on the extent to which, between 2000 and 2005, patients with various conditions received specific services appropriate for their condition. In one section, the authors discuss elements of comprehensive diabetes care. Diabetes is an important disease because large numbers of Americans have it; the numbers seem to be growing; and, although it is treatable, many patients do not have it under control. In addition, since it is a chronic condition, patients with diabetes must be monitored, and the effects of treatment must be assessed regularly. Finally, since it is so widespread and the treatment continues for many years, it results in very large expenditures both for individuals and in the aggregate. NCQA reports that over fourteen million Americans have been diagnosed with the disease, and another six million have the disease but have not yet had it diagnosed. Expenditures for an average patient with diabetes were $13,243 in 2002, more than $10,000 higher than for patients without diabetes. Most treatment is an effort to prevent long-term complications associated with it, including heart disease, blindness, kidney disease, and stroke.[25]

The good news is that of seven measures for comprehensive diabetes care, virtually all improved between 2000 and 2005 because the percentage of patients with the disease who obtained the particular test or whose

LDL cholesterol was under control increased. (Those with poor HbA1c control declined, another good result.) On the other hand, the measures also showed a lot of room for improvement. In 2005, just over half (55.1 percent) of patients in commercially available plans were monitored for diabetic nephropathy, a unique injury to the kidney resulting from diabetes that, as it progresses, can lead up to and include the need for dialysis. In addition, although 88 percent had HbA1c testing, 30 percent were still in poor HbA1c control. Moreover, all of these averages masked wide variation among insurance plans. Finally, some authorities believe that the most appropriate measures would be those that combine the original seven elements into a single indicator because, for example, some people might have had an HbA1c test, but not LDL screening or eye exams. In other words, some argue that, instead of the individual measures, "all or none" measures that combine data on the full range of recommended services are the most accurate indicator of the extent to which a condition like diabetes is under control.[26] In one of the few studies that report all-or-none measures, colleagues and I showed that the proportion of patients with good quality care is much lower than the figures shown here.[27]

Data for other conditions presented in the 2006 NCQA report show similar trends, although the percentages vary by diagnosis.

So not only is there much left to do, but individual studies show that, despite evidence of successes here and there, in the aggregate the unsatisfactory quality-of-care situation has not changed much going back even before the year 2000. For example, a recent study by Ma and Stafford, which compared two national surveys of ambulatory care for 1992 and 2002, found only "modest" changes in utilization rates during that ten-year period.[28]

In 2001, the Institute of Medicine issued a second report, *Crossing the Quality Chasm: A New Health System for the 21st Century,*[29] which emphasized the need to redesign the health care system. The authors chose the word *chasm* to emphasize the wide space between the system we have now and the better one we could have. Essentially the report argued that the current health care system has not adequately adapted to the changes it has faced. Rapid advances in medical science and technology have increased the potential benefits but also caused growing complexity in health care delivery. At the same time, the insurance system meant to pay for the improved care has changed only at the margins. Fundamentally, it is little different from what it was thirty or more years ago. Partly as a result, the delivery of health care today can be characterized as complex and uncoordinated, requiring many handoffs from one professional to another within the system. Because health care providers are mainly organized in separate "silos," the structure is not well equipped to handle the rapid growth of chronic diseases that demand increasingly coordinated care among many components in the health care system.[30]

Although *Crossing the Quality Chasm* described necessary changes, progress toward implementing these changes has been slow. Frustrated by this slow response, Dr. Donald Berwick, who helped write both reports, took action into his own hands. As president and CEO of the Institute for Healthcare Improvement (IHI), he launched the 100,000 Lives Campaign in December 2004. The campaign sought to save 100,000 lives by implementing six highly feasible interventions for which efficacy had been established in the scientific literature.[31] The six interventions included the following:

1. Deploy medical emergency teams to address patients who would otherwise experience a cardiac arrest by making changes to prevent arrest or facilitating transfer to an intensive care unit.

2. Deliver reliable evidence-based care for acute myocardial infarction.

3. Prevent adverse drug events through medication reconciliation at the interfaces of care. (Medication reconciliation is a process by which a clinician reviews the patient's medication orders and tracks the medications actually administered before and after the transition of care from one site to another, for example when transferred from the emergency department to an inpatient bed).

4. Prevent central-line infections.

5. Prevent surgical site infections.

6. Prevent ventilator-associated pneumonia.

The essence of the campaign was a belief that 100,000 lives could be saved by consistently following a few well-known processes and procedures. The campaign enrolled more than three thousand hospitals, representing 75 percent of U.S. hospital beds, and in eighteen months prevented an estimated 122,300 deaths.[32]

The need for special initiatives like the IHI Campaign to implement known solutions should give one pause. If the strategies for improvement are so well known, why isn't their absence more the exception than the rule? In other words, if these are things clinicians *should* be doing, why are they *not* doing them routinely? We will take up that question in more detail in Chapter 6, but for now, let me just say that there is little in our current system beyond moral suasion to lead clinicians and the organizations in which they work to adopt the changes required to improve quality systematically. In its various reports and proposals, the Commonwealth Fund's Commission on a High Performance Health System recognizes that reality. It notes, for example, that incentives are misaligned so that providers tend to bear the costs (of, for example, information technology and the reorganization of clinical work) and others, including patients and insurers, reap the benefits in the form of improved quality and lower costs. In addition, while teams and coordinated care are generally considered to be important ingredients of quality reform, such clinical teams exist in few places to date, and the delivery system tends to be characterized not by coordination and cooperation but by isolation and fragmentation.[33]

The IHI list of interventions raises another concern. Item 2 targets increased use of "evidence-based" care for patients experiencing a heart attack. Why isn't evidence-based care already being used? And why is so much of what clinicians do *not* supported by persuasive evidence of its value? And what is "evidence-based" care, anyway?

Evidence-based assessment consists of a formal review of the scientific literature using standardized techniques with special emphasis on data from randomized controlled trials.[34] This approach has been offered as an antidote to the fact that many widely used clinical practices and procedures lacked support in the scientific literature and in some cases were found to be either of questionable value or even harmful to patients.

Why wasn't the information already contained in the scientific literature being used? One reason is that the volume of studies showing whether new ideas work has grown enormously.[35] In response to this explosion of knowledge, a variety of tools have been developed to help busy doctors find what they need easily and in an easily accessible format. One is the *ACP Journal Club,* a compendium put out by the American College of Physicians of one-page summaries of research literature relevant to particular clinical problems. Additional tools are available on the Web. Still other activities intended to increase the use of scientific data in actual medical practice include NIH consensus panels, blue-ribbon meta-analyses, and longitudinal comparative studies. All of these require, first, that their results are disseminated widely in the clinical community and then that practicing physicians actually access them. Computers and electronic information systems can help spread this knowledge more widely among practicing physicians. Yet Liang estimated that the U.S. health care system delivers evidence-based care only 55 percent of the time.[36] And elsewhere it was estimated to take an average of seventeen years for what is known to be effective to be incorporated into common practice (exceptions are some new technologies and pharmaceuticals).[37]

Another part of the answer, to be taken up in Chapter 6, reflects the absence of effective incentives on providers of care to adopt these practices and the pressures that result from the dysfunctional incentives they do face.

Satisfaction with the U.S. Health Care System

What I have presented so far in Chapters 2 and 3 are objective data regarding various aspects of the U.S. health care system—rates of spending, rates of insurance and uninsurance, effects of high costs on both coverage and use of services, quality and safety of care available in the United States, and comparisons with other developed countries on spending and a number of other relevant measures. It does not overstate the case to say that, on all these dimensions, the United States leaves much to be desired. To what extent are these problems visible to the naked eye? Many of them have existed for years, and we have not done much to solve—or even reduce—them. Is that because Americans don't recognize them? After all, in a democracy, the presumption is that policy follows the needs and wishes of the people—otherwise, they will replace elected officials with ones who will serve them more effectively. At least, that is the theory. So what do Americans think of their health care system?

Robert Blendon, a professor at Harvard University, has been conducting surveys about the health care system for years, and among other questions, he has asked about the extent to which citizens—and in some cases, special subgroups such as people who have been sick and professionals in the system—are satisfied with the system. Here is some of what he found.

In 2000, he and his colleagues discovered that only 40 percent of U.S. respondents were "fairly or very satisfied" with their health care system.[38] He presented that result with responses to the same question asked of citizens in sixteen other countries. The U.S. ranked fourteenth. Only Italy, Portugal, and Greece were ranked lower by their citizens. More than 90 percent of Danes, 70 percent of Dutch, and even 57 percent of British citizens—the latter from a country whose health system is often compared unfavorably to the American system by opponents of a public-sector approach to reform—were satisfied with their systems[39] (Table 3.1).

Blendon and his colleagues began their surveys of the public in 1988 and 1990, and have asked some of the same questions in several additional surveys since then to reveal trends in attitudes. The interesting result about the United States is that at least as far back as 1988—twenty years ago—few Americans were satisfied with the health care system. In the interim, some of the other countries have lost support among their citizens, but between 1988 and 2001, among Americans, the percentage who thought that fundamental changes were needed or the system needed to be rebuilt completely was never less than 79 percent. And in all three years, Americans were most likely among the seventeen countries to think their system needed to be rebuilt completely.

In 2001, citizens in five countries were asked some specific questions regarding access to care, and again, although citizens of other countries also reported problems, Americans tended to be the least satisfied. Americans were more likely to report that access was worse than two years ago, that it was difficult to get care in the evening or on weekends, and that they

TABLE 3.1

Citizen satisfaction with their own health care
system, seventeen countries, 1998 and 2000

Country	Percent Satisfied with System
Denmark	91
Finland	81
Austria	73
Netherlands	70
Luxembourg	67
France	65
Belgium	63
Ireland	58
Germany	58
Sweden	58
United Kingdom	57
Canada	46
Spain	43
United States	**40**
Italy	20
Portugal	16
Greece	16

SOURCE: Taken from Robert J. Blendon, Minah Kim,
and John M. Benson, "The Public Versus the World Health
Organization on Health System Performance," *Health Affairs*
20(3) (May–June 2001), p. 16.

were sometimes or often unable to get care because it is not available where they live. In addition, the United States registered the largest *gaps* between those whose income was below average and those whose income was above average. For example, while people with below-average incomes in all five countries were more likely to have difficulty seeing a specialist than people with above-average incomes, *the difference in the United States was 22 percentage points*—and this in a country in which almost two-thirds of the physicians are specialists! The country with the second highest difference was New Zealand, where the gap was 15 percentage points. In the other three countries, the difference ranged from only 3 percentage points to 7 percentage points.[40]

Finally, when cost was the reason for access problems, the situation in the United States was reported to be particularly stark (Table 3.2). Thus, for example, 39 percent of Americans with below-average incomes—that is, about two out of every five such respondents—reported not filling a prescription or not getting a recommended test, treatment, or follow-up due to cost. And even among those with above-average incomes, 18 percent did not fill a prescription due to cost, 15 percent with a medical problem did not even visit a doctor because of the cost, and 14 percent did not get a test, treatment, or follow-up due to cost. By contrast, in the United Kingdom, no more than 7 percent of either group failed to get a service because of cost.

The fair conclusion to draw from these figures is that Americans have been dissatisfied with the U.S. health care system for a long time—at least since 1988—and that, while none of the other countries reporting data is without problems, their citizens tend to be more satisfied with their systems than Americans are with theirs on most dimensions.

TABLE 3.2

Access problems due to cost and medical-bill problems in the past year, by income group, five countries, 2001

Country/ Income level	Did not fill a prescription due to cost (percentage)	Did not get recommended test, treatment, or follow-up due to cost (percentage)	Had a medical problem but did not visit doctor due to cost (percentage)	Problems paying medical bills (percentage)
Australia				
Below average	21	17	14	17
Above average	18	14	10	8
Canada				
Below average	22	9	9	14
Above average	7	4	3	3
New Zealand				
Below average	20	18	24	20
Above average	11	11	18	7
United Kingdom				
Below average	7	4	4	4
Above average	7	1	2	2
United States				
Below average	39	39	36	35
Above average	18	14	15	11

SOURCE: Excerpted from Robert J. Blendon, Cathy Schoen, Catherine M. DesRoches, Robin Osborn, Kimberly L. Scoles, and Kinga Zapert, "Inequities in Health Care: A Five-Country Survey," *Health Affairs* 21(3) (May-June 2002): p. 185.

Before leaving this section, it is worth noting Americans' attitudes toward some proposed changes. In other Blendon studies since 1980, at least half of the population (and sometimes as high as 66 percent) favored "national health insurance, financed by tax money, and paying for most forms of care."[41] On the other hand, when asked if they favored "a national health plan, financed by taxpayers, in which all Americans would get their insurance from a single government plan," only 38 percent answered yes.[42]

Thus, although Americans express high rates of dissatisfaction with the current system and are willing to accept, if not embrace, a publicly financed national plan, they have reservations about the nature of the government's role. That was the situation in the year 2000. Since then, if anything, the situation has deteriorated—as countless newspaper stories, as well as scholarly articles, attest. In addition, we have been in a period since the late 1970s or early 1980s in which even public officials have been critical of the government and have promoted the idea that the market is good and the government's role should be limited. The second Bush administration did a lot both to strengthen that idea and to undermine confidence in the role of government in general—some of it out of conviction that the best government is the least government, but some, apparently, out of sheer incompetence (for example, their handling of Hurricane Katrina and its aftermath).

Against this background, it is reasonable to believe that three developments might lead Americans to be willing to accept an even larger role for government in health care reform than reported in 2000. One is that confidence in the present health care system has dropped in recent years as more and more Americans are losing insurance. Second, the new administration may begin to restore confidence in government as an institution. And third, as specific proposals enter the debate—especially if they are supported by and promoted by an enthusiastic national administration and the public learns more of the kinds of facts presented here—more people may be willing to entertain the possibility of a large role for government. That said, the public's support of reform proposals is only one ingredient in the political mix. The interest groups that expect to be worse off under particular types of reform—for example, private health insurers; doctors, hospitals, and other providers of care; and small business owners—will exert their political muscle, and experience tells us they can be formidable protectors of their interests. We will discuss these issues in more detail beginning in Chapter 9.

Conclusion

In this chapter, we saw that while contemporary health care in the United States is capable of producing much good for Americans, many are unable to access the services they need. In addition, the quality of care for those who do have access to it is uneven and, in the aggregate, has not improved much over many years. Finally, for at least twenty years, survey after survey has shown not only that Americans are unhappy about this situation, but also that substantial majorities accept the need for big changes in the health care system, including a much larger role for government.

The failure to solve these problems, which have persisted for so many years, has consequences. In the next chapter, we consider evidence about one of them: that the delivery subsystem all Americans rely on to actually provide the services we need is deteriorating.

Chapter 4

Trouble in the Delivery Subsystem

THE MOST IMPORTANT point in the previous chapter may be not that the U.S. health care system has serious quality and safety issues, but that these issues have proved so intractable over so many years. Little progress is evident in published data. Is it possible that the delivery subsystem—in which the problems reside and the solutions must be implemented—cannot respond to the challenge? Is it possible that, after almost fifty years of failing to solve the health system problems discussed in previous pages, the delivery subsystem has begun to deteriorate as a result of the accumulated neglect and is no longer capable of righting itself?

Fundamentally, what we all want from a health care system is confidence that when we as individuals need services to diagnose or treat a developing clinical condition, we not only can gain access to appropriate medical care providers but also can know that the care provided will be the most appropriate for the circumstances and of good quality. Unfortunately, that confidence has been undermined by the growing commercialization of the health care system, which Arnold Relman, long-time editor of the prestigious *New England Journal of Medicine,* argues has replaced the professionalism that used to be a hallmark of physicians and leaders and medical institutions.[1] This trend, which began to grow in the 1970s, has been buttressed by the contemporary writings of economists who seem to have ignored Kenneth Arrow's insights about the ways in which the markets for health insurance and medical care differ from typical markets.[2] (I will have more to say about this in Chapter 7.) These developments have also been supported by a number of judicial decisions and the actions of the Federal Trade Commission, which removed long-standing obstacles to treating medical care as a market. One result is that the quest for more revenue has replaced the fiduciary responsibility in behalf of their patients that used to govern the actions of physicians, hospitals, and other providers of care.[3] Relman writes that "[m]any physicians in their office practice have become more focused on defending and enhancing their income than ever before, and their entrepreneurial behavior contributes to the growing influence of business incentives on medical costs."[4]

The main challenges facing the U.S. health care system have been grouped into three categories—access, cost, and quality—for more than thirty years, but I believe a fourth problem has developed more recently, partly as a result of the dynamics Relman describes. Our failure to solve these perennial health system problems is resulting, I believe, in the slow erosion of the vaunted U.S. health care delivery system itself, resulting in its inability to assure us that the confidence in it that we want is justified throughout the system. This phenomenon, if it can be documented, has implications both for our efforts as a society finally to reform the health care system and for our ability as patients to obtain good care when we need it.

As we saw in Chapter 3, the health care delivery system's quality problems have been well established for some time.[5] Why have we not made more progress in overcoming them? I believe a major part of the answer is system characteristics that not only contribute to creating the problems but also—perhaps more important—erect obstacles to solving them.

In this chapter, I have two main goals: (1) to explore the evidence pointing to delivery system erosion and to characterize its relation to the access, cost, and quality problems; and (2) to identify the built-in barriers to improvement and how they affect reform efforts.

We can start with a related question: Why has health care information technology (HIT) not transformed the health care system as proponents have been predicting for at least thirty years? Part of the answer is that not enough medical care organizations have adopted HIT for it to have produced system-wide effects.[6] But then, why have so few providers bought it even though studies suggest it could help to make them better doctors and perhaps give them a "competitive advantage" in our largely market-oriented system? Are they not interested in increasing the probability that they will choose the right diagnosis or treatment for their patients? Do they not care about "competitive advantage"? Are they driven more by short-term financial imperatives—such as avoiding unnecessary costs or bringing in revenues by attracting as many patients as possible and providing as many services as possible—than by the objective of offering their patients the best care they can?

Part of the explanation can be found in the power of incentives on individuals. Adam Smith argued that each individual pursuing his own interests "frequently promotes that of society more effectually than when he really intends to promote it."[7] Does that argument hold true in health care? Can we expect improved quality of care to result when providers of medical services pursue their own interests? After looking at the evidence, a colleague and I concluded several years ago that "the evidence to date offers little support for the view that competition among health plans improves quality to a substantial degree."[8]

The juxtaposition of these points suggests that, if we assume that provider organizations tend to follow their self-interest, their perceived self-interest apparently does not include investing seriously in either HIT or quality-enhancement methods, probably because it provides them no direct benefit—even though it may be good for their patients. If they are right, then to solve the quality problems requires identifying and removing the barriers to delivery-system improvement, including perhaps the absence of any compelling self-interest in doing so.

As we have seen, the growth of third-party payment beginning in the 1960s caused expenditures to rise to the point that the United States spends about 16 percent of GDP on health care.[9] That spending growth has led public- and private-sector payers to introduce numerous strategies to contain those expenditures, but without much success. Their efforts included restricting coverage and access to services, increasing employees' share of premiums and cost-sharing at the point of service, limiting payment rates to providers, offering to pay for second opinions prior to surgery, prior authorization requirements, and managed care. Yet even though some had the effect of limiting payments for certain services or to individual providers for a time, total spending has continued to grow at rates higher than those in most other countries.[10] Payers' efforts to limit spending put great pressure on providers, but ultimately they failed because providers and patients found ways to negate them. Under these conditions, it should not be surprising to learn that quality and safety problems, among others, have surfaced, at least partly as a result of provider and patient efforts to cope with the constraints being placed on them in the unsuccessful attempt to contain spending.

Why haven't their coping strategies led organizations to adopt the changes successfully introduced by the Institute for Healthcare Improvement (IHI) in parts of some facilities?[11] If they had done so, we would see results in the form of improved quality measures and reduced safety problems, as well as greater efficiency and more consistent effectiveness of the care provided. On the other hand, to the extent that causes of the problems and obstacles to diffusion of effective remedies are found in characteristics of the larger health care *system,* then *systemwide* interventions are needed before reliably good care can be expected throughout.

So to what extent does evidence support such a picture? Are systemic obstacles working against efforts aimed at improving the quality and safety of medical care in the United States? We turn to these questions next.

Setting the Stage: The Mission of the Health Care Delivery Subsystem

The mission of the health care delivery subsystem is to provide care that meets the clinical needs of individuals for preventive services, acute care, and the treatment of chronic conditions. Achieving the mission requires two conditions. First, services must meet contemporary standards of excellence that change with scientific developments. Practitioners must keep up their knowledge and skills, and the offices or organizations in which they work must be able both to adopt proven innovations and to support continued skill development of clinicians. To pay for these, they need revenues that exceed the expenses incurred in delivering services. Yet practice revenues have been under increasing pressure for some time. Two indicators of the financial constraints they face are that physicians' real income has declined in recent years[12] and hospitals' share of the health care dollar has dropped by 10 percentage points over the past twenty years.[13]

The second condition needed to achieve the health care delivery subsystem's mission is that individuals must have access to that good care. Care is expensive, incomes have been stagnant except at the very top of the income distribution, and most people need third-party coverage to pay for it. That is eroding, too. Further, providers must be willing and able to serve individuals for the payments and under the conditions set by the payers—which aim to limit their own expenditures. To the extent that patients lose the ability to pay for services, utilization tends to decrease and pressure on caregiver income increases still more. If the professionals and organizations that constitute the delivery subsystem do not keep up with developments, partly because patient access to services is reduced and their own income fails to keep up with costs, the care they provide no longer meets evolving standards, the system erodes, and it is less able to achieve its mission. Moreover, if they divert their energies from caregiving to other activities to make up for revenue shortfalls, their ability to provide excellent care may suffer still more.

Signs that are consistent with the view that the delivery subsystem as a whole is in trouble are becoming increasingly common. What follows next is a sampling. Although the number of these stories is small, I believe that they are not isolated, unconnected events, but indicators of systemic issues and that, if they continue to grow unabated, the delivery subsystem as a whole will continue to deteriorate.

The working assumption is that, if the problems are widespread and pervasive, the cause is in the system and therefore the solution must be at the system level as well. Relman believes they developed—or at least became much worse—because of the increasing commercialization of insurance and care. He may be right, but whatever the main culprit, the bottom-line conclusion is clear: even those people with health insurance cannot always count on the adequacy of the care they obtain—even if medical research has developed good tests and treatments for people with their conditions.

Examples Indicating Erosion of the Health Care Delivery Subsystem

This section contains a brief catalogue of some of those events and organizational policies that undermine the health care delivery subsystem. They are arranged into several key types (summarized in the following list), which will help to uncover and articulate a coherent story.

Preliminary List of Delivery System Problem Types

1. Erosion of providers' fiduciary responsibility to their patients
2. Failure to invest in innovations and adopt quality-enhancing activities
3. Quality deficits resulting from denial of care to nonpaying patients
4. Quality deficits resulting from inattention to detail and unresponsiveness
5. Quality deficits resulting from treatment delays caused by paperwork related to payment (that is, failure to put patient care ahead of administrative matters)
6. Insurance provisions that undermine provider ability to deliver quality care
7. Deterioration in health statistics (for example, increases in infant mortality)
8. Deterioration of care from hospital diversification to supplement inadequate income
9. Deterioration of quality as a result of conflicts of interest

EROSION OF PROVIDERS' FIDUCIARY RESPONSIBILITY TO THEIR PATIENTS

Providers continuing to treat patients who need more advanced care than they can offer in order to continue to generate needed income.   Much is known about what is needed to treat heart attacks when they occur, how quickly that treatment must be received, and the consequences of failing to obtain it in time. The *New York Times* reported that "people have only about an hour to get their arteries open during a heart attack if they are to avoid permanent heart damage. Yet, . . . fewer than 10 percent get to a hospital that fast."[14]

Another statement in the article was even more worrisome, however: most patients who do "reach the hospital quickly do not receive the optimal treatment [because] many American hospitals are not fully equipped to provide it but are reluctant to give up heart patients because they are so profitable."[15] Although we do not know the extent to which providers fail to refer patients to more appropriate sources of care—to the detriment of those patients—in order to retain income for themselves, the considerable financial pressure on both doctors and hospitals makes plausible the assumption that it is not an insignificant phenomenon.

Providing services in which the physician has invested. A firm offering "an expensive patented device for the treatment of back pain (list price $149,000)" made its machine available to physicians. It offered both sale and leasing arrangements, which the company asserted could increase practice income by "several hundred thousand dollars a year. Under the lease arrangement, the company will install and service the device without charge in exchange for a per-treatment fee from the doctor, who can then charge the patient's medical insurance enough to make a substantial profit. The company recommends a series of twenty or thirty treatments for each patient, . . . [for] a fee of $5,000 to $7,000 for each patient. . . . The company also provides marketing advice and materials designed to recruit new patients and generate referrals from other doctors." Although the Food and Drug Administration has approved the device as "safe and effective," it has not systematically compared this device with "the many other techniques" for treating back pain. "The company and the physician are in effect business partners in promoting the use of an expensive medical device that has not been adequately evaluated."[16] Under these conditions, how much confidence can a patient have in a physician's recommendation to use the device?

FAILURE TO INVEST IN INNOVATIONS AND ADOPT QUALITY-ENHANCING ACTIVITIES

Because of cuts in payment rates or failure of payment rates to keep up with costs, some provider organizations lack the income to either invest in new equipment that may improve quality and safety or adequately maintain existing equipment. Pressure on practice income may also increase when patients reduce their utilization because they lose or are forced to drop their employer-sponsored health insurance or because their cost-sharing amounts increased.

Some innovations result in entirely new services while others improve existing services. Recognizing the need for investment, the Medicare program "uses add-on payments to reimburse hospitals for using innovative clinical technologies."[17] For add-on payments to be used, the device or drug must be new and represent a substantial clinical improvement, and the current payment must be inadequate because costs exceed the diagnosis-related-group (DRG) payment[18] by a specified amount. Add-ons are used for two to three years, after which the costs are incorporated into the DRG payment. According to the American Hospital Association, however, by 2007 the Center for Medicare and Medicaid Services (CMS), the federal agency responsible for those two large public-sector payment programs, rejected most applications for add-on payments, having approved only seven new technologies for them. Moreover, "add-on payments do not reflect the majority of hospitals' costs when adopting new inpatient technologies."[19] Although Medicare used somewhat different payment mechanisms for outpatient services, the result was said to be the same: payments did not cover the cost of the innovations.

Especially in view of the enthusiastic promotion of information technology for health care (HIT) by many in both the private and public sectors, its slow spread is an unobtrusive measure of, among other things, the difficulty of paying for these expensive systems. The failure of clinical information technology applications to diffuse throughout the medical care system deprives clinicians and patients of an important tool for improving quality and reducing errors. Further, HIT may be an example of a larger class of available quality-enhancing innovations that care organizations decide not to adopt because of their cost.

In most other industries, technology often "directly improves productivity, generates savings and thus builds profitability for the entity that invested in the new technology."[20] In health care, by contrast, most of the benefits accrue to payers and patients. That is true of clinical innovations, and it is also part of the IT story: those who bear the substantial financial burden of installing, upgrading, and maintaining hardware and software do not benefit directly under present conditions. As a Maryland internist put it, "I can't capture the economics [sic] of scale as a sole practitioner. Electronic health records may well be a good thing, as a collective good, but why should I make the investment if I don't get any of the gains?"[21]

Another example of the failure to invest in improving quality is the fact that many physicians are no longer willing to attend continuing medical education (CME) programs. Facing reduced real income,[22] they may believe either they cannot afford to lose the income they would earn during the days spent at CME programs or they cannot afford the outlay for the course tuition,[23] travel, and other associated expenses. These results occur among practices that are under financial pressure resulting from the reduced income from third-party payments and the reduced number of patients, especially those who either lost their insurance or reduced their physician visits to avoid higher out-of-pocket expenses.

QUALITY DEFICITS RESULTING FROM DENIAL OF CARE
TO NONPAYING PATIENTS

Although national health care expenditures continue to rise at substantial rates, individual hospitals and physicians are under increasing financial pressure. Hospitals are in a particularly difficult position. Their emergency departments (EDs) are a vital community resource, providing not only the care needed by people suffering true emergencies—such as sudden heart attacks or serious auto accidents—but also the more routine services needed by the growing numbers of uninsured and others who can find no one else to treat them. EDs are expensive to operate because they must have the sophisticated equipment and highly trained staff needed for true emergencies, even though these may occur infrequently, as well as the capacity to serve what may be a much larger number of patients with less serious episodic needs. As a result, they can add to the financial burdens shouldered by hospitals, which have "less flexibility to respond to these pressures" than physicians do. Part of the reason is the requirement in the Emergency Medical Treatment and Active Labor Act (EMTALA) that hospitals provide emergency care to patients "around the clock, regardless of the ability to pay, and to maintain access to physician services to support that care."[24] Neither physicians nor the ambulatory facilities they may own are subject to those provisions. On the other hand, since physicians, too, are under financial pressure, many are less willing than they once may have been to help hospitals meet their EMTALA obligations by staffing those emergency departments, especially as volunteers. Moreover, these financial pressures contribute to reduced physician willingness to spend time on charity care in general. Given the growing numbers of uninsured and increased strain on free-care funds where they exist, this example raises the question of the extent to which financial pressures are keeping hospitals and others from serving the growing numbers of patients who cannot pay for the care they need.[25]

QUALITY DEFICITS RESULTING FROM INATTENTION TO
DETAIL AND UNRESPONSIVENESS

Donald Berwick's frightening description of his wife's experience as a patient in several renowned teaching hospitals[26] is a particularly graphic example of a subset of such stories: quality problems that occur to family members of physicians who are knowledgeable enough to recognize they are occurring but who, even though experts themselves with a direct stake in the outcome, find practitioners and the "system" unresponsive.

In December 1999, Berwick, a national leader in the quality measurement and quality improvement movement, told the story of six hospitalizations for a total of sixty inpatient days over a six-month period that his wife had spent in three of the best hospitals in the country. As he put it, "In early

March, Ann competed in a 28-kilometer cross-country ski race in Alaska. Two months later, she couldn't walk across our bedroom. . . . [S]he gradually experienced increasing pain, lost the ability to walk, and became essentially bed-ridden." Although she has substantially recovered by now, "[f]or most of that time, nobody could tell us what exactly was happening or what her prognosis was." The mysterious nature of her illness was not the main issue, however. Rather, it was the care she received in the attempt to diagnose and treat it.

Medication errors "were not rare; they were the norm." Medications were regularly brought to his wife even after her physicians had cancelled orders for them. In other cases, drugs that physicians ordered "to start immediately" did not come for two-and-a-half days.

"As far as I know, the only person who ever drew a graph of Ann's fevers or white blood cell counts was me, and the data were so complex and crossed so many settings that, short of a graph, no rational interpretation was possible. As a result, physicians often reached erroneous conclusions, such as assuming that Ann had improved after a specific treatment when, in fact, she had improved before it, or not at all. The experience of patienthood, or patient-spousehood, as the case may be, was often one of trying to get the attention of decision-makers to correct their impressions or their assumptions. Sociologically, this proved very tough, as we felt time and again our migration to the edge of the label 'difficult patient.'"

"On at least three occasions, Ann waited alone for over an hour, cold and frightened on a gurney in the waiting area outside an MRI unit in a sub-basement in the middle of the night."

"Times of transition of responsibility, such as the first of the month, were especially trying. On one such 'first of the month,' the new senior attending physician walked into Ann's room, cheerfully introduced himself, and asked, 'So how long have you had MS?' Ann doesn't have MS."

"One after another, caregivers told us of their own distress. The occupational therapist apologized for cutting back Ann's treatment, explaining that 17 OTs had been laid off the week before. The doctors told us about insurance forms and fights for needed hospital days. The nurses complained that the transport service never came."

"And the bills were astounding." Although, fortunately, their insurance covered them, he wrote, "I cannot reconcile what happened with the fees. The doctor discontinued one of the drugs on the first day of a 14-day hospitalization, but a nurse brought it every day of that stay." And the bill included "[p]ill by pill charges for all the days on which the nurse opened the unneeded packet and threw it in the garbage." He estimated that of the care his wife received, "billed at perhaps $150,000 so far, . . . a remarkably small percentage—half at best, probably much less—stood any chance at all of helping her. The rest has been pure waste."

As the patient's husband, he reported, "I am deeply, deeply grateful for the people, and I respect the institutions a great deal." And, then, as a quality-improvement leader, he continued, "But we have so much left to do. We are causing harm, and we need to stop it." Many individuals in those hospitals were kind, empathetic, and technically expert, but the system in which they worked fails many patients. As Berwick concluded, if all this occurred "in our best institutions, I wonder more than ever before what the average must be like."

QUALITY DEFICITS RESULTING FROM TREATMENT DELAYS CAUSED BY PAPERWORK RELATED TO PAYMENT

First, fill out the forms!   *Health Affairs,* a leading health policy journal, occasionally publishes personal narratives of experiences that health professionals or members of their families had as patients in the health care delivery system. They often describe the staff's preoccupation with how people will pay for services before even determining what the patient's health care needs are. One such story was recounted by a health economist who, while picking up something from his daughter's school, noticed a workman who came out of a house across the street and had trouble getting into his van. The author wrote "he appeared to be having a heart attack right there." He ran to the man, grabbed his keys, lifted him into the passenger seat, and drove his van to a nearby "prestigious academic hospital." There he left the van in front, "half-walked, half-dragged" the man into the emergency department, put him into a chair, and went to the desk, where he told the receptionist that he thought the man was dying. Instead of responding to the obvious urgency of the situation, the clerk began to ask ordinary intake questions, including his name, social security number, and how he planned to pay for his care. The only way the good Samaritan could get her to focus on the patient was by saying "loudly enough for everyone in the waiting room to hear, 'Lady, if you let him die here, you're going to be the second person to die in this emergency room this afternoon!'" This particular story had a happy ending—the man got appropriate care in time to save his life.[27] What we don't know is whether the clerk was a particularly insensitive young woman, or whether no one in the management of the unnamed institution trained her to recognize people in obvious distress and behave accordingly. Regardless, this is a dramatic example of a common occurrence in which clerical personnel keep patients from care until the requisite forms are filled out.

Cash before chemotherapy.   Hospital bad debts are a growing problem. "Uncompensated care cost the hospital industry $31.2 billion in 2006, up 44 percent from $21.6 billion in 2000."[28] This is a serious problem for patients and hospitals alike. It is driven by the growing number of Americans who are uninsured or underinsured and cannot pay for the services they use.

To cope with this problem, apparently a substantial number of hospitals—14 percent in a 2006 survey by the Internal Revenue Service—are insisting that patients pay cash before agreeing to admit them or to provide expensive services. Those tactics have, apparently, reduced the bad debt problem, at least for those institutions, though it is still a widespread phenomenon. What is not clear is the extent to which that result has been achieved because people have been able to come up with the cash or because they have been denied needed care.

But the situation is even more complicated than that. Some of the hospitals that are taking this hard-nosed approach and denying services to sick people who are underinsured and without the necessary cash are not only not-for-profit institutions but facilities that operate well into the black. One such institution is the M. D. Anderson Cancer Center in Houston, one of the nation's leading cancer institutions and a part of the University of Texas system.[29] In 2006, it refused to admit a Texas woman with leukemia until she paid $105,000. Though she had been in good health, when she left her job she bought insurance because "you never know what's going to happen." But the coverage she bought in the nongroup market was a "limited-benefit plan" provided by the AARP and underwritten by United Health Group, one of the largest sellers of such plans. Her insurance was limited to an amount that was about 30 percent of the hospital's expected charge, so the hospital refused to accept it. The woman brought a certified check for $45,000, as requested, and had some tests; but before admitting her, hospital staff "demanded" another $60,000. Eventually, after much wrangling, she was admitted that day as a result of an "override." In subsequent months, she had to provide additional large sums of cash in order to get treatment. In one case, "nurses would not change the chemotherapy bag in her pump until her husband made a new payment. She says she sat for an hour hooked up to a pump that beeped that it was out of medicine, until he returned with proof of payment." Although her insurer reimbursed them almost $40,000, the woman and her husband paid many more thousands of dollars by borrowing funds from a retirement trust and suffered countless indignities in the process. Yet they were among the fortunate ones who had resources they could draw on.

The hospital says it acted appropriately in this case because "she wasn't indigent, but underinsured."[30] While that is a matter of debate—Uwe Reinhardt, a health care economist at Princeton, said that a not-for-profit institution with net income of $310 million and a substantial endowment "shouldn't behave this way"—the real issue is that the system permits this to happen. The woman had been insured through her job until she left it three years earlier to care for her ailing mother. Her husband was retired. Because they were no longer connected to a job—one that had provided coverage—they did not have adequate insurance. She developed cancer and lived near one of the great cancer centers in the world. Yet she was subjected to repeated indignities in order to get care that, in any other developed country in the world, would have been provided without any of these hassles. The bottom line is that no matter how good a place M. D. Anderson is clinically, it did not provide optimal care to this Texas woman. The question the story raises is, Is this the kind of health care system in which we want to be treated? How do we know when we choose an insurance policy—whether one offered by our employer or one bought in the nongroup market—that it will be accepted by the hospital in which we seek care next year or the year after?

Summary of progress after five years.   An article about progress made in the first five years following publication of the IOM report[31] on quality summed up the authors' serious concerns. In it Leape and Berwick write that "the groundwork for improving safety has been laid these past 5 years but progress is frustratingly slow . . . and the barriers are formidable."[32] They ask, "Why has it proved so difficult to implement the practices and policies needed to deliver safe patient care? Why are so many physicians not actively involved in patient safety efforts?" They attribute much of the blame to complexity, professional fragmentation, individualism ("the culture of medicine"), hierarchical authority structures, and diffuse accountability. Their description of forces in the medical care system that make it difficult to ensure a high level of quality nationally suggest these follow-up questions: What countervailing forces can be adopted to overcome these systemic obstacles? What will it take to implement those forces *throughout the system?* Much of the rest of this book is an attempt to answer these questions.

INSURANCE PROVISIONS THAT UNDERMINE PROVIDER ABILITY TO DELIVER QUALITY CARE

Coverage of prescription drugs.   Insurers are placing limits on coverage of prescription drugs in order to earn more and to keep from raising premiums (or to limit the amount of increases). They have taken these steps as a result of both their desire to keep their costs (and therefore their premiums) down and the high prices charged by drug companies to finance their attempts to bring to market an unending supply of "blockbuster" drugs and to add to their bottom line.

In one example, a physician prescribes a particular dosage of a drug presumably to meet the needs of his or her patient. The insurer approves a dose which is less than the doctor ordered, and asserts to the patient that it is the "recommended" dosage. By that action the insurer's pharmacy benefits manager (PBM) interposes itself between the doctor and patient. An unintended consequence of doing so is to undermine the patient's confidence in her physician, whose judgment has been challenged by a computer in a different state.

The way it works is that an employer or insurer contracts with a distant PBM to monitor the use of prescription drugs by covered patients and to offer people with chronic conditions the option to actually obtain the drugs by mail from the PBM instead of from the neighborhood pharmacy. The PBM does two things to encourage the patient to accept the opportunity: it offers a ninety-day supply instead of the thirty-day supply patients can typically obtain from their neighborhood pharmacy, and a reduced co-payment, since the prescription needs to be filled only once instead of three times during that period. When the patient uses his local pharmacy as the dispenser of the drugs rather than the PBM, the pharmacist must get authorization from the PBM using the computer. Sometimes she must actually talk to a PBM representative on the phone to try to override a computer's denial.

Another example is the practice of some insurers to cover a sixty-day supply of a drug prescribed for a ninety-day period (or fifteen pills instead of a full month's supply of thirty). The patient may still be able to get the rest of the dosage, but at much greater out-of-pocket cost. Quality of care may be compromised when patients who cannot afford the uncovered portion cut their use of the medication in order to stretch their supply for the full ninety (or thirty) days. Alternatively, they may take the doctor-recommended amount for the first sixty days, stop, and after ninety days, refill the prescription.

Yet another PBM example: a patient was given two prescriptions by his physician for prostate problems. When the pharmacist entered them into the computer for approval, Medco, the PBM used by the patient's insurer, agreed to pay for one but not the other, saying the physician would need to submit a justification for it. After five weeks and several resubmissions of the physician's original request, approval was finally granted. Then the patient received a letter informing him that the request had been approved. The letter indicated that the "Date of Request" was February 20, 2008, at 2:44 P.M. and that the "Date of Decision" was February 23, 2008. In reality, the first request was submitted on the same day the prescription was issued and approval was granted for one drug but denied for the other—one day short of *five weeks earlier.* Since, like many drugs, the compound in this case takes weeks to achieve its effect, quality was reduced, and the only "benefit" is that the insurer saved the cost of about five weeks' worth of capsules. These examples also raise the question of what benefits, if any, the additional costs associated with inserting a PBM between a patient and his neighborhood pharmacy really produce.

Assuming that the physician is competent and knows what the individual patient needs, then this kind of regulation—by private insurers, not the government—may reduce quality in three ways: the effectiveness of the drugs is diminished, the physician loses control of patient care to the insurance company, and the patient's confidence in his doctor is undermined because the insurer refers to the approved dosage as "recommended," implying that the physician does not know as much as the insurer or PBM.

Despite the point just made, I should note that another justification often advanced for the role of the PBM in examples like these is to improve quality of care. The assumption is that the PBM's computers have more complete and accurate information to help physicians choose appropriate drugs. Among other things, they may include data about drugs' effects, recommended dosages, and interactions with other drugs. Undoubtedly, there is some truth in the view that ordinary community-based physicians can have trouble keeping up with the latest research on drugs. On the other hand, when physicians' own computers connect them to reliable, Web-based drug information sites, this justification for PBMs will disappear. Some physicians—especially those who are part of large integrated systems, some of which are affiliated with academic medical centers—already have that kind of accessibility, but the PBMs do not differentiate between them and the isolated solo practitioner.

Insurance coverage for university students.   A different kind of insurance-reduces-quality story was recounted by a physician who wrote about his niece, a graduate student who purchased health insurance from her university.[33] It turned out that when she went to her primary doctor about a growth that developed on her leg, she was referred to a surgeon to have it removed and was urged to have an MRI before the surgery. Because of limitations in the policy, however, the student insurance only covered $1,000 in x-rays in a year, so the MRI would have cost her about $2,000 out-of-pocket. The surgery itself cost only $200 after insurance. Since she had been advised that the growth was probably benign and she had limited funds, she opted to have the procedure without getting the MRI. It turned out, however, that below the fatty tumor on her leg the surgeon discovered "a big bloody mass . . . the size of my fist," which he also removed and sent to a lab for analysis. The report that came back identified the second mass as "a synovial sarcoma, a rare, aggressive, malignant tumor." The young graduate student had a second surgery to produce "clean margins" as well as radiation and "quarterly MRI scans and physician visits, for at least the next two years, then every six months after that" to monitor her condition against the possibility of metastasis to the lungs, which probably would have been fatal. Although she seemed to be doing well at the time the article describing her story appeared, several points are of concern. One is that limitations in the coverage caused her to focus on the substantial out-of-pocket cost of the MRI instead of its potential benefits (even though at the time of the decision no one knew of the existence of the second mass or that it was malignant). As a result, she declined the MRI, which not only would have revealed the second mass, but would have provided guidance to the surgeon as to the cancerous margins and thus avoided the need for the second surgery. A second point is that, as she went through the early months of the care process, knowing she was accumulating large medical bills, she could not get answers from her insurance company as to what bills would be covered by her policy and for how much. She called and talked to company representatives but they would not or could not give her answers. So at the same time she worried about the possible recurrence of her cancer—she had been told if it did recur, it would likely be fatal—she had to worry about how she would pay for the care. She considered filing for personal bankruptcy and giving up her graduate studies in order to take a job that would provide the cash to pay the bills. In addition, if she survived, she worried that future insurance coverage might either be hard to get or have exclusions for her preexisting condition. In the end, with help from her expert physician-uncle, she was able to get her share of the cost down to about $3,500, which she paid off in monthly installments.

DETERIORATION IN HEALTH STATISTICS

A front-page *New York Times* story on April 22, 2007, reported increasing infant mortality rates in the southern United States after many years of declining rates.[34] Because the trend was observed in six states, it could not be attributed to factors peculiar to a single one. One contributor was thought to be lack of prenatal care, which either was not available for many at-risk women or, though available, was not accessible because of financial ineligibility or other factors that kept them from taking advantage of the services. Prenatal care, especially for at-risk women, is one of the services most likely to produce clinical benefit. Yet enough women encountered decisive obstacles to its use that a measurable increase in infant mortality was registered in six states!

DETERIORATION OF CARE FROM HOSPITAL DIVERSIFICATION TO SUPPLEMENT INADEQUATE INCOME

Some hospitals that have been unable to earn as much income as they think they need have "diversified" into other areas to add to their revenues. Many justify these efforts as necessary in order to be able to continue to achieve their primary mission of providing needed medical services to patients. However, these activities may have the additional effect of diverting resources (people, space, energy, equipment, money) from care to other activities.

For example, some academic medical centers have created lucrative organizations to operate drug trials. Not only may these activities divert resources from their primary missions of education, research, and direct patient care, but to the extent they give clinicians or the institution a stake in a particular drug or protocol or pharmaceutical company, they may also compromise the care their patients receive.

Non-academic practices have a growing role in clinical trials as well, largely mediated by the drug companies. A multidoctor practice often assigns the youngest, most recently trained member to be the liaison. The practice gets paid for each patient recruited to the trial, the patient gets free medications, and the drug company gets larger numbers of patients. Some groups make a specialty of it and advertise in local newspapers or on local radio stations for subjects.

In this context, a medical professor, Richard Deyo, put it this way in the *New York Times:* "More people are interested in getting on the gravy train than on stopping the gravy train."[35] Indeed, these relationships between drug and device firms, on the one hand, and physician-scientists and the hospitals where they work, as well as community-based physician practices, on the other, are examples of the commercialization of the medical care system that Arnold Relman decries with such passion.

DETERIORATION IN QUALITY AS A RESULT OF CONFLICTS OF INTEREST

Physician ownership of medical facilities.   A recent trend has seen the creation of about 140 physician-owned specialty hospitals.[36] Proponents argue that these facilities are able to provide exceptional quality by concentrating on only a limited number of procedures and developing expertise in them. Critics such as Senator Charles Grassley of Iowa, however, believe that "decision-making is more likely to be driven by financial interest rather than patient interest." Among other things, the physician-owners, in their role as clinicians, are thought to "cherry pick" the patients they send to their own hospital. They are especially likely to choose those with good private insurance and to refer others to nearby general hospitals where, incidentally, they may also have operating privileges.

The *New York Times* reported two examples of patients kept in small specialty hospitals overnight following surgery after which they developed complications. Because no physician was on duty, and the facilities were exempted from provisions of EMTALA, the federal law that requires full-service hospitals to provide emergency care, in each case, staff called 911 for an ambulance to take the patient to a full-service hospital in the area. Both patients died. An investment in emergency services—facilities, equipment, and personnel—would represent a major, perhaps impossible, financial commitment by a small, fourteen-bed specialty institution. It may not be justified on efficiency grounds since, chances are, it would not be needed often. The point is, however, that things can go wrong unexpectedly no matter how expert the physician or how sophisticated the institution. In such a situation, whose interest should prevail when a need for emergency care arises: that of the patients, whose interest is nothing less than their lives, or that of the facility, which, for economic reasons, does not have the capacity to deal with it? To put the question differently: knowing these stories, would you want to have cardiac surgery in a small specialty facility with no capacity to respond to complications or in a general hospital with a fully staffed emergency room?

Medical research. A related issue is represented by the conflicts of interest that have surfaced involving medical researchers. In the space of little more than a week, three different articles appeared in the *New York Times* about conflicts of interest related to scientific trials of drugs and medical devices. One reported that a study of 240 patients with lower back pain revealed that an artificial spinal disk "worked much better than conventional surgery in which patients' vertebrae were fused."[37] The problem is that the "well-known spine specialist" who was one of the study's lead researchers had a financial stake in the company that made the artificial disk. Moreover, so did doctors at about half of the seventeen research centers involved in the study. That stake gave them an interest in finding a positive outcome that competed with their interest in doing good research. It also raised doubts about which interest was paramount and whether the reported results were valid.

Another example of the same phenomenon involves a "world-renowned Harvard child psychiatrist" who "earned at least $1.6 million in consulting fees from drug makers from 2000 to 2007. . . ."[38] Two of his colleagues earned similar amounts. Moreover, none of them reported these payments, which came to light only as the result of an investigation led by Senator Grassley of Iowa. The work of the physician involved, Dr. Joseph Biederman, "helped to fuel a controversial 40-fold increase from 1994 to 2003 in the diagnosis of pediatric bipolar disorder which is characterized by severe mood swings, and a rapid rise in the use of antipsychotic medicines in children."

Similar stories have implicated researchers at other leading universities. Not surprisingly, the researchers claim that the money taken from firms with a stake in the outcome of their studies did not influence their research. Dr. Biederman's statement was typical: "My interests are solely in the advancement of medical treatment through rigorous and objective study." The problem is, having an equity interest in a company that produces the drug being studied or taking large fees to promote a company's drugs *creates* conflicts of interest. This is because the scientist in question now has two interests:

one is in the quality of the research and the other is in earning the drug or device company's money. When the physician has two interests, we can never be sure which one is primary at any given time. Indeed, the physicians themselves may not know. What is even more disturbing is that, in virtually all cases, the researchers failed to recognize the existence of the conflict. To illustrate the nature of the conflict: when the results of a study are inconclusive, the investigator may present them in the most positive light or, worse, may withhold some of the findings that cast doubt on the preferred outcome. Journal editors may have trouble even knowing when the potential for such a problem exists.

The issue is not whether the research is scientifically sound. It is often very difficult to tell from a published article how the samples of patients were chosen, how similar the experimental and control groups were, or whether other factors could have been controlled in the data analysis. The real question is whether or not a reader—including a practicing physician who might be influenced by the articles to prescribe the drug or use the device for his own patients—can have confidence in the conclusions of the study. Another *Times* article showed that "a prominent diabetes expert" had greater loyalty to the drug company than to the medical journal for which he reviewed an article. Papers being considered for publication and communications about them with the editors are supposed to be kept confidential. In this case, however, the University of Texas physician leaked to the drug company the article he reviewed, which had raised questions about the safety of the firm's diabetes drug.

A physician commentary in *The New England Journal of Medicine* put the issue this way: "Although for-profit companies' primary responsibility is to their shareholders, and physicians' primary responsibility is to their patients, doctors can collaborate with industry to improve patient care. . . . These relationships, however, can influence prescribing behavior and the use of medical devices and supplies, increase the cost of care, create a mind-set of entitlement among doctors, and undermine the independence and integrity of the profession."[39] That it is happening so often suggests it has become a characteristic of the health care system that compromises physicians' commitment to patients.

Sharing research data and related issues.   One of the cardinal rules of academic research is that the data on which research reports are based must be made available to other researchers so that they may either attempt to validate the original findings or carry them forward. In another recent essay in the *Times,* a statistician who designs and analyzes cancer studies reported that he had asked another cancer researcher for the raw data from a trial the researcher had recently published.[40] He was denied the data because the other researcher thought new analyses might "cast doubt" on the original results. The author wrote that "given the enormous physical, emotional and financial toll of cancer, one might expect researchers to promote the free and open exchange of information." Patients volunteer for cancer trials, after all, but instead of treating the data they provide as in the public domain, "cancer researchers typically treat it as their personal property." And this occurs even when the studies are paid for with public money.

Still another recent article reported that drug makers routinely draft papers that appear in prestigious medical journals under the names of respected academic physician-scientists. Even if the named author does some editing of the paper, the practice calls into question the credibility of the research reports.[41]

Together these stories not only raise doubts about the validity of the studies being reported but also undermine confidence in patient care. If physician-scientists in the most prestigious academic medical centers have a substantial financial interest in drug and device companies on whose products they conduct clinical trials, how can patients in those institutions have confidence in the care choices made by those same doctors and the colleagues they persuaded to use the tested drug or device? And how can other doctors reading those articles have confidence in the recommendations for their patients? The conflicts multiply when it is recognized that some of these same institutions have themselves—as institutions—created thriving businesses to run clinical trials.

Continuing medical education.   The "transformation of continuing medical education (CME) into an enterprise for drug marketing" may have undermined its integrity.[42] It is reported that drug industry financing of CME has nearly quadrupled in less than ten years, and half of all CME courses are now paid for by drug companies. Moreover, there is evidence that speakers in such programs tend to emphasize the sponsoring drug company's products over those of competitors and to downplay side effects and other risks. Under such circumstances, it is reasonable to infer that the quality of CME has degraded since the days when universities and medical associations produced most of the courses.

The Importance of These Questions

The issues raised by the preceding examples are important for several reasons: one is that they represent responses of various groups in the delivery system to the conditions they encounter in the contemporary practice of medicine. And those responses undermine the system's ability to provide us with the care that we need and want. This discussion revealed signs that the health care delivery system is less robust and less reliable than it should be and many believe it used to be and that, as a result, it is less able to meet the needs of its patients.

Another reason is that, if the problem is as widespread as it appears and if the trends are downward, then the situation they reveal provides a compelling reason all by itself for reforming the health care system. Otherwise, when we finally do solve the access, cost, and quality problems that students of the health care system have described for many years, the delivery subsystem may be so damaged that it will need to be rebuilt so that we can all benefit from the reforms.

Two further questions follow from this last point: Is the insurance system the culprit? That is, do the problems arise from the responses of providers to conditions they find in the health insurance system? Would the trends reverse if health insurance were universal and stable? And, if so, would that be enough, or is universal coverage a necessary but not sufficient condition to produce and sustain the desired changes in behavior? Does the coverage need to have particular features in order to correct the problems?

The second question is, even if the insurance system is not the main *cause* of the problems (but, rather, poor training, carelessness, and lax standards are), can those causes be fixed without changing the insurance system? In other words, do conditions in the present system work against organizations' making serious efforts to improve? Does the insurance system need to be changed in order to introduce more effective incentives or other inducements or "nudges" for patients, providers, and others to act in ways that are more beneficial?[43] We know that even under present conditions, some hospitals, physician practices, and other care organizations *do* introduce improvements, but what is less certain is why *they* choose to do so and so many others do not. What will it take to make implementation of improvements the general case among provider organizations? What can be done to improve the system as a whole enough to justify an average patient's confidence that, in a typical medical encounter, he or she will benefit from the care received without accident or error?

Conclusion

In the past three chapters, I have presented data demonstrating the existence of problems in the U.S. health care system that cannot be denied. In the next chapter, I will begin to discuss what, if anything, we should do about them and why.

The principal challenge is to understand why these problems occur, because a strategy to overcome them can succeed only if it is designed to attack the causes. Otherwise, we may do little more than reduce the most egregious effects—at least for some people and for a short time. We turn next to that effort.

Part Two

Solutions

Chapter 5

Why the Problems Need to Be
Solved and the Goals of Reform

WE HAVE BIG PROBLEMS in the U.S. health care sector. But that recognition is not the same as saying that we must make a concerted, focused effort to solve them. After all, other sectors of the economy occasionally run into trouble too. For example, the U.S. automobile industry over the years has faced big challenges, first from Europe, then from Asia. Many people were losing jobs, and the economies of whole states suffered. Yet until the catastrophic economy-wide debacle in the fall of 2008, and with the notable exception of Chrysler in the 1980s, Washington was not tempted—and few suggested it—to bail out the auto industry.

Over the years, the steel industry, the textile industry, and others also have faced such challenges. In the fall of 2008, massive problems in the finance sector spilled over into other areas. Companies could not borrow the cash they needed to operate; consumers could not borrow to buy homes, cars, and other big-ticket items; many Americans lost jobs and homes; large numbers of companies disappeared—financial problems on this scale had not been seen since the Great Depression. Times were so unusual that even a conservative Republican administration proposed large-scale government intervention, a measure of how remarkable the situation had become.

Normally, economic difficulties affected companies one at a time. Some had the political clout to induce the Congress to impose tariffs on foreign imports of competing products. Doing so, they argued, would, among other things, give the affected industry time to adjust so that it could compete more effectively with foreign firms. One successful example—notable because it was an exception to the general rule—occurred after the American motorcycle maker Harley-Davidson lost substantial market share in the early 1960s when the Japanese firm Honda introduced lighter, more versatile motorcycles into a market that previously Harley had had largely to itself. Having made several unsuccessful attempts at recovery, the company persuaded the Congress in 1983 to increase the tariff on imported cycles to 45 percent (up from 4 percent) for a period of five years. With a combination of improved product design; restored confidence in product quality; and an innovative, multipronged promotional campaign, Harley-Davidson recovered so successfully and so quickly that it asked the Congress to remove the tariff in late 1986, more than a year early.[1] But usually, companies either succeed in overcoming competitive challenges on their own—that is, they adapt, innovate, change in various ways, emerging stronger in the process— or they succumb and disappear as individual companies. Life goes on. The economy as a whole continues to expand. Workers get new jobs. Capital finds new investments.

So why not let organizations in the health sector—insurers, hospitals, physician group practices, among others—continue to muddle through? Innovating as they can to adapt to new challenges, some will become more efficient and more productive and will provide consistent high-quality care. Others that do not adapt successfully will disappear. In fact, recent years have seen changes. Hospitals have diversified, greatly expanding outpatient services, including ambulatory surgery. One result is that hospital inpatients as a group now tend to be sicker than in years past. In fact, inpatient services, once the defining characteristic of hospitals along with their emergency departments, now represent a smaller portion of their activity. In addition, the 1980s saw the substantial growth of for-profit chains of hospitals. Further, during this period, many hospitals have closed or merged, and some have bought physician practices, partly in an effort to secure needed referrals.

For their part, physician practices have grown in size, with many practices including physicians of several specialties. The insurance sector, too, has seen the emergence of new products, such as preferred provider arrangements and managed care, and a massive wave of consolidation.[2]

Yet while these changes may have benefited individual organizations and groups, the fact is that the health system as a whole continues to embody the problems described in Chapters 2, 3, and 4.

Why Health System Problems Cannot Be Ignored

The reasons for intervention in the health care system are numerous. First, nothing has worked. Over the past thirty years or more, spending has continued to increase at rates greater than inflation, the rolls of uninsured have continued to grow, and quality problems have continued to multiply. Private initiatives, undertaken on a company-by-company basis, have targeted discrete aspects of the health insurance problems. One example is that insurers agreed to pay for second opinions for patients for whom surgery was recommended in the hope of reducing the incidence of unneeded surgeries.[3] Later they introduced requirements that patients get prior authorization before paying for certain services. Again, because the assumption was that some services were being provided unnecessarily, perhaps so a doctor or hospital could earn additional fees, insurers insisted on examining certain physician recommendations before agreeing to pay for them.[4]

A variant of this mechanism was the development of a new type of organization, the pharmacy benefit management companies introduced in Chapter 4 to "manage" use of prescription drugs. These large national firms were expected to save money in two ways. First, given their volume and supposed efficiency, they were able to charge less for prescriptions they filled, which they did by mail, often for three months at a time. Typically, they offered lower co-payments as an inducement to patients to use their services instead of the neighborhood pharmacy. Second, they scrutinized the doctors' orders and, in some cases, refused to pay for prescribed medications on the grounds that either another, less expensive drug was more appropriate or the drug was unnecessary altogether to treat the patient's condition. Often, however, they would reverse their decisions if the patients' doctor took the time to write a persuasive appeal.

The managed care movement was still another attempt to save money. Here the idea was to change the incentives that economists argued encouraged physicians to provide services of marginal value in order to generate additional fees. By paying a health plan on the basis of the number of people it enrolled[5] instead of fees for the services provided and by limiting the number of approved providers, who preferably worked only for a single plan, managed care organizations (MCOs) would retain more income if they could find ways to induce physicians to spend less on services provided or ordered.[6] In other words, managed care realigned the incentives to facilitate and support the provision of good care without waste. Not only would MCOs gain financially by being both effective and efficient, but also they had the means to transform medical practice to do so. The model on which the "health maintenance" movement was based was the Kaiser Permanente plan on the West Coast.[7]

Yet although the growth of managed care in the early and middle 1990s coincided with a period in which the growth in health care expenditures slowed somewhat, it is not at all clear that the reason for the slowdown was that managed care plans had found reliable ways to control utilization without sacrificing quality. Moreover, such a conclusion is doubtful, given that one of the selling points for the most popular plans during that growth period was that patients could retain their doctors, who would continue to be paid fees for the services they provided. In other words, managed care's dramatic growth occurred after two of its most distinctive characteristics—prepayment and a limited group of dedicated providers—were discarded.

Public-sector initiatives, too, had little if any effect. An early example grew out of the Experimental Medical Care Review Organizations experiments in the early 1970s, which reviewed recommendations for care with the goal of reducing unnecessary services. Although originally introduced as demonstrations in several states, the concept was later embodied in the Professional Standards Review Organizations and Peer Review Organizations, which the federal government required each state to establish.[8]

Almost from the beginning of the Medicaid program, states paid physicians reduced fees for treating Medicaid-eligible patients. And then they refused to increase the fees to keep pace with either inflation or the fees paid by other third parties, including Medicare. The most direct effect was to drive large numbers of office-based private physicians from the program.[9] In state after state, doctors protected themselves from losing money by refusing to treat Medicaid patients because, they argued, it cost them more to provide care than the state paid. Yet state Medicaid expenditures continued to grow, in part because eligible patients who could no longer visit relatively low-cost private physician offices got the care they needed in hospital emergency departments—at much greater expense.

So despite many attempts—some of which, such as second opinions for surgery, were supported by evaluation research—the experience of the past provides no reason for optimism that similar efforts will work now.

In addition to the fact that past innovations have failed to have an impact on the system as a whole, a second reason for intervention is that failure to rein in the costs of care and expenditures for services used leads, inexorably, to higher prices for insurance. Employers that continue to offer coverage to their employees put themselves at a disadvantage vis-a-vis their international competitors. Others drop insurance altogether or increase premiums and cost-sharing, which in turn leads individual employees to either drop their coverage, too, or forgo services they should use. As a result, those decisions reduce the numbers of Americans with insurance coverage and increase the out-of-pocket costs to those lucky enough to retain it. In this context, a medical care system with great doctors and other well-trained clinicians, great hospitals, innovative surgical techniques, new medical devices, and more powerful medications is unsustainable because fewer and fewer people will be able to pay for them. Moreover, as a result of these trends, hospitals and other medical organizations, as well as individual providers, have fewer insured patients providing the income they need to maintain or sharpen their abilities or obtain new equipment or modernize their physical plant. Ironically, it may turn out that the only people left who have insurance are those healthy enough that their premiums can be low and thus affordable, but who don't get sick often enough to provide the revenues that provider organizations need to survive.

One might think that, if increasing proportions of the population do not have good (or any) health insurance and therefore cut down on the medical care they use, expenditures would be reduced. In fact, however, those left without coverage may tend to reduce their use of routine care, but they do use services when they cannot avoid them. In that event, they tend to go to sources—especially hospital emergency departments—that, though more expensive, cost them less out of pocket. Finally, in a fee-for-service system, providers tend to provide more services of uncertain value to the insured in order to compensate both for reduced aggregate utilization and lower prices paid by insurers.[10]

Third, our rates of uninsurance, which already are highest in the developed world, mean that more Americans get sick than need to, many who are sick do not get the care they need to help them get better, and many with chronic conditions continue to decline instead of being able to cope with their condition and remain productive. Not only are many not getting the benefits of the great innovations in American medicine, but those who do increasingly are the privileged among us. Partly as a result, disparities between the various segments of our one society are growing. Thus the top 1 percent of households had 21.8 percent of pre-tax income in 2005 compared to only 8.9 percent in 1976. And since 1979, the change in after-tax income for the top fifth of households grew by 69 percent while that for the middle fifth grew by only 21 percent.[11]

The importance of differences like these was highlighted by Arthur Okun, an economist, who wrote in the 1970s of the inherent conflict between equality and efficiency in American society. He noted that the American democracy as a political system depends on equality before the law and at the ballot box, while a capitalist economy thrives because of the promise of great rewards for creative people who work hard and succeed—that is, it promotes inequality.[12] The rewards that successful entrepreneurs earn create greater wealth for them, as intended, but if those lower on the income scale have too little, the degree of equality needed to nourish the democracy may be diminished to the point that the vitality of the political system is threatened. The idea is not that everyone should have exactly what everyone else has, but that everyone should have an equal chance to compete for—and achieve—the benefits offered by a capitalist economy. Also, the gap between those at the upper and lower ends of the income scale should be narrow enough not only for the two groups to understand that they share much, but also for those in the lower half who are so inclined to reasonably aspire to improve their lot. The growing disparities in health insurance, which make access to appropriate health care unavailable to more and more Americans, are a powerful indicator that the ties that bind us together are weakening.

Fourth, apart from the practical effects identified in the first two points above and the normative ones, in the third, the fact is that we can do better. The health care system we now have does not represent our best in any sense—many get good care, but many get none despite their need; many clinical professionals are trained well enough to provide good care, but many of the organizations or systems they work in inadvertently undermine their ability to do so; and too much of what determines whether we get the care we need depends on how much money or what type of insurance we have. That is not the United States that embodies the ideals we learn in school to admire and which we were taught as students to continue to perfect. Indeed, most other developed countries, even those with a lot less wealth, do much better on virtually all health-related measures.

Finally—perhaps this should come first—is a two-part reason: first, health is central to life and to all the important activities that people must engage in for the society to function most effectively. And second, medical care can support health, if not ensure it, by helping to prevent illness, cure illness, and make chronic conditions manageable so that people can continue to function at reasonably high levels. Therefore it is in our collective interest to maximize the benefits of modern medicine for both individuals and the society.

Being in our interest and within our grasp, it can also be argued it becomes our responsibility to make the health care system as good as it can be.

So there are good reasons for attempting to solve the health system problems. To put the argument a different way: How would we justify *not* doing what it takes to *solve* the problems with our health care system? Do we really want a system in which patient access to needed—perhaps even life-saving—services is determined not by their medical conditions but by their ability to show a provider's clerical staff that they have an acceptable means to pay for them?

Certainly, providers of medical care need to earn "enough," but—apart from the ethics of the situation[13]—making access to the services they offer depend on the patient's demonstrated ability to pay affects everyone in predictable but not always desirable ways.

It reduces access to care—many have no coverage or other means to pay for services. Growing numbers who had coverage in the past no longer do and, if trends continue, still more will lose coverage in the future. For some the coverage may not pay for the services they need. Some with coverage may not be able to prove it to the clerk's satisfaction (if, for example, they left home without an insurance card, and the insurer's 800 number cannot verify coverage because it is overloaded and does not answer). And still others may have coverage that some providers will not accept. (The latter has long been a fact of life for Medicaid patients.[14] It is becoming a larger issue for elderly and disabled Medicare patients and even for patients covered by some private insurers.)

Since fewer patients will have coverage, providers will earn less income and, perhaps just to cover their costs, will need to charge more to patients who *do* continue to have coverage. That will increase premiums and cost-sharing and, eventually, reduce still further the number of privately insured people. Ultimately, the care subsystem itself will shrink, fewer services will be available, and the only ones able to access them will be those with enough cash to pay for them. Indeed, although insurance is not likely to disappear altogether, it will become too expensive for growing numbers of employers and their employees to afford, and the group of employers who might be willing to continue to offer or obtain it won't be large enough or diverse enough to spread the risk effectively. And since the rich will be able to pay for most of the services they use out of their own resources, they will tend increasingly to buy coverage with high deductibles, contributing lower premiums to the pool of funds used to pay for care, if indeed they buy any coverage at all.

Given these observations, the fact that spending on health care is so high and growing so fast means that failure to solve these problems will make the good that the medical care system *can* do largely irrelevant for more and more Americans because they and their employers will be unable to continue to pay for insurance. As a result, the numbers of people with no access to good medical care will grow even more. The companies that employ them will not be as productive as international competitors in countries where health insurance and medical care are seen as social goods that benefit the society and the national economy, not as commodities to be purchased in the marketplace by those who can. And without the income that insurance expenditures provide to hospitals, doctors, nursing homes, and other caregivers, more and more of those professionals and health care institutions will be threatened with going out of business.

It is a vicious cycle and perhaps the best evidence, despite commentators who decry our "nonsystem," that we really do have a health care *system* in the sense that the parts are inextricably linked and interdependent. The failure of health insurance threatens the delivery subsystem itself.

For all these reasons, therefore, the problems *need* to be solved—not just for the benefit of individuals who struggle with personal health challenges they cannot overcome on their own, but also for the society as a whole and its economy. Yet even though so many Americans have said for years that they were unhappy with the health care system and wanted to see it changed dramatically, one of the main obstacles to reform in the past has been fear on the part of people *with* insurance—who are more likely to be voters than those without insurance—that any *new* system would be worse for *them* than the present one. So as long as they expected the health care system to continue to serve them—even if they acknowledged that, as a whole, it had problems—they were afraid to support actual reforms.

Given recent developments and current trends, however, no one can be confident that the good coverage he or she had in the past will continue into the indefinite future or that the medical care professionals and institutions that served them well in the past will continue to be able to do so. As a result, confidence that the system will continue to serve them well is misplaced. That is, even those with good coverage should worry about their continued ability to access the care they will need in the future. The health care system they have used with such assurance in the past is in jeopardy. So in addition to the importance of health to life and the ability of medical care to improve health in so many ways—which, for many people, would be enough reason to reform the system—the fact is that the system is in danger of being unable to serve even the majority of the population who still have some form of third-party coverage.

Having established that the U.S. health care system has numerous—and serious—problems and that we need *finally* to solve them, we need to take some additional preliminary steps before putting forth a plan for reform. We need, first, to articulate the end state we would like to reach as a result of the reform effort so that we know what we want to accomplish. And then, second, we also need to figure out whether we can address either of the two main problems—cost containment and deteriorating access to both coverage and care—separately. That is, can we attack one and then, having succeeded at that, turn attention to the other? We take up these two questions next.

What Reform Should Accomplish

This is what I believe the well-functioning health care system should be like following reform: everyone should have access to the care they need to keep them healthy, return them to health, or help them manage their chronic conditions. Sufficient services should be available and distributed throughout the society in such a way that everyone can actually obtain the care they need. Further, those services should be of reliably good quality. The system should avoid any features that discourage people from seeking appropriate care from the most appropriate source at the most appropriate time. At the same time, it should avoid other features that encourage providers to reject some patients or discourage them from providing the care they believe those patients really need. Patients should get services that benefit them, but not services that do not. And, finally, providers should not only be efficient in the delivery of those services so that we don't waste money, but also be knowledgeable enough to provide the best care (which may result in less spending than it does now) and organized so that the care we receive from all our providers is coordinated.

To reach this end state, we need to achieve the following:

1. Everyone must have financial access to the health care they need through comprehensive health insurance.

2. Everyone should have access to a personal primary care physician and early access to needed care.

3. The appropriate provider should be the key decision maker, along with the patient, in a system that maximizes the opportunities for coordination and teamwork among caregivers, and in which neither provider nor patient achieves additional material benefit from providing or obtaining less or more than is needed.

4. Costs—from insurance premiums, cost-sharing, and utilization— must be kept under control.

5. System-generated obstacles to good-quality, safe care—including the ready availability of electronically generated, clinically useful information—must be eliminated.[15]

Other formulations of the desired end state have been offered by thoughtful observers, including The Commonwealth Fund Commission on a High Performance Health System.[16] No matter what solution is ultimately adopted, however, it will not serve us in perpetuity. Rather, it will need adjustments because conditions change over time and whatever works now and for the near future will work less well as the years pass. Medicare provides a good example. In 1965, when it became law, the biggest problem for the elderly was coverage for acute care, especially in hospitals. They were more likely to need those services than the rest of the population simply by virtue of their age, and Medicare was designed to protect them against the costs of that care, thus enabling them to have access to what they needed. By 2008, the health issue that differentiates the elderly from other groups is the presence of chronic conditions. So a program that protected them well—and still does—against the financial risk of needing acute care services is no longer adequate because it does not provide good protection against the financial implications of care for chronic conditions. What was good public policy in 1965 now requires adjustments. The needs of its beneficiaries have changed, and medical professionals can do a lot more to treat chronic conditions now than they could in the mid-1960s.

Nonetheless, if we are serious about actually *solving* today's problems, we need to recognize that the rising cost of care and the large numbers of uninsured are two components of the same problem and need to be attacked together. Some argue that we can—indeed, must—solve one first and only then take on the other. I disagree and explain why next.

The Affordability of Care

Some characterize the health policy debates as a contest between those who consider that the main challenge is to provide universal coverage because 16 percent of Americans have no health insurance and those who believe that cost containment is the primary problem.[17] The latter group tends to believe that if costs can be brought down, people will be able to afford to buy coverage from private insurers, their preferred solution.

In fact, however, the real challenge can be characterized as *the affordability of health care,* a single issue with two parts—containing the cost of care and guaranteeing that everyone has health insurance—both of which must be dealt with together (even if they are implemented or phased-in on different schedules) because neither can be solved alone. Moreover, there is evidence that this is how a growing number of Americans see the issue. A recent Kaiser Family Foundation poll showed that early in the 2008 election year the economy became the issue that most voters wanted the presidential candidates to talk about.[18] It replaced Iraq as the predominant issue and appeared to demote "health care" from a close second to a more distant third place. As surveyors probed, however, they discovered that, in fact, one of the most serious effects of "recent changes in the economy" experienced by respondent families was "problems paying for health care and health insurance." It was virtually indistinguishable from the numbers who had "problems getting a good-paying job or a raise in pay."

Indeed, the two parts of "affordability" are linked, not just by the public but also by logic. *High health care spending* drives up the price of health insurance. When that coverage comes from employment, it means that fewer firms can afford to offer comprehensive family coverage and fewer people can take up the coverage even when offered by their employers. When that coverage comes from government programs such as Medicare and Medicaid, eligibility for which is established by law and regulation, managers of the programs adjust in ways that either effectively reduce benefits or, in the case of Medicaid, make it harder to qualify for coverage. So unless health care spending in the United States, already the highest in the world, comes down, fewer people will have coverage and the exclusions in the insurance policies they do have will reduce their value.

Having *comprehensive health insurance coverage* is the other part of the affordability equation. Insurance spreads the financial risk of covered events (here, the use of services) over all who are insured. Rates are kept affordable because, while some people will need a lot of services, others will not need much at all. In other words, the healthy subsidize the sick. For insurance to work, therefore, a lot of healthy people need to sign up. What they get out of the deal is peace of mind in the event, unlikely though it may be, that they, too, need care—for example, if they are hit by a car driven by an uninsured drunk who runs a red light. The probability might not be high, but *if* it happens, the cost will be large. And no one wants to have the adequacy of treatment in that situation determined by how good his or her insurance is or, worse, by whether or not he or she has it at all.

So to keep the price of coverage affordable, the risk pools need to grow, not shrink, and to include lots of healthy people. And if the denominator reflecting the size of the risk pool is not both large and diverse enough to include lots of healthy people, then utilization *rates* will be high, the next year's premiums will rise to cover them, and fewer companies and individuals will be able to afford it.

Expenditures link to coverage and access in another way as well, as a result of the peculiar reality of the U.S. health insurance market. Instead of having one huge risk pool, we have many smaller ones, typically organized company by company. Private insurers compete in the market trying to sell policies to firms, each of which seeks coverage for its employees, which often number under one hundred. Moreover, those competing health insurance companies deliberately segment the market, trying to cover disproportionate numbers of healthy people who will not need much care and thus will not require them to pay many bills.[19] In that way, insurers can offer an employer premiums that are low enough for them to be chosen as the company's carrier. Indeed, that is the way many markets work—sellers offer their products or services at lower prices than their competitors in order to attract more business. To offer low prices, they want to keep down their costs. Because health insurance costs are determined largely by the utilization of services, the key to low premiums in an employment-based, competitive market is low utilization rates. And the most reliable way for insurers to have low utilization rates is to enroll healthy people, a proxy for which is age (since young, employed adults tend to use few services).

For a society, a problem arises because of the people who do *not* fall into a favored market segment. They include workers in well-established manufacturing industries in the rust belt of the upper Midwest whose members tend to be older and in need of more care than the younger, better educated workforces in Silicon Valley startups. Since, as they age, folks in startups too are likely to need more—as well as more expensive—services, the premiums to cover their expected higher spending naturally will grow. Indeed, for many firms, they grow to levels that are unaffordable—so, as we saw earlier, some companies drop coverage while others increase employees' share of the premium and cost-sharing provisions. And for some employees, their higher share becomes unaffordable. So the ranks of the uninsured grow.

But it does not end there. Back at the companies with younger, healthier workforces, what rates do insurers set? It turns out that they set prices not simply to cover the estimated payout for care (plus profit) but also in relation to the prices charged by competitors. They might go to a firm with a young workforce and say, "Since your workers are young and do not use many services, there is no reason for you to pay the higher rates charged by our competitors for covering more diverse groups. We will charge you only $x per member per month." And they set that $x at a level high enough to cover anticipated costs and low enough to differentiate themselves from their competitors. They might reduce it still further, but why be satisfied with a lower profit? So they set it just enough below the level of competitors to make themselves the favored bidder. This phenomenon was described many years ago as the practice of "snuggling under" the rate set by higher-cost competitors.[20]

The final piece of the puzzle is represented by the public-sector programs, such as Medicare and Medicaid, that cover special populations. In the case of Medicare, these are the elderly and disabled—both of which are expected to use many services simply because of their age or because their eligibility is actually determined by their need for care (that is, by their status as "disabled"). In the case of Medicaid, they are the poor and, by a quirk of history, many are residents of nursing homes. Many studies show that the poor tend to be less healthy than more well-to-do people and therefore can be expected to need relatively higher rates of service.[21] Since Medicaid eligibility is determined largely by low income, and an individual may qualify by "spending down" a certain amount of an otherwise higher income on covered medical services, state Medicaid programs tend to enroll large numbers of people with rather great need for services (although, for a variety of reasons we will review later in this chapter, some do not use all the services they really need). As the years passed, the spend-down provision has come to affect large numbers of older people who have required the services of nursing homes. So even though they may enter the home paying for care out of their own pocket, many become eligible for Medicaid after they have spent a certain amount of their own money over a specified period of time (usually eighteen months). Although need varies even within those groups at higher risk of needing care, it tends to be at a higher level of expenditure. The result of all this is that Medicare and Medicaid will always tend to be expensive because they cover people with greater-than-average need for services.

The bottom line is that everyone pays more. The firms with older workers pay more because their risk pools have larger numbers of high users of service. The firms with younger workers pay less than those firms if they continue to offer coverage, but more than they would if insurers were satisfied with lower profits. The workers pay a higher share of premiums if their employers offer coverage and they can afford their share. And public programs have higher expenditure rates because they tend to be defined by the characteristics of their clientele, who tend to need high rates of service.

Thus, although the reform task will be more difficult as a result, it is unrealistic to think that we can solve the cost problem first and then expect that the coverage problem either will take care of itself (because prices will be lower and most people will be able to afford coverage) or will be smaller and therefore more manageable. Similarly, it is unrealistic to think we can solve the coverage problem and then expect costs to come down enough to sustain a program of covering everyone. The reason is that, although we call it a "cost" problem, it is really "spending" that is the difficulty, and spending is determined primarily by utilization. So if utilization rates go up—and they would because insurance lowers the price of care to the user—indeed, that is the intent—expenditures, too, would go up. The trick is to keep that increase manageable by increasing services used early in an illness episode—they tend to be less costly and often keep illness from escalating so that additional, more expensive care will not be needed—and by reducing the amount of unneeded care provided. We also must pay attention to the methods and rates of pay for providers because they influence provider willingness to furnish the needed care. In our present system, one way that providers cope with lower payment rates is by providing services of only marginal value in order to earn additional fees. In other words, when a provider concerned about low payment rates is not sure about the benefit of a particular service, he or she may be tempted to provide it anyway because the patient is covered and, in the process, the provider earns another fee.

For all these reasons, we should define the problem as *the affordability of needed care* and recognize that its solution has two components that need to be tackled together—bringing down the high rates of spending on services and ensuring coverage for everyone.

Utilization Drives Expenditures

Implicit in the previous section is the defining importance of the *utilization of services*. It is the key driving force resulting in most of the problems discussed in Chapters 2 and 3, and redirecting it is the key to the new outcomes we want to produce. Appropriate utilization confers the benefits of medical science on individual patients. Access problems that cause suboptimal utilization patterns result in the need to catch up or repair the damage. Those suboptimal patterns tend to result in higher per capita expenditures than would be required if people were able to avail themselves of services early in an illness episode. Utilization also provides income to physicians, hospitals, and other providers and revenues to medical device and pharmaceutical companies. And, of course, it results in expenditures incurred by private insurers, Medicare, and Medicaid.

Because the driver of expenditures is utilization of services—appropriate care provided in the most appropriate site by the most appropriate professional as well as care that, for one reason or another, is not optimal by that definition—that must be the primary target of reform. We must eliminate those factors that deter people from seeking beneficial services or from using ones that are recommended. We must also rid the system of factors that discourage physicians, hospitals, and others from providing useful services or encourage them to provide ones that are of marginal value (or less).

To accomplish those goals, we need to understand the factors that determine whether a person uses medical services and, if so, which services and when. Fortunately, many years ago Ronald Andersen, a former colleague at the University of Chicago, now at UCLA, developed a framework that helps us to accomplish that important task.

He identified three groups of factors to be considered in sequence.[22] First, a set of *predisposing* characteristics that, as the term suggests, affects the probability that a person will need services. Some of those characteristics, which are immutable, include age, gender, and race and ethnicity. It is not that all old people need services and all young people don't, but a typical person who is seventy is *more likely* to use services and to use more services than a typical twenty-year-old, simply because of the difference in their ages. Similarly, women between twenty and forty are more likely to need obstetrical services than fifty-year-old women because of their age, and men, because of their gender, will never need those services (have zero probability). It is also true that use of services is higher among some racial and ethnic groups than others and, though race and ethnicity are immutable, other characteristics that also influence use of services (such as education levels and income) may change and thus alter the probability that people of particular racial or ethnic groups would use services.

Predisposing conditions that affect the probability of utilization but that can change (are mutable) include education, occupation, general health care beliefs and attitudes, and knowledge of health care information. A person who is part of an ethnic group that, for whatever reason, has had little experience with modern medicine may not use services because he or she does not understand the potential benefits of care or the clinical symptoms for which it might be useful. Julie Salamon offers an example about the role of a modern hospital. Maimonides Medical Center in Brooklyn serves a polyglot area with many foreign-born residents, and new Chinese immigrants were the fastest-growing segment of the local population. While a typical American-born person living in a big city with a television set, not to mention a college degree, is likely to know about the role of a modern hospital as a place where sick people can get better, that is not always the case with residents of that same city who come from other cultures. Salamon tells a story that illustrates the point. Hospital staff wondered why so few Chinese people were using their services. After some exploration, they figured out that because white is the mark of death in Chinese culture, the white blankets used in the emergency rooms were keeping Chinese people away. The word spread in the community that the hospital was the place to go to die, not a place to obtain treatment to cure serious illness. Taking knowledge of this cultural predisposition into account, staff neutralized it by ordering new beige blankets for the entire hospital.[23]

Even those who are more likely to use services do not do so willy-nilly. Two other conditions need to be present. Thus the second set of Andersen's factors affecting access to care is *enabling* conditions. These make it *possible* for a person who is predisposed to use services to do so. A well-educated employee may have a higher predisposition because he knows what medical care can do for him, but may not be able to use it because his company's insurance policy is too expensive for him to purchase. Among others, enabling conditions include factors that affect a person's ability to pay for care. Family income is an obvious one. People with high incomes are better able to pay for services than people below the poverty line. Similarly, the type and extent of third-party coverage, *if any,* also affects the ability to pay and, even more, so do the terms and conditions under which insurance payments will be made. So, for example, if an insurance plan requires that a patient obtain needed care through a specified network of providers, then care received from even well-trained, licensed practitioners who are outside that network may not be covered. Plans that require a patient to be referred to a specialist by her primary care physician may not pay for covered specialty services in the absence of such a referral. Some plans require that people working for the insurer, perhaps in another city or even in another country, approve some services before they are rendered in order for them to be covered. And the rates that the insurer pays may affect the willingness of physicians and other providers to treat the patient unless the patient can guarantee payment. (She might, later, be able to get partial reimbursement from the insurer.) Finally, those people with no insurance at all are less likely to use services—even when they know they could benefit—because they cannot come up with the cash to pay for them. So they are likely to avoid using services or at least to delay until their condition makes it impossible for them to continue to do so. Recall the Orozcos from Chapter 2.

Finally, the probability that people with the income or insurance to access services actually do use them is also affected by where they live and the availability of appropriate care nearby. Or, to put it in the negative, by the difficulty of finding appropriate providers and the difficulty of getting to them. The fact is that physicians, hospitals, and other health care personnel and facilities are not distributed uniformly throughout the nation.

Because decisions to seek or provide care are made by individuals in the thousands of cities and towns throughout America, it is worth taking a minute to examine trends in the availability of services nationally. It turns out that they, too, help explain expenditure trends. What has happened to the numbers of physicians and hospitals, for example, in the past thirty years?

Tables 5.1 and 5.2 reveal several important points about the distribution of practicing physicians. For one, their number has increased dramatically since 1975 in both absolute numbers and in numbers per 10,000 population. That means more doctors should be available when people need them. But it also means a lot more doctors needed enough patients to serve (both to fill their time and to generate the income they needed) in 2005 than in 1975. So, for both reasons, the increased number of doctors undoubtedly contributes to the growth in utilization and expenditures.

TABLE 5.1

Trends in numbers of physicians in nonfederal patient care,* 1975–2005

	1975	1985	1995	2005
Primary Care Physicians				
General and family practice	46,347	53,862	59,932	74,999
Internal medicine	28,188	52,712	72,612	107,028
Pediatrics	12,687	22,392	33,890	51,854
Total Primary Care Physicians	87,222	128,966	166,434	233,881
Specialists	200,615	302,561	397,640	484,592
Specialists as % of MDs and DOs in nonfederal patient care	69.7%	70.1%	70.5%	67.4%
Total physicians in nonfederal patient care	287,837	431,527	564,074	718,473
Physicians in nonfederal patient care per 10,000 civilian population	15.3	20.7	24.2	26.9

*Includes medical doctors and doctors of osteopathy.

SOURCE: National Center for Health Statistics, *Health, United States, 2007* (Hyattsville, MD: NCHS, 2007).

TABLE 5.2

Geographic distribution of physicians in patient care,* 2005

Region	Patient Care Physicians/10,000 pop.
New England (CT, ME, MA, NH, RI, VT)	37.5
Middle Atlantic (NJ, NY, PA)	35.0
East North Central (IL, IN, MI, OH, WI)	26.6
West North Central (IA, KS, MN, MO, NE, ND, SD)	25.0
South Atlantic (DE, DC, FL, GA, MD, NC, SC, VA, WV)	26.7
East South Central (AL, KY, MS TN)	22.8
West South Central (AR, LA, OK, TX)	21.8
Mountain (AZ, CO, ID, MT, NM, NV, UT, WY)	22.8
Pacific (AK, CA, HA, OR, WA)	26.0
United States	26.9

*Excludes doctors of osteopathy.

SOURCE: National Center for Health Statistics, *Health, United States, 2007* (Hyattsville, MD: NCHS, 2007).

Although the supply of physician services has increased substantially, Table 5.2 shows us that they are not distributed evenly throughout the country, which means that people living in some states are much more likely to be able to access a physician than those living in other states. While the number of patient care physicians per 10,000 population for the nation as a whole is 26.9, the ratios in New England and the Mid-Atlantic states are about 10 physicians per 10,000 higher than that figure, and in the southern and mountain states, about 5 physicians per 10,000 below it. If we looked at data for individual states, we would see even more variation both between the states and within them. Residents of urban areas, for example, are likely to find more physicians available to serve them than their rural neighbors.

Perhaps even more important than the numbers and the geographic distribution is the fact that throughout the period, more than two-thirds of those physicians have been specialists, who earn higher fees than primary care physicians even when they provide similar services. This generalist-specialist mix is an important reason for the frequent complaints of a shortage of primary care physicians in the United States. Other developed countries tend to have at least as many primary care physicians as specialists.[24] The distribution in those countries reflects a two-part view: first, that patients should have easy access to first-contact care, saving specialists for situations in which their expertise is needed to diagnose or treat conditions that are beyond the experience of primary care physicians. And second, that patients do not really need specialists' expertise in most cases.

In the 1970s, Walsh McDermott described a secondary effect of the peculiar U.S. distribution, which he called the "hidden system of general care." These were primary care services provided by specialists that patients receive "as a sort of dividend for their once having received some other kind of care." McDermott wrote that one of the reasons specialists continued to respond to primary care needs was "because it is just plain easier to speed the patient on his way . . . by *solving* his problem than by *referring* it" (emphasis in original).[25] But the fact is these specialists were able to become the primary care physicians for those patients because they did not have enough demand for true specialty services to keep them busy.[26] Subsequent research showed that such specialist-provided primary care was still part of the picture twenty years later.[27] A study of Medicare patients in Washington state found that about 15 percent saw only specialists during the two study years, 1994 and 1995. Moreover, the care provided met at least some of the characteristics of primary care in that it was continuous, was reasonably comprehensive, and included some preventive services. Medical Outcomes Study research-ers showed "that at least some specialists used more resources than gen-eral internists and family physicians, indicating that even when adjusted for patient mix, the care they provide is more expensive."[28]

When we look at trends in hospital services, a very different picture emerges (Table 5.3). The availability of both nonfederal community hospi-tals and hospital beds declined substantially in the thirty years between 1975 and 2005. Part of that reduction was the result of technological advances that made it possible to provide many services to outpatients that previously could be provided only to hospital inpatients—including brain surgery. In fact, the nature of the hospital has changed in that period from an institu-tion known primarily for complex emergency services and inpatient care, much of which was related to surgery. Indeed, while tradition leads us to report data on numbers of hospitals, their bed capacity, and occupancy rates, a strong case can be made that those figures no longer provide an adequate picture of hospital sector capacity and use. While hospitals still have—and the public needs—inpatient beds and the ability to provide inpatient ser-vices, most hospitals have diversified to the point that much of their clinical activity—not to mention their income—occurs in outpatient clinics.

It is worth noting that not only did the number of hospitals and beds decline by 15 to 16 percent in that period, but the number of beds per 1,000 population also fell. Even with the decline of inpatient capacity, occupancy rates—that is, the extent to which the hospitals' remaining beds are filled throughout the year—also dropped by almost 8 percentage points to less than 70 percent. Although the reduction in hospitals can be seen across the board, the rate of decline is somewhat higher among the smallest hospitals, which is a proxy for small-town hospitals. Perhaps surprisingly, the largest

TABLE 5.3

Trends in numbers of nonfederal community hospitals,
beds, and occupancy rates, selected years, 1975–2005

	1975	1980	1990	1995	2000	2005	Percent Change 1975–2005
Capacity							
Number	5,875	5,830	5,384	5,194	4,915	4,936	−16.0%
Beds	941,844	988,387	927,360	872,736	823,560	802,311	−14.8%
Beds/1,000	4.36	4.34	3.71	3.27	2.92	2.70	−1.66/1000
Occ. Rate	75	75.6	66.8	62.8	63.9	67.3	−7.7 pctage. pts.
Ownership							
Nonprofit	3,339	3,322	3,191	3,092	3,003	2,958	−11.4%
For profit	775	730	749	752	749	868	12.0%
St-local gov.	1,761	1,778	1,444	1,350	1,163	1,110	−37.0%
Size							
6–99 beds	2,935	2,750	2,424	2,339	2,253	2,403	−18.1%
100–499	2,649	2,763	2,675	2,591	2,415	2,289	−13.6%
500 or more	291	317	285	264	247	244	−16.2%
Population (000)	215,973	227,726	250,132	266,557	282,430	296,940	

SOURCE: National Center for Health Statistics, *Health, United States, 2007* (Hyattsville, MD: NCHS, 2007). Population figures are from U.S. Census Bureau, *Statistical Abstract of the United States: 2008* (Washington, DC: U.S. Census Bureau, 2008).

facilities declined almost as much as the smallest. That trend, accounted for largely by big-city teaching hospitals, probably masks the fact that some of those institutions did not close but reduced the number of their beds, placing them now in the next smaller category, as they diversified into more lucrative outpatient services.

One might think that the reduction in use of inpatient services, which invariably are expensive, would have led to reduced spending. In fact, however, spending has not fallen, in part because acuity of illness is higher now for hospital inpatients and therefore the care they need is more advanced and more expensive. In addition, the volume of outpatient services has increased dramatically (Table 5.4). And, not surprisingly, the prices hospitals charged are higher than the same services provided by community-based physician practices because hospital overhead costs are spread over all hospital services.

Before leaving the subject of ambulatory care, it is worth calling attention to several additional points. First, although not shown in the table, total ambulatory visits increased from 861,000 in 1995 to 1,123,000 in 2006.[29] That

TABLE 5.4

Age-adjusted physician visits per 100 persons, 1995–2006

Location	1995	2000	2003	2006
All places	334	374	391	380
Physician offices	271	304	317	305
Hospital outpatient depts. (OPDs)	26	31	33	35
Hospital emergency depts. (ERs)	37	40	40	41

SOURCE: National Center for Health Statistics, Health, United States, 2008 (Hyattsville, MD, 2008), Table 94, pp. 375–377.

30 percent increase is accounted for in part by the increase in population. But second, the 14 percent increase in the *rate* per 100 persons between 1995 and 2006 (an additional forty-six visits per 100 in eleven years) should be juxtaposed against increases in the numbers of physicians and decreases in the number and bed-capacity of hospitals. Third, while the number of total visits per 100 dropped 3 percent between 2003 and 2006, the numbers in hospital OPDs and ERs continued to grow (6 percent and 2.5 percent, respectively) (Table 5.4). The latter suggests at least some substitution of hospital-based ambulatory care for that provided in doctors' offices and helps to explain the increased rates of hospital spending.

So while numbers of key personnel have grown in the aggregate, people living in a large city with many doctors in primary care and many specialties are likely to have more to choose from than people living in small towns or rural areas. Moreover, even if they have trouble paying for the care, they are more likely to be able to access services, for example, in a federally qualified Community Health Center. And beyond primary care, people living in the same cities as medical schools and academic medical centers have available more and better care to treat their cancer or their heart condition than people living in small towns or rural areas. They may also have better access to hospital emergency departments, which, though expensive, have become a principal source of first-contact care for people with no other alternatives, as we saw earlier. Although those facilities may have trouble covering their costs with paying patients, they depend on the patients who appear at the emergency department to provide some of the supervised clinical experience that medical students, interns, and residents need to complete their clinical training. Given these data, it may seem counterintuitive that, even if they have insurance, urban residents sometimes have difficulty accessing services because their preferred physician has no opening for several weeks.[30] Residents of medium-sized cities, small towns, and rural areas, too, are likely to have difficulty accessing the care they need but for a different reason: there simply are fewer providers of those services near where they live or work.

The third set of factors that affect access to care and the use of services is *need*. Andersen and his colleagues describe two types of need. One is the need for care as *perceived* by the would-be patient. Many of us wake up in the morning after a night of fitful sleep with headaches or stomach aches or feeling feverish. When we do, some will recognize symptoms they have had before and that, in the past, have disappeared on their own—usually following rest, a healthy intake of fluids, and the proverbial "chicken soup." Those people know they are "under the weather" but do not call their family doctor because, reasonably, they believe she cannot do much more than a day or two of rest can do for them. Sometimes, however, they do not get better in a couple of days, by which time they define their problem differently and do call the doctor.

Others, perhaps because they cannot afford to lose a day's income by staying home from work, will try to "tough it out" and go to work anyway. If their symptoms occur on a Friday and they make it through the day without getting sicker, perhaps, for them, the weekend will provide the chance to take care of themselves with rest and fluids, and they will be better by Monday. If, on the other hand, their symptoms occur early in the week and they get worse instead of better, then, like it or not, they may decide not only to miss work but to seek care. By then, they may be sicker and need more aggressive medical intervention than they would have if they had been able to take care of the problem early. By that time, they perceive that they cannot avoid going to a doctor, whether she is their family doctor in a private office or another one in a hospital emergency department.

When the doctor examines the patient and performs whatever tests are relevant given the patient's symptoms, the patient's need is *evaluated* by a professional, Andersen's second type of need. That cannot happen, of course, until the individual actually becomes a patient, having perceived he has a need and called or visited the doctor. Mark Pauly, the University of Pennsylvania health economist, many years ago advised us that, at bottom, the reason we go to a doctor is for expertise.[31] The doctor has it; patients usually don't. And, having determined what the patient's ailment is, the doctor is able to prescribe a course of treatment to reverse it or, where warranted, to refer the patient to a specialist who is better able to do that.

Obviously, there are other scenarios. A patient has tightness in the chest that does not clear up for a week even though he took some over-the-counter medication he saw advertised on television. He perceived a need for the medication and treated himself. But then, if his condition does not improve, he calls his doctor. A woman discovers a lump in her breast and calls a doctor to check it out. A young person is playing ball and hurts himself, but toughs it out, waits a week before calling a doctor and, following tests, discovers the pain he has been having in his foot is from a broken bone.

The Andersen formulation shows us, first, that many factors determine whether a person uses services in the most appropriate, most beneficial way. Some are characteristics of the person—predisposing factors and symptoms; others—enabling factors—are characteristics of the environment or community in which the person lives or more personal ones that affect how easy it is to access services; and the most proximate factors are the patient's need—first, as he or she perceives it (which may be affected by the difficulty of accessing services) and then, as the professional clinician evaluates it. Some factors cannot be changed; others can.

The framework, second, can provide a guide to understanding the vast amounts of research that have been done on the related questions of access to and utilization of health care services. So it can help us not only to demonstrate that the individual patient examples found in earlier chapters are more than just anecdotes but also to understand what about them must change in order to produce more appropriate utilization patterns and better clinical outcomes. It shows us that the stories put a human face on a well-documented aggregate picture of dysfunctional utilization patterns. Those patterns include large deficits, especially of primary care utilization, among the uninsured and increasingly among those with insurance, as well; widespread delays (because of high out-of-pocket costs and geographically dispersed services); and even *over*-utilization of some services (perhaps as doctors try to compensate for their reduced income resulting from lower utilization rates and reduced insurance payments). Finally, it helps us explain the *origins* of the well-documented problems so that we can know how to deal with them.

Much of our focus has been on the insurance system, an enabling condition, and it too affects utilization in multiple ways. Obviously, and most directly, it affects an individual's ability to pay for care, and therefore the probability that he or she will seek services when they can be of benefit. But also, in the aggregate, it affects the providers' ability to survive economically and therefore the distribution of available services. In turn, it affects the ability of patients, even those with good coverage, to access care. So insurance influences utilization in both directions—by affecting the ability of individuals to pay for it and, as a result, the willingness of professional clinicians and organizational providers alike to furnish care, in part because of their desire to remain financially viable. This helps us to understand the decisions made by both groups when insurance does not do what they need it to do.

Conclusion

In this chapter, I have argued that we cannot afford to ignore the problems described earlier and instead must not only tackle but this time really solve them. Then I described an end state that we should try to reach through reform; that is, a health care system that would provide all of us with justifiable confidence that we are able to get good care when we need it. I also showed that the problems of high spending and inadequate access need to be attacked together because both affect the affordability of care. And finally, I argued that what we really need to change are the utilization decisions made by patients and their providers of care. It is those decisions that provide the benefits of modern medicine to patients, income to professional and institutional providers of care, and revenues to medical device and pharmaceutical companies. So to change the unsatisfying outcomes on those dimensions, we need to find ways to induce people to make better decisions. To do that we need to understand why people are making poor decisions now. Then strategies can be designed to change the conditions that cause them to make those unfortunate choices. We turn to that question in the next chapter.

Chapter 6

What Caused These Problems, and How Can We Attack Them?

HAVING ESTABLISHED that the U.S. health care system has numerous and serious problems and that we need *finally* to solve them, the natural question to ask is, What caused the problems? To put it another way, while we usually think of high rates of uninsurance and runaway expenditures as the main problems, in this context, we should see them as the *results* of other causes. If we want to change the outcomes, we need to identify the underlying causes because they are what we need to overcome. Otherwise, we run the risk of solving only part of the problem or of doing little more than making some of the health system's parts worse even if other parts temporarily appear to be better. For example, if we try to solve the uninsurance part of the problem without also tackling the high rates of spending on care, we may create for ourselves a system in which everyone is "covered" but the only affordable coverage leaves out so much or requires such high out-of-pocket payments that too many still will be unable to access the care they need. In other words, we may solve the "uninsurance" part of the problem by creating a new generation of *under*insured.

It Is the Incentives, Stupid

The first thing to notice is that the problems that I have described are really the aggregate result of millions of separate decisions made by individuals acting either for their own benefit (for example, in their roles as patients or doctors in solo practice) or as representatives of various groups or organizations. That being the case, we need to find ways to induce people—or "nudge" them, using Thaler and Sunstein's term[1]—to make different choices than they have been making in recent years. To do that, first we need to discover what caused people to decide as they have.

For Americans accustomed to thinking about markets, it will come as no surprise to learn that, although other factors played a role, the main answer, in a word, is *incentives.* Yet although people *are* influenced by the incentives they face, they do not always make "rational" decisions based on an assessment, however informal, of costs and benefits. And while they know they will need to pay a cost-sharing amount (deductible, co-payment, or coinsurance) even if they do not know the total dollar price of the services, most people do not have a clear sense of the benefits those payments are likely to produce. Under these circumstances—that is, when the price is known but the value of either the insurance or the service is uncertain—many people forgo the insurance or the service in order to avoid having to spend their limited supply of dollars for it. The aggregation of all the independent decisions they have made to buy or not buy insurance or to use or not use services, partly in response to those incentives, has created the problems I have described. Moreover, as the decisions of one group enter the system, other groups make choices that take those prior decisions into account. It is like a circle, which can be entered at any point (Figure 6.1).

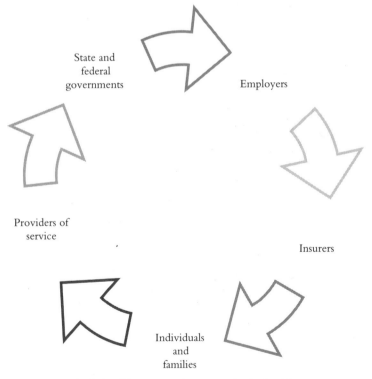

FIGURE 6.1. Relationships among key actors in the health care system

Incentives for Employers

Most health insurance for non-elderly Americans comes from their employers, who offer coverage as a fringe benefit in addition to wages. Before 1910, the only types of health "insurance" were medical care provided by some industrial firms in isolated areas and disability insurance, whose primary benefit was replacement of lost earnings.[2] Even though most European countries had introduced some form of public-sector health insurance by then, and a national health insurance plank was included in the Progressive Party's 1912 presidential campaign platform, even private health insurance lagged in the United States. Paul Starr wrote that in addition to the vehement opposition of the American Medical Association (AMA) that had emerged by the late 1910s, the main obstacles were technical ones, including "the difficulty in monitoring abuse, the high acquisition and collection costs, . . . and the likelihood of 'adverse selection.'"[3] Two of these issues could largely be solved by a strategy of selling insurance through employers to large groups of workers (which avoided adverse selection) and having employers deduct premiums from workers' pay (which greatly reduced collection costs).[4] Even so, most of the protection in these policies was for lost income associated with injury and illness. Starr cites a 1930 study which showed that only about 10 percent of benefits paid out under these policies was for medical expenses.

The rising costs of hospital care and the new salience of those costs for middle-class families increased interest in health insurance in the 1920s, and these factors created the potential for health insurance as it later developed. By the start of the Depression, however, they had not yet changed the face of health insurance. "During the 1920s there was growing recognition of the need for some mechanism by which middle-income people could finance extraordinary costs of hospitalization. Hospital insurance was virtually nonexistent."[5] During the early 1930s, the worsening Depression was taking a toll on hospital income and led to the development of the national Blue Cross network of health insurance plans, which were started by hospitals as "small, voluntary plans for prepayment of medical expenses, particularly the predictable expenses incident to childbirth."[6] The Baylor University plan, which is generally considered to be the beginning of Blue Cross, enrolled 1,250 Dallas school teachers for fifty cents a month in a plan to prepay hospitalization at the Baylor University Hospital.[7]

Other hospitals duplicated Baylor's success, and multihospital plans were created as well. Over the next few years, city-wide or county-wide plans appeared in various parts of the country, and the national Blue Cross system of not-for-profit hospital-insurance plans began to develop during the Depression. In the early years, organized medicine, through the AMA, insisted that these plans "confine themselves to provision of hospital facilities and should not include any type of medical care."[8] In fact, however, physicians benefited because "once insurance paid the hospital bills, patients were more likely to be able to pay their physician."[9] What later became Blue Shield plans that paid for physicians' services began to appear in the late 1930s and early 1940s.

During World War II wages were frozen, but the "War Labor Board in 1942 established that employer-provided health insurance coverage to workers did not represent a violation of wage controls. Collective bargaining expanded in the late 1940s and early 1950s, and as a result employee health insurance coverage became a negotiable item. The period following World War II was characterized by expanding health insurance coverage, particularly for workers and their dependents."[10] Firms were further encouraged to offer coverage by the fact that the cost of the insurance was a tax-deductible expense. As a result, the employment-based insurance system grew to be the primary source of health insurance for the under-sixty-five-year-old population. Even so, in 1960, only 21 percent of personal health care expenditures were paid for by private health insurance. More than half, 55 percent, came directly out of the pockets of patients and their families.[11]

Today, however, the employment-based system, with its roots extending back to the late 19th century, is eroding. As health care expenditures have been rising, insurance premiums have risen as well, forcing some firms to drop coverage or to shift more of the cost to their employees. For their part, more employees are opting out of health insurance because they believe they do not need it or cannot afford the premiums. Firms that retain coverage tend to be larger (99 percent of those with more than two hundred employees offer coverage[12]) and need to do so to attract or retain their employees. They may have union contracts that require it or be in a sector of the economy with highly trained or educated employees and whose competitors offer it (for example, financial services firms, hospitals, and universities).

The first line of defense against higher spending for organizations offering coverage is to attempt to contain their outlays by making changes to the plans they offer their employees. The simplest change, which may help to control the firm's spending without eliminating covered services, is just to increase the amount paid by the employees. They can do that in two main ways. First, they can increase the share of premium costs paid by employees. So instead of shouldering the entire premium themselves, as many large companies did in the past, they require their employees to pay 10 percent or 20 percent or some other amount. The difficulty is that some employees will decide they cannot afford to pay that amount and will take a chance that they will remain healthy. If they give up their insurance, the employer's outlays will be reduced still more, but the ranks of the uninsured will increase at the same time.

At this point, it is important to point out that although it looks as if employers pay a large share of insurance premiums, the reality is different. As Emanuel and Fuchs write, "employers do not bear the cost of employment-based insurance; workers and households pay for health insurance through lower wages and higher prices. Moreover, government has no source of funds other than taxes or borrowing to pay for health care" so the people are paying for public-sector programs too, even if they do not qualify for the programs' benefits. Among the evidence the authors cite are data showing that over the past thirty years, health insurance premiums increased "by about 300% after adjustment for inflation. Corporate profits per employee have flourished, with inflation-adjusted increases of 150% before taxes and 200% after taxes. By contrast, average hourly earnings of workers . . . have been stagnant, actually decreasing by 4% after adjustment for inflation." Emanuel and Fuchs conclude that "Shared responsibility [among individuals, employers, and government] is a myth."[13] This point is relevant for when we begin to discuss particular reform plans and the extent to which publicly funded insurance represents a change in individuals' payments for coverage.

The second main device for reducing an employer's own costs without eliminating covered services is to increase cost-sharing amounts to be paid by employees and their families at the point of service for the care they actually receive.

The three types of cost-sharing are deductibles, coinsurance, or co-payments. The purpose of these cost-sharing devices is to encourage people to use fewer services (presumably ones that add little or no medical benefit) in order to reduce the amounts insurance companies need to lay out for them. Insurers that spend less on services will have lower costs to cover when policies come up for renewal and therefore will be able to keep down premium increases.

Indeed, cost-sharing does work to reduce utilization. As the RAND Health Insurance Experiment (HIE) showed more than thirty years ago, out-of-pocket costs do indeed influence behavior. Random samples of people faced with cost-sharing used fewer services than similar people who faced no cost-sharing.[14] Moreover, the primary impact tended to be on the decision to initiate an episode of service or not rather than on the costs of services incurred during an episode once it began. Yet individuals tend to have trouble differentiating between services that are beneficial and those that are not necessary. So although they may spend less—at least in the short run—their health may decline. Ironically, if that happens, the cost of services used to try to restore the patient's health may be higher than if the original service had been used at the start of the episode. This is a reason to keep barriers to use of primary care services low.[15]

Deductibles are the amounts that people spend of their own money before the insurance even kicks in. If a policy calls for an annual deductible of, say, $400, then the employee must spend that amount out of his own pocket before the insurance pays anything. At the start of the year, before a person has used any services, the deductible acts as a disincentive to using services, even ones that provide benefit, because the individual must come up with the entire amount in cash or on a credit card. As payments for services used get closer to the maximum deductible—that $400, for example—the incentives change, however. If a person has spent $300 by May, let's say, and has a reason to use other services that cost another $300, then in essence, he will be getting $300 worth of care for only $100 (the rest of the deductible) plus whatever co-payments or coinsurance are required. We will talk about them shortly. Further, when late in the year a person has already surpassed the deductible, it is advantageous—purely from a financial point of view—to use more services before the year ends instead of waiting until the new year begins because a new deductible will begin then as well. So in November, instead of putting off a recommended prostate-specific antigen test or a pap test or even a complete physical examination, from a financial point of view, it may be a good idea to have them before year's end. Doctors and their staffs are aware of these dynamics, too, and often encourage patients to consider these financial realities in making their decisions.

Co-payments are amounts that a patient must pay each time she uses the particular service to which they are applied. They are expressed as dollars and usually are relatively small amounts. They are intended to get patients to think more carefully about whether or not to use a service without presenting an insurmountable barrier to needed care. So, for example, a patient may need to pay $10 or $15 each time she fills a prescription. The insurance pays the rest of the cost. Although co-payments like this have been used for many years, recently, insurers have created several tiers of co-payments to influence patient decisions even more narrowly. For example, a typical plan may have three tiers. Drugs in the first tier are generics that require the smallest co-payment (for example, $10) because they cost the insurer less and thus are preferred. Tier-two drugs are brand-name medications, used especially when no generic exists. The employer or insurer prefers these because they cost less than other branded drugs that could serve the same therapeutic purpose—perhaps because they are purchased in larger volume and the manufacturer is willing to negotiate lower prices (for them, the co-payment might be $20). When no comparable generic exists, the effect is simply to shift some of the cost to the patient—as long as the co-payment is not so much that it keeps the patient from using the drug at all. Tier-three drugs are for other brand-name drugs that are not preferred (with a co-payment of, say, $40). Patients have their choice of drugs, but the variable co-payments encourage them to choose lower-tier drugs.

Some insurers have upped the ante and tried to add a more controversial fourth tier, which they attempt to justify by saying that this allows them to keep costs of coverage lower for other subscribers. Critics such as James Robinson, a health economist at the University of California at Berkeley, argue that the new system, in effect, negates the insurance principle by saddling people who have serious illnesses with huge bills. "It is very unfortunate social policy. The more the sick person pays, the less the healthy person pays."[16] Several similar stories in a *New York Times* article illustrate the situation. Here is one: a woman who had had the same insurance for seventeen years through her husband's employment developed multiple sclerosis in the year 2000 and had been taking an expensive drug called Copaxone since then. Early in 2008, shortly after renewing the insurance policy, she refilled the prescription for another thirty-day supply, but instead of being charged a $20 co-payment, as in the past, she was charged $325. Over twelve months, the charges would have added up to $3,900, a huge increase over the previous $240 in annual out-of-pocket payments for the drug. Following an appeal and intervention by the employer, the insurer, Kaiser Permanente in Washington, D.C., agreed to suspend the change for the rest of the year and review the new policy. The story is dramatic evidence of the destructive power of rising medical costs. It negates the insurance principle under which the well subsidize the sick, who are supposed to be protected by insurance against the financial implications of serious illness. It shows that in the current system health plans and providers are not able to manage care effectively enough to keep costs down to an acceptable level and, as a result, resort to draconian measures that fall most heavily on the sick. This particular example had another unfortunate side effect in that it debased the reputation of Kaiser Permanente, the quintessential not-for-profit prepaid group practice that served as the model for the plans contemplated under the Health Maintenance Organization Act of 1973.

Coinsurance is the share of the charge, expressed not in dollars but as a percentage of the total, that the individual must pay himself or herself. Frequently, it is 20 percent. If the service is expensive, the patient's share can be large as well. The Orozcos' plan (see Chapter 2) paid 80 percent of the cost of diagnostic tests and surgery. It left them an out-of-pocket charge they could not pay and, as a result, they were unable to use some services they really needed.

In addition to changing the financial arrangements for employees, employers can use other devices to keep their health insurance costs down. They can eliminate coverage altogether for certain services, limit the amounts of services covered (such as the number of physician visits in a year), put a ceiling on expenditures (for example, $5,000 in a year), and drop family members from the coverage or at least stop paying some or all of the premium for others in the worker's family. Finally, of course, as growing numbers are already doing, they can decide simply to drop the coverage they have offered in the past.[17]

And then there are the many companies that have never offered health insurance—especially small firms with high turnover of unskilled workers.

The latter may be a case of the chicken and egg. Do employers not offer insurance because their workforce turns over frequently, or are employees more likely to leave because they find a job elsewhere that offers coverage?

The point is that many employers, wanting to limit operating costs, follow their short-term incentives and either do not offer coverage at all or find ways like the ones described here to contain their own expenditures. That may not be good for their employees, whose access to useful services thereby is reduced if not placed completely beyond their financial reach. In the long run it also may not be good for the employers themselves because it can lead to higher rates of absenteeism, lower productivity, or higher employee turnover. Finally, it clearly is not good for society—our main concern—that a substantial proportion of residents do not have affordable access to low-cost, timely medical care. Before discussing the responses of individuals and their providers of care who together make the utilization decisions we want to change, we turn next to consider the incentives for insurers, because their actions influence patients and providers directly.

Incentives for Insurers

Insurers, too, face incentives that influence their decisions. All insurers want to end their fiscal years with money in the bank. At the very least, they need to cover their expenses, and investor-owned, for-profit firms need also to earn profits for shareholders so the shares will rise in value.[18] As the outlays for covered services increase—both because provider costs (and charges) rise and because utilization rates increase—insurers must find ways to end the year profitably. That so many have succeeded "despite the erosion of employment-based coverage"[19] is revealed in data on operating earnings margin, return on equity, and stock price growth.[20]

A critical element in insurers' success is their ability to estimate trends in utilization and costs for the period of the upcoming contract, a task made more difficult by the fact that the data get old fast. For insurance contracts that come up for renewal on January 1, the insurer needs to release its prices to potential customers by November 1, perhaps earlier for large contracts. But because the lag from the date of service to the date of payment typically was 90 to 120 days, the paid-claim experience that an underwriter could use to predict future outlays would end in August.[21] It took that long because, first, the provider would need to submit the claim to the insurer, the insurer would need to "adjudicate" it—that is confirm that the patient was covered on that date, then determine whether the service was a covered one and, if so, what rate was included in the patient's contract and whether any non-financial requirements (like prior authorization) applied. If a question arose about a claim, resolving it would take additional time.

The cycle could be lengthened if the provider insists that the patient pay the bill directly and submit a claim to the insurer, not for the doctor to be paid but for the patient to be reimbursed for the amount already paid to the doctor. In that case, patients may not get the necessary forms from the provider quickly, may not get them filled out and signed promptly, and may delay still longer in actually submitting the bills to the insurer. Further, in contrast to providers whose livelihoods depend on the smooth operation of these procedures and who have lots of experience with them, patients tend not only to be inexperienced at these tasks but also to have other priorities—including recovering from illness—and thus are at a disadvantage. Despite the imprecision of these processes and the potential lag time before claims are actually settled and paid, the rates based on that experience will be good for the entire following year—through December 31, more than sixteen months after the last event on which the new rates are based. And these are the rates insurers count on to produce a surplus or profit.

In setting their rates, health insurance plans forecast cost trends and set a price. That rate not only covers the costs but also reflects the chosen strategy of either sacrificing market share to increase profitability (setting prices higher) or gaining share at the expense of profitability (lowering prices).[22]

A fundamental problem is that it is very difficult to predict what will happen to utilization. It is affected by secular trends in the distribution of illness (a flu epidemic, for example, can throw off predictions); by changes in available treatment choices, including new drugs heavily marketed by manufacturers and new medical technology; or by characteristics of the insurance itself. Among the latter are the out-of-pocket costs faced by the patient, and the insurer's payment rates to providers, which, if too low to cover their increasing costs, may lead clinicians to adjust by providing more services where they can.

The difficulty of predicting underwriting gains and losses, coupled with the competitive dynamics in the insurance industry, gave rise to the health insurance underwriting cycle, described by Gabel and others in 1991.[23] This is typically a six-year period characterized by three years of gains followed by three years of losses, which was observed from the mid-1960s through at least the early 1990s.[24] Here is how it works.

Knowing the inherent difficulty of predicting expenditures on covered services eighteen months in advance, insurers tended to set their rates higher than turned out to be necessary. As a result, they made substantial profits, which "attracted new plans and led to efforts by incumbent plans to expand market share. As these plans priced their products below those of competitors to gain enrollment, this triggered price wars, which depressed profitability and eventually led to industry-wide losses. If plans priced aggressively while cost trends—unbeknownst to them—were turning up, then the losses were magnified. The losses, in turn, caused plans to exit the market. With reduced competition, premium trends increased, leading to increased profitability and starting the cycle anew."[25]

There is some evidence to support the view that the underwriting cycle has moderated in recent years in part because insurers have taken steps to reduce the effects of some of the factors that fueled it. For example, the claims payment cycle has been reduced somewhat, and contract renewal dates are spaced more evenly throughout the year.[26] At the same time, however, other trends have emerged, which point to continuing volatility in the industry.

As insurance premiums have risen and more employers have dropped coverage for their employees, employment-based health insurance has eroded. From the peak in 2000, when 67 percent of the non-elderly population was covered by employment-based insurance, the proportion fell by 5 percentage points (to 62 percent) in 2007.[27] Yet the industry has remained profitable. The major firms "have consistently raised premiums ahead of claims costs, reducing medical cost ratios and expanding operating margins and overall earnings."[28] However, its continued success "is threatened by three related trends in the employment-based sector. First and most obviously, the industry remains reliant on employment-based business for the majority of its overall earnings."[29] Individual firms may moderate premium increases, thus reestablishing the underwriting cycle. Second, the nonprofit Blue Cross and Blue Shield plans "have accrued financial reserves far in excess of mandated minimums and now face regulatory pressure to offer premium relief."[30] And third, the gradual shift from insured to self-insured funding and from comprehensive to high-deductible benefit plans reduces insurers' margins. Large companies that self-insure hire an insurance company not to bear the financial risk associated with utilization of services, but only to perform administrative functions, such as processing claims for payment and maintaining records. "Insurers' earnings per enrollee for their self-insured business—that is, administrative services only (ASO)—are only one-third the level for their insured members, while their earnings per enrollee in high-deductible plans are 30 percent lower than in comprehensive plans."[31]

The industry is responding to these trends in two main ways. First, it has consolidated dramatically to the point that it "now comprises four national plans (United, WellPoint, Aetna, and CIGNA); state-specific Blue Cross and Blue Shield plans; a few regional for-profit plans (such as Humana, HealthNet, and Coventry); and, in some markets, regional nonprofit plans (such as Kaiser Permanente, Tufts Health Plan, and HealthPartners)."[32]

Second, it is diversifying into the public sector. Medicaid and Medicare are the only segments of the health insurance world that are growing—in part because the private sector is shrinking—so the only programmatic way to diversify is to partner with either or both of them.[33] This is not the first time that commercial insurers and public officials have joined forces. Previous efforts proved contentious, however, and there is no reason to think that current efforts will be different. Nonetheless, for the time being, state-level Medicaid Managed Care plans and the Medicare Prescription Drug, Improvement, and Modernization Act (MMA) of 2003 offer inviting opportunities. Regarding Medicaid, some states, frustrated by their failure to contain escalating costs and the poor financial performance of local managed care plans, turned to commercial insurers for help. And for Medicare, the "MMA authorized the creation of freestanding prescription drug plans (PDPs) for beneficiaries enrolled in FFS Medicare and expanded funding for the full-service Medicare Advantage with prescription drug (MA-PD) products."[34]

The extent to which the private-sector insurance companies have been able to perform better than their public-sector counterparts became a hot political issue again in the spring of 2008. Bruce Vladeck, when he headed the Health Care Financing Authority, the predecessor agency to the Center for Medicare and Medicaid Services, lamented the higher costs of managed care. In connection with the debate over Medicare reform, it was revealed that Medicare in 2008 still paid substantially more per capita for beneficiaries enrolled in private Medicare Advantage managed care plans than for those in the regular Medicare program. And this occurred even though the selection bias, as in previous periods too, worked in the plans' favor.[35] On the other hand, Medicare officials have a vocal, well-organized constituency of elderly Americans who are accustomed to turning to their elected representatives to ensure that they receive the services they expect. And state officials continue to be concerned about rising Medicaid expenditures and, especially, their impact on state taxes. So the endemic tension between public-sector obligations and goals and the private-sector drive for profits may rear its ugly head again.

Whether or not they find a way to succeed in the public sector this time, the insurance companies' primary business is in the private sector, and it is therefore in their interest to try to protect it. Unfortunately, they have only a limited range of tools available to them as they pursue profits in a difficult environment. They can (1) vary price; (2) limit availability (that is, the groups to whom they sell their policies); and (3) affect quality (that is, they can vary what they cover and the terms of that coverage).[36] Given that they are limited to these three options, what can they do to solidify their financial position?

One possibility is that they can raise premiums, which as we have seen, will cause still more employers to either drop coverage for their employees or increase the employee share of premiums. When the latter happens, still more employees will give up coverage, even if their employers continue to offer it. That this is happening already can be seen in the figures shown earlier that demonstrate the erosion of the employment-based segment of the insurance industry. Insurers gain because those most likely to drop coverage are people with lower incomes who also tend to be less healthy than those with higher incomes.

Ironically, therefore, those employees who expect to need services tend to be less likely to drop insurance than healthy people who do not. Knowing their enhanced risk, those with limited incomes are more likely than those in similar financial circumstances to stretch their resources to be able to afford some coverage. When that occurs, the insurance principle of spreading the risk over large numbers of people, many of whom do not use services, is further undermined, and premiums will increase still further.

Second, insurers can try to influence subscribers to use fewer services by raising cost-sharing provisions, which makes services more expensive at the point of service. As noted, although cost-sharing does reduce utilization, patients often have trouble differentiating between services they need and those they don't. One result is that by deciding not to use services in order to avoid the out-of-pocket payments, people can undermine their health status. And another is that, when they guess wrong and wind up very ill, they will need not only more services but ones that are more costly than if they had used appropriate care early in an episode. Moreover, if those services are not covered, they will place additional burdens on safety-net providers, especially hospital emergency services.

Third, insurers can also respond to cost pressures by imposing constraints on utilization directly. They may limit the number of services covered or require prior authorization by administrative personnel of some services, especially big-ticket items. They may even retroactively deny payments for services already used that, after the fact, they decide were unnecessary.[37]

Finally, insurers can find ways to discourage people who are expected to use relatively large numbers of services from subscribing in the first place. They can either drop high-cost plans by not renewing policies for companies with high proportions of older workers who tend to be high users or quote prices they know are too high for those firms to absorb. They can reject applications from people with prior serious illness or exclude coverage for specific preexisting conditions. Or they can further segment the market by imposing higher prices or administrative hurdles—such as physical exams—before offering coverage to individuals expected to incur utilization expenditures. A companion to this negative strategy is a more positive one in which they encourage younger, healthy people to subscribe by offering bonuses that they value, such as membership in a health club. Such benefits will be of little interest to older people with a variety of other risk factors likely to increase their propensity to use services, but they may be very attractive to young adults who like to exercise regularly and won't use many medical services.

Although all these tactics do constrain insurer spending—even though they may also require additional administrative expenses—they tend to undermine the value of insurance both to individuals and the society. The bottom line is that the response of both employers and insurance companies to the incentives they face tends to exacerbate the problems we are trying to solve. We turn next to the actual makers of utilization decisions: first, individuals and their families and then the providers of care.

Incentives for Individuals and Families

Individuals make two types of health-related decisions of concern to us here. One is to buy insurance coverage or not; and the other is to use services or not.

When considering whether or not to take the insurance offered by his employer, an employee makes an informal calculation that includes both assumptions about the probability that he (or family members when the policy covers them) will need services and the options for obtaining those services should the need arise. In other words, a generally healthy individual for whom cash is limited may assume the chances he will need care are small and decide it is more important to be able to buy food or pay the rent than to buy insurance against the unlikely possibility that sometime during the year he will need services. Further, he may also figure that if that need does arise, either the services will be relatively inexpensive (a doctor visit, perhaps, and a prescription) or he can always obtain care in a hospital emergency department (ED), which since 1986 has been obligated under federal law to treat him.[38] The Emergency Medical Treatment and Active Labor Act (EMTALA) was designed mainly to address the problem of "patient dumping," the practice by which hospital emergency rooms deny treatment to uninsured patients, either by refusing care outright or by transferring them to other facilities. That problem, in turn, arose because emergency rooms "for people without medical insurance, [had] become the doctor's office." One measure of the scale of the issue is revealed in this quote about Maimonides Medical Center in Brooklyn: "In the hallway leading to the ER, it was routine to find patients backed up like airplanes on a runway in lousy weather."[39] The person who declines insurance expecting to receive care in an ED if he needs it probably does not have that image in mind.

Nonetheless, as premium costs rise, more employees will decide they cannot afford the coverage given their other obligations and will "go bare." Indeed, large numbers already have reached that point and made that decision. In 2002, 15 percent of the uninsured (representing almost six-and-a-half million people) had been offered coverage but declined it.[40] An individual's threshold for that choice will be determined by factors such as the amount of family income, the nature and size of the family, the probability that she will need services, and family attitudes about the importance of medical care. An employee with a spouse and children may make different decisions in this regard than one of the same age who is responsible only for herself.

An individual who makes a different choice and decides that insurance *is* important enough to justify the premium cost—even if he does not expect to need services—will have an easier time paying for care if the need arises than a person in similar financial circumstances without insurance. Nonetheless, financial incentives may lead him to make other dysfunctional decisions regarding the use of services. Think about it as an individual's propensity to exercise restraint (or not) in his or her use of services. At one extreme is the well-insured (or well-to-do) hypochondriac who seeks care for every minor ache or pain and cannot seem to differentiate potentially serious symptoms from trivial ones. At the other is the person who, in addition to having a stoic personality, also is worried about every expenditure. That person may have trouble recognizing potentially serious symptoms at the same time that, in contrast to the hypochondriac, he has no temptation to seek care for minor ones. The nature of coverage can influence the care-seeking behavior of both—as well as the majority in between the two extremes.

If the coverage includes no cost-sharing at the point of service, the insured person faces only the cost of getting to the service—that is, lost wages, transportation, and perhaps the cost of a babysitter to keep an eye on young children—as well as the opportunity cost of the time spent in the effort. If, however, the policy also includes deductibles, co-payments, or coinsurance, then to use services requires coming up with additional out-of-pocket payments. A person with such an insurance plan may set a higher threshold for seeking care than the person with no cost-sharing in order to avoid incurring those additional outlays (or the entire cost of care if he has no insurance). Typically, doctors' staff asks a patient about insurance coverage during the check-in process at the office and collects whatever co-payment or coinsurance is due at the time.

Finally, in states that allow "balance billing," patients may face still additional outlays if the insurer's payment to the doctor does not cover the full difference between the billed charge and the coinsurance or co-payment. All these ways to increase out-of-pocket costs to the patient are intended to reduce *unnecessary* utilization. But, as already indicated, patients tend not to be very good at differentiating between services that are beneficial and those that are unnecessary.

A 2003 study on the effects of incentive-based drug formularies substantiates this point.[41] Spending on prescription drugs, which accounted for a little more than 10 percent of national health expenditures in 2006, has been growing in recent years even more than other segments of the health care sector, though the rate of increase appears to have slowed more recently.[42] The use of incentive-based formularies may have played a role.

"The goal of incentive-based formularies is to encourage people to choose lower-cost prescription drugs, thereby creating cost savings for the health plan, which can, in theory, then be passed on to the consumers."[43] Indeed, as described earlier in this chapter, many insurance plans now include several tiers of prescription drugs, each of which requires a different out-of-pocket payment for patients. The objective is to direct consumer demand to the least expensive appropriate drugs given the nature of the patients' condition and the available choices. Researchers found that specific effects depend on the exact nature of the incentive plan as well as on the arrangements it replaced. In the case of an employer that switched from "a one-tier to a three-tier formulary involving across-the-board increases in cost sharing," they reported "a shift in the distribution of spending from the plan to the enrollee in all classes of drugs."[44] On the other hand, they also found evidence that sizeable proportions of covered patients discontinued "the use of medications such as statins and ACE inhibitors that are needed for the treatment of chronic illnesses [which] raises important questions about potentially harmful effects of formulary changes and the associated changes in copayments."[45]

Cost-sharing is, perhaps, most defensible in the case of discretionary services, but it has also been applied to preventive services that, by permitting disease to be detected early, may improve survival rates. One such example was reported in a study of the increased use of cost-sharing for mammography among Medicare-eligible women between the ages of sixty-five and sixty-nine.[46] In this study, cost-sharing was defined as requiring a co-payment of more than $10 or coinsurance of more than 10 percent for a screening mammography. In plans with this level of cost-sharing, the researchers found that "biennial screening rates were 8.3 percentage points lower in cost-sharing plans than in plans with full coverage."[47] They also found that "screening rates decreased by 5.5 percentage points in plans that instituted cost sharing and increased by 3.4 percentage points in matched control plans that retained full coverage."[48] Because accepted clinical guidelines support a biennial mammography in this age population, the depressing effect of even small co-payments on screening rates is worrisome.

But the fact is that these are just recent examples of an old story. The RAND health insurance experiment, the landmark study mentioned earlier that occurred between November 1974 and January 1982 in six sites around the country, some urban and others rural, demonstrated that patient cost-sharing can indeed reduce both utilization and expenditures, at least in the short run.[49] The study randomly assigned more than 7,700 non-aged people to one of several different insurance plans. In the fee-for-service

(FFS) portion of the study, which is most relevant to this discussion, 5,814 individuals from 2,005 families were enrolled. In all, fourteen different plans were introduced. One was a free-care plan in which the family received all care without any out-of-pocket payments. Thirteen other plans had different coinsurance rates: nine had either a 25 percent or 50 percent rate on all services up to a maximum expenditure of $1,000 in 1973 dollars or 5 percent, 10 percent, or 15 percent of family income, whichever was less. Three additional plans had a 95 percent coinsurance rate up to the same maximum expenditure. An individual deductible plan imposed the coinsurance only on ambulatory expenditures up to a maximum out-of-pocket amount of $150 per person or $450 per family. All outpatient care beyond that amount and all inpatient care required no out-of-pocket payments.[50]

The authors summarized their findings by saying that "as expected, cost-sharing lowered the likelihood that HIE participants would obtain care for numerous individual diagnoses. The decreased probability of contact during a year appeared to be more likely for the acute and preventive diagnostic categories than for the chronic conditions. It appeared to be stronger for children than for adults, although this did not lead to measurable decrements in general health status."[51] Although the cost-sharing plans were designed to take account of family income, "they affected use more among the poor than among the nonpoor. The deterrent effect was greatest for children from low-income families."[52] Finally, the RAND researchers at the time found that "cost-sharing did not lead to rates of care seeking that were more 'appropriate' from a clinical perspective. That is, cost-sharing did not seem to have a selective effect in prompting people to forego care only or mainly in circumstances when such care probably would be of relatively little value."[53]

Proponents of cost-sharing justify it because of the assumption that, given moral hazard, insured people are likely to over-use services (that is, use services that are of little or no value) when there is no out-of-pocket cost. In other words, without insurance, consumers face the entire cost of services and will be careful to use only those of clear benefit. With insurance and facing no additional payment to use services, they are likely to use even those with little or no benefit simply because the cost is so low. Therefore, raising the price they must pay by imposing cost-sharing at the point of service should reduce their use of services.

But, as Thomas Rice argues, a problem occurs in economic terms only when insurance causes people to use services that cost more than "the utility that people derive from consuming them."[54] So that raises two questions. One concerns the size of the problem: How much is spent on services of little or no value? The other is, Assuming it is big enough to be concerned about, will cost-sharing reduce it?

Rice and John Nyman both show that previous estimates suggesting the problem was a large one need to be reconsidered because, as Rice put it, the studies were "based on assumptions about consumer behavior that are not supported by the available empirical evidence."[55] And Nyman shows that previous estimates overstated the welfare loss because, among other things, they included the effects of income transfers on consumption of health care services.[56]

Regarding the second question, the HIE showed that instead of causing people to reduce only the use of services that provide them with little or no value, cost-sharing "reduced their demand for care that was most likely to improve their health as much as they did for care that provided the fewest benefits."[57]

Why would people do that? One reason is they do not know enough "to make the right choices for themselves." And another is that they "may be misled by providers who have their own objectives, which may deviate from those of their patients."[58] And still another is that even insured people may not be able to afford beneficial services because cost-sharing tends to have a bigger effect on people with less income.[59]

Yet research does suggest that a nontrivial amount of utilization represents waste in the sense that it is unrelated to clinical need. That idea originated with two widely cited studies. One, from the late 1950s, showed that in the presence of insurance both hospital admissions and length of stay increased when a community in upstate New York had a sudden increase in hospital beds. In the community being studied, Milton Roemer examined the impact on hospital utilization associated with the addition of 58 new hospital beds to the community, which increased the bed-to-population ratio from 2.8 beds per 1,000 residents to 3.8 beds per 1,000. Comparing hospital utilization in the year before the new hospital opened and the year after it opened, Roemer found that admissions and length of stay both grew even though the population was practically the same and there was no substantial increase in the incidence of any major disease category. The rates continued to increase in the following year, as well. The study gave rise to "Roemer's Law," which asserts that, under conditions of widespread insurance, a built bed tends to be filled.[60]

The other study—really, a long series of studies—led to a health services research subfield of "small-area variations." In the early 1970s, John Wennberg and his colleagues discovered that contiguous small areas in Vermont had widely differing rates of certain surgical procedures, which could not be explained by differences in the incidence of conditions for which those procedures were appropriate. Indeed, the only factor they found that covaried with the rates of surgery was the availability of surgeons. Moreover,

Wennberg was able to replicate these findings in other states and for other services. The assumption was that because surgery was performed at higher rates in areas with more surgeons for a given level of population, some of that surgery must be unnecessary.[61]

Roemer's Law and Wennberg's small-area studies gave rise to efforts to reduce the amount of unnecessary utilization. In the first instance, states passed laws requiring approval before hospitals could add to their bed capacity. And the second result was used as a justification for patient cost-sharing, which was touted as a means to put a damper on consumer "demand" for unnecessary procedures. In the end, however, neither did much to contain spending.

Although the primary rationale of cost-sharing is to encourage patients to be *prudent consumers* and thus use only the services they need, an important problem is that—whatever form it takes—cost-sharing can distort utilization decisions in ways that encourage not prudence but penuriousness. One implication of this fact is that, as we noted earlier, a utilization decision—even one involving a person with good health insurance—is made by two people, the patient and the physician. So a utilization-reducing and cost-saving strategy aimed only at the patient is likely to produce unwanted distortions, as RAND and other researchers have shown.

That is likely to be the case because, even with the rise of Internet sites providing medical information, most patients tend to know only two things about their illness: they know where the pain is, and they know that, if they use services, they will need to pay for them. They usually do not know the value of what they will get for that money, however. Often, what people who are concerned about their finances do is to hold out as long as they can in order to avoid having to spend the money.

In fact, as noted at the end of Chapter 5, because of their relative ignorance on clinical matters, what people want from a doctor, primarily, is expertise.[62] When a patient is not sure of the diagnosis, the "care" he seeks "consists primarily of information," especially "an assessment of what *his* symptoms and test results suggest" (emphasis in original). Then, on the basis of the physician's general knowledge of diseases and treatments, the patient wants more information, this time about "the outcome of various courses of treatment on individuals" with his diagnosis. And only then does care consist of an "active-therapeutic" action, perhaps an injection or a surgical procedure.[63]

When, instead of going to the doctor, the patient waits to see if the symptoms will get better on their own, sometimes the delay can turn out to be too long. For example, community-acquired MRSA (methicillin-resistant staph aureus) is a potentially deadly "superbug" if not treated in time.[64] In fact, many have died from it in recent years because they did not seek care soon enough. An uninsured patient with achiness and a fever (what we often think of as flu-like symptoms) may try to avoid the co-payment at the doctor's office, thinking the symptoms will go away in a day or two with rest and plenty of fluids. And many times they do. On the other hand, patients whose aches and fever are caused by MRSA infections may not survive if they delay more than that day or two. That is another reason why it is a good idea—for both the patient and the society—for barriers to primary care to be low even if access to specialty care or the hospital is made more difficult.

It is worth noting again in passing that the ability to pay for care, important though it is, is not the only determinant of whether or not people use services (see Chapter 5). Next we turn to the other half of the utilization-determining pair, the providers, to see how they respond to the incentives they face.

Incentives for Providers

Providers of care—physicians, hospitals, and others—are under enormous financial pressure primarily from three causes: (1) efforts by third parties (private insurers, certainly, but also public programs such as Medicare and Medicaid) to limit their expenditures; (2) the reduced numbers of people with insurance leading to both fewer patients and less demand for services that generate income; and (3) delays in payment and bad debts resulting when those patients who do come must shoulder a larger share of the bill themselves and have difficulty doing so. In ordinary markets of nonessential items, consumers tend to wait until they can afford to purchase the items they want.

To reduce their outlays, as we have already seen, third-party payers not only reduce their payment rates to providers, they impose prior authorization requirements and use other administrative tactics that cause physicians and other providers to spend more time coping with them and, among other things, require them to hire more staff and thus increase their administrative costs. Ironically, a competitive market with many insurers, each of which offers a variety of plans with different provisions and payment rates, not to mention different claim forms, leads to even higher administrative outlays for providers.[65] One estimate is that administrative costs absorb 31 percent of health care expenditures in the United States, just under twice as much as a comparable figure for Canada.[66]

Another way physicians try to cope is to become specialists because they can charge higher prices for at least some of the services they offer. Even before the current crisis, a much higher proportion of U.S. physicians were specialists than those of any other developed country (see Chapter 5). Doctors can also limit the average amount of time spent with individual patients so they can see more patients per hour and collect more fees.[67] Providers who are paid fee-for-service based on their charges may also try to provide additional services per patient to earn the income they think they need. To do so, they may provide tests or other services of limited clinical value or ask patients to return for unnecessary follow-up visits. This possibility gave rise years ago to the concepts of "physician-induced demand" and "the target-income hypothesis."[68] "Physicians can control their income-earning activities better than most individuals" by, for example, working more hours or altering the amount and types of services they furnish (that is, by inducing extra demand). This has led some economists to hypothesize that physicians who earn less than their target or reference incomes will adjust their behavior to meet those targets. Many empirical tests of the hypothesis have found "that physicians respond to financial pressures by increasing prices or quantities of services provided."[69]

The net effects of these pressures and provider efforts to cope with them can be seen in the fact that, between 1995 and 2003, average physician net income from medical practice actually declined by 7 percent in real terms (that is, taking account of inflation).[70] Among the key reasons for the drop in physician income were a 4 percent reduction in hours spent on medically related activities, though significantly not on patient care, and "flat or declining fees" from third-party payers. Time spent on patient care has not declined because not only is seeing patients one way to cope with falling fees and reduced real income, but also 70 percent of physicians face financial incentives tied to productivity (that is, to seeing more patients or providing more services).[71] At the same time, these financial pressures contribute to reduced physician willingness to spend time on noncompensated medical activities (for example, being on call to a community hospital's emergency department, as we saw in Chapter 4).

Hospitals are under financial pressure, too. In the past twenty-five years, the hospital sector's share of overall health spending fell by 9 percentage points, from almost 40 percent to just under 31 percent.[72] One reason is the technological developments that have made it possible to do surgery outside the hospital on patients who no longer need to be admitted to a hospital bed. Another, as Goldsmith points out, is that, although they adapted by creating their own outpatient surgery services, hospitals have steadily lost market share in the resulting "lucrative ambulatory surgery and imaging markets to physician-sponsored enterprises."[73] Physician-owned specialty hospitals more than doubled in just the five years between 2002 and 2007.[74]

These specialty hospitals reflect the market at work, but they have raised a number of important issues that cast doubt on the proposition that, on balance, they represent a net gain for the society. One is the potential conflict of interest that results when physicians refer to a hospital in which they have an ownership interest. In those cases, they gain not just from the fee they earn for the surgery they perform but also by sharing in the hospital's profits.[75] A number of studies provide evidence that "physicians at physician-owned facilities are more likely than other physicians to refer well-insured patients to their facilities and to route Medicaid patients to hospital outpatient clinics."[76] In general, they are more likely to treat a healthier population that requires less complex procedures, has fewer complications and higher rates of success, and pays higher fees.[77]

There is also evidence that self-referral increases utilization of health care services and that at least some of that increased utilization is not medically appropriate.[78] Finally, although comparisons of surgeries performed in physician-owned and other hospitals do not suggest that the quality of the operations is lower, many physician-owned facilities lack emergency departments and are less likely to have physicians on site all the time. As we saw in Chapter 4, the *New York Times* reported several cases in which patients experienced complications following surgery and staff had to call 911 to have the patients transferred to full-service hospitals because the specialty hospital where the procedure was performed was not able to provide appropriate care.[79]

Because, as Goldsmith and many others believe, the growing financial pressure on both hospitals and physicians is largely an "artifact" of the dramatic increase in the numbers of uninsured, it is critically important that the uninsurance part of the health system problem be solved. Until then, it is likely that these conditions will continue for the foreseeable future and that providers of all kinds, following their incentives, will make dysfunctional decisions that undermine the ability of patients to get needed care.

Another, perhaps secondary, result of these increased pressures is growing tensions between hospitals and doctors—with the potential for patients to be caught in the middle. That relations between hospitals and doctors are increasingly strained is well established. One piece of evidence is that in 2001 only 15 percent of respondents to a survey of the Center for Studying Health System Change indicated hospital-physician relations were a major issue, whereas by 2005 that percentage had tripled to almost half (46 percent).[80]

Moreover, hospitals are in a particularly difficult position because they have EMTALA obligations to provide emergency care to patients "around the clock, regardless of the ability to pay,"[81] while neither physicians nor the ambulatory facilities they own are subject to those provisions. Further, since physicians too are under financial pressure, as noted in Chapter 4, many are less willing than they once may have been to help hospitals meet their EMTALA obligations. The growing tensions between hospitals and physicians are exacerbated by some of the steps that physicians have taken to increase their incomes (for example, by forming competing organizations, such as imaging centers or outpatient surgery facilities) and those that hospitals have taken either in response to doctors' actions or in anticipation of other trends. Finally, although some physicians may be willing to trade their independence for the apparent stability of hospital employment, hospital executives will need to engage even employed physicians in a concerted effort to ensure they serve the interests of the institution at the same time they care for their patients.

While these forces tend to feed a resurgent "medical arms race"[82] that increases total health care spending and exacerbates the financial stresses, our primary concern is with their impact on patients' ability to obtain the care they need. We have already seen in this chapter some of the ways physicians cope with these pressures, which sometimes result in poorer care for patients. Julie Salamon's book *Hospital*[83] describes incidents in which Maimonides Medical Center in Brooklyn stabilized patients who came to the emergency department and then, "walked them to the door." While hospitals must treat all who come to the ED, "treat" is not defined.

Why should we be concerned if doctors or hospitals earn less than they used to or have trouble covering their costs? Isn't that the way markets are supposed to work? Lower prices will lead them to become more efficient and reduce their costs in order to survive. Those that are unable to do so will, in the case of physicians, retire early and in the case of institutions, like hospitals, go out of business. The survivors will be stronger, and newcomers entering the market will build efficient practices to begin with. Perhaps. But another result will be that people who live in areas with reduced numbers of providers will lack the ability to access services easily enough to meet their medical needs. It may be okay for other sectors to function in that way. Retailers can close unprofitable stores when they sell nonessentials whose purchase can be put off until consumers plan a shopping trip to another store in a nearby community.

Access to medical care is different, however. I already said that one of our goals is to facilitate easy access at least to primary care and that services should be available when people happen to get sick and need them. If providers disappear from the community, that becomes impossible. Providers whose income suffers may be able to survive short of closing their doors. But it would also be good for them to invest in enhancements (such as information technology or new clinical equipment) that may improve quality of care, increase efficiency, and lower costs; to maintain their facilities; and, in the case of physicians, to keep up with the latest developments by attending continuing education programs. If they do not earn enough to do those things, but they survive, the standard of care they provide will be lower than we would like.

Incentives for State and Federal Governments

In the private-public American system, the public sector is intended to play a residual role. That is, federal and state governments provide coverage to people who do not get private insurance through their employment and cannot buy it on their own. Some of those people are eligible for benefits permanently—because they are sixty-five or older in the case of Medicare, or because they are veterans in the case of the Veterans Administration—but others become eligible temporarily as a result of circumstances. Either they suffer an illness or disability that keeps them from working for a time or their employer drops coverage or raises the price higher than they can afford. Their condition can change, as when they get a better-paying job with another employer that still offers affordable coverage. The public programs that provide coverage to those people are counter-cyclical because they tend to expand when the economy is down and shrink when it comes back up again. Although all health insurance is redistributive—from the healthy to the sick—these programs are also redistributive from those with more income to those with less. The problem is they are funded by taxes, which also decline when the economy is down.

Moreover, public-sector payers are subject to many of the same forces that act on private payers, as well. And they too need to cope. Medicare and Medicaid, over the years, have attempted to limit utilization through devices that are strikingly similar to those used by the private insurance sector. They have even tried to increase cost-sharing, which imposes a particularly large burden on their beneficiaries, who are among those least able to afford it. The Department of Veterans Affairs, which provides medical services directly to eligible patients, uses different tactics (such as employing salaried staff and a system-wide electronic medical record), but it too needs to be concerned about the financial effects of utilization.

Although the Congress decided many years ago that it was in the public interest to provide a health insurance safety net for people who cannot obtain private-sector coverage, the states are having trouble continuing to fill that role. Medicaid is the primary program in that effort, but because it is a means-tested program (people qualify by demonstrating that their incomes are low enough), many working people have too much income to be eligible for it. Yet they either may not have enough to buy insurance or may have a disqualifying preexisting medical condition that causes private insurers to reject their applications. One example is a Maryland couple who were cancer survivors rejected by twenty-five different commercial insurers. Richard and Susan Logan were able to obtain insurance for themselves and their daughter from the Maryland Health Insurance Plan, one of thirty-five state programs for high-risk applicants unable to obtain coverage from private firms.[84] The annual cost was $22,232 which, fortunately for them, they were able to afford.

Chaim Benamor, another Maryland resident with a preexisting medical condition, was not so lucky. The fifty-two-year-old self-employed renovator had recently suffered a mild heart attack, and he too was rejected by private insurers. He earned only $35,000, however, and though it was too much for him to be eligible for state subsidies, he decided he could not afford the premium of $4,572 for a plan with "heavy deductibles."[85] Yet even though these premiums and those in similar programs offered by other states are high, they leave about 40 percent of the cost uncovered, which the states themselves need to pay. Funds for them to do so come "usually through assessments on insurance premiums that are often passed on to consumers."[86] Even so, it is estimated that although 47 million Americans are uninsured, only 207,000 such people are covered by these state programs for high-risk residents, which like other third-party payers are under enormous financial pressure. The result is that these types of safety-net programs—which fifteen states do not even have—are able to address only a small part of the need they were created to fill, in part because, to cope with their own rising costs, they make it too expensive for many to afford.

Perhaps the quintessential example of dysfunctional policies in a safety-net program is a story that began many years ago in Medicaid. Although Medicaid is jointly funded by state and federal governments, the states set many of the rules, including most eligibility criteria and payment rates to providers. The program was created in 1965 by Title XIX of the Social Security Act, at the same time that Medicare, Title XVIII, became law, and it went into effect in 1966 in the first states to pass enabling legislation. Its spending quickly exceeded projections, and states faced the challenge of finding ways to keep its costs under control. One method was to reduce the prices paid to providers for services rendered to Medicaid eligibles. They could do little with hospital rates, however, since the federal law required that hospitals be paid on the basis of their costs, which were determined using elaborate formulas embedded in federal regulations. Physicians, however, made an inviting target. Since they were assumed to be high earners anyway, cutting payment rates to physicians was expected not to hurt them much and to save the states money in the bargain. Unfortunately, the reality turned out differently.

Low fees tended to drive many doctors from the program—they either refused to treat Medicaid patients or they moved from neighborhoods with large numbers of Medicaid eligibles so that they would be less likely to have Medicaid patients in the first place. Yet those patients, the most numerous of whom were children, still needed care when they became ill. (Children also need immunizations and other well-child care, which too often they did not get.) So if private doctors were not available, where did these patients get care? Large numbers were taken to hospital emergency departments where, typically, they waited long hours to be seen—especially if other patients had more serious clinical needs. In addition, of course, hospital emergency departments' costs are much higher than those of a community-based physician in private practice, and Medicaid payments were based on ED costs. The result was that the state paid lower physician fees, fewer community-based physicians were willing to treat Medicaid patients, patients got the care they needed in expensive hospital EDs, and the program's expenditures continued to rise.

Medicare, the federal program for the aged and disabled, has also adopted dysfunctional policies in response to fiscal pressures. Perhaps the most dramatic recent example is the Medicare Prescription Drug Program, Part D of Title XVIII. Among other things, it creates a "donut hole" for beneficiaries who reach a threshold amount in Medicare prescription drug spending and then, incredibly, get no additional benefits at all until they spend another several thousand dollars on prescriptions out of pocket. At that point, the program kicks in again and pays part of the drug costs for the rest of the year. On the one hand, this bizarre measure saves cash for the program at the expense of the hardships it creates for Medicare beneficiaries with illnesses needing expensive drugs. On the other, a more conventional money-saving provision—to allow Medicare officials to negotiate lower prices with drug manufacturers—was rejected. (This plan is discussed later in the book.)

Conclusion

To eliminate *throughout the entire health care system* the serious problems that have been described, the incentives that produced them need to change. It is not enough simply to introduce advances—such as information technology—to improve quality or to find ways to deliver services more efficiently so the cost of each service can be reduced. One reason is that, even if information technology can do all the things its advocates claim (and there is growing evidence that it may not be able to do so),[87] most providers are still not adopting it. Another is that spending is the product of quantity times price. So even if prices for some services come down, unless the quantity stops growing too, spending will continue to rise. Recall the discussion of the target-income hypothesis for physicians. That is just one piece of evidence that the system itself must change. Unless it does, not enough medical care organizations will adopt information technology, and the greater efficiencies will not materialize in sufficient quantity or scale to pay the expected dividends.

The task therefore is to change the incentives in order to change utilization patterns and increase the chances that

- Everyone will have comprehensive health insurance—so that employers, individuals, insurers, and government officials will not make decisions that create our high rates of uninsurance and underinsurance.
- Individuals will use services appropriately—primary care early in an episode of illness, preventive services, chronic care management; will fill prescriptions; and will follow other physician recommendations.
- Providers will locate in areas that currently are underserved because they have high rates of uninsurance and thus a reduced likelihood that providers will be paid for their work.
- Providers will furnish appropriate care—not too much in response to low fees or too little out of fear that they will not be paid at all.

To accomplish these goals, we face a choice between two main approaches: one is to find ways to remove imperfections in the market so the incentives stimulate (or "nudge") the various actors to make decisions that serve the society as well as themselves. The other is to rely on the public sector to do those things because the market cannot. In the next chapter, we examine this challenge, considering the private-sector option first.

Chapter 7

Competition and the Market
or the Public Sector?

IN THE UNITED STATES, when problems surface that need the society's attention, we tend to prefer solutions that minimize the public-sector role and maximize reliance on the private sector.[1] This view seems to be fueled by the idea that self-interest is the most reliable engine to progress. The thinking, which traces back to Adam Smith, goes something like this: to succeed, each individual and organization will need to develop improved products and services, which will be not only more effective at what they do but also more efficiently produced and therefore less expensive. And in the end, that innovation will make us all better off.

Even when we do turn to public policy, moreover, whether to try to improve private-sector performance or to achieve other goals, we tend to move slowly, one step at a time. The appeal of such incremental improvements is two-fold. First, they are easier to enact into law because, while they can indeed produce real change, they limit the "losses" of key interest groups. Second, because the steps are relatively small, they tend to be manageable, allowing the changes to be absorbed more readily by the underlying social or economic system than more ambitious or far-reaching changes can. If we move forward steadily, that approach produces continual progress which, over time, ensures that whatever system is the focus of our attention remains vibrant and effective.[2]

Using an incremental public policy approach to increase the extent of effective competition in the marketplace has long been proposed as a solution for the ailing health care system. In 1980, Alain Enthoven published *Health Plan*,[3] a major element of which was "a positive program on the part of government to make the market work."[4] These ideas, somewhat elaborated and expanded, reappeared as managed competition in the Clinton era.[5] They continue to attract support in the first decade of the 21st century, as witness, for example, John McCain's statements as a presidential candidate in 2008 about his hopes and plans for the health sector.[6]

The primary question being addressed in this chapter is whether an incremental approach that uses improved competition to produce the desired change can really achieve the goals of health care reform enunciated earlier. On the basis of the analysis presented here, my conclusion is not only that enhanced price competition will *not* enable us to accomplish those goals, but that, in fact, it is an obstacle to achieving them. What follows is a statement of the evidence and reasoning that led me to this position.

Health Care Issues

Health care reform is on the agenda again for many reasons, as we saw in earlier chapters, and there is growing consensus about the two primary problems that must be overcome. One is *expenditures*—we spend too much on health care, and that spending has been rising too fast and for too long. The other is *access*—too many people lack financial access to health care because either they are without health insurance altogether or the coverage they do have is inadequate, creating insurmountable barriers to their clinically appropriate use of services. The two are intertwined inextricably, as shown in Chapter 5.

We face these problems because what started out as a simple insurance strategy to protect people against the financial consequences of relatively rare but expensive events, primarily hospitalization and surgery, has been transformed over the years into something different. In some of its parts, the complex system that has evolved from these simple beginnings resembles prepayment for relatively common events more than insurance. That is not necessarily bad, but we need to recognize it as different from conventional insurance in which the driving forces are the risks and consequences—especially the financial ones—of rare, random events.

The system grew the way it did because (1) the decisions made by physicians and patients alike—both following their own perceived interests in a system paid for by a distinctively American combination of private and public third parties—led to certain anomalies, and (2) the adjustments made to correct them, in an apparently unending chain, have created still more problems. As an example, old-style hospital insurance policies typically covered services provided to hospital inpatients and to outpatients treated in emergency rooms. Most did not cover services—whether to treat illness or to prevent it—if they were provided in a doctor's office. The rationale was that patients went to hospitals for serious problems that arose unexpectedly and were expensive to treat. In those cases, the need for care was not discretionary, but people could not afford the necessary services without insurance. Not incidentally, insurance increased the chances that hospitals would actually receive payments for the care they provided and thus enable them to earn enough income to survive.

Over time, however, patients began to use emergency rooms and were admitted to hospital beds not only for treatment of serious, unexpected conditions but also because services provided in those sites were covered by insurance. Patients could thereby avoid or limit out-of-pocket expense, and providers could be certain of payment. I recall attending a committee meeting of the American Academy of Pediatrics at which a member related a story told by one of his colleagues. He said the colleague was in his office on a Sunday doing some paperwork when he got a call from the nearby hospital emergency room asking if a child whose father had brought him there was a patient of his. When he said yes, the person at the ER said he was sending the child over. When they got to the pediatrician's office, the father said he was upset that the pediatrician was there that day because now he would have to pay for the service himself instead of relying on insurance. It should be noted in passing that, given the nature of his insurance and the needs of his child that day, the father was acting rationally in following his financial incentives.

Moreover, financial incentives faced by both hospitals and physicians exacerbated the tendency toward higher utilization. Providers were paid separately for each service offered and at rates that, for the most part, they set themselves. Not only did they have no reason to restrain utilization, they had a powerful financial reason to increase it.

Thus insurance provisions contained incentives (1) to use or provide services even when no service would be a clinically appropriate option and (2) to use the hospital even when other sites would be clinically preferable and less expensive. To correct this condition, insurance policies became more inclusive in the services covered (for example, many policies added coverage of services in physician offices) so that patients would no longer have incentives to use unnecessarily expensive sources for the services they needed and instead could choose clinically more appropriate, less expensive providers. Typically, however, the method of paying the provider remained unchanged, volume continued to grow, expenditures rose, premiums increased to cover them, and, finally, some of the efforts to contain those rising expenditures resulted in the actual or threatened loss of coverage for many Americans.

In the early 1970s, the concept of managed care entered the national lexicon as Paul Ellwood, a physician in the Minneapolis area, began to promote it as a way to change the incentives and align them for all the parties. The goal was to increase the probability that people would get good care delivered efficiently. As noted in Chapter 5, the approach was based on the distinguished history of the Kaiser Permanente Health System on the West Coast. The health insurance offered by Kaiser entitled subscribers to receive care from Permanente physicians, a large multispecialty group practice that contracted to provide care only to Kaiser subscribers and in Kaiser hospitals.

The plan had several distinctive features: the Permanente organizations were partnerships of physicians and were paid an annual capitation amount to provide all ambulatory care needed by the patients who signed up with them. Capitation, from the Latin for "head," paid the practice for each patient ("head") who enrolled rather than a separate fee for each service provided. The Permanente physicians, in turn, earned salaries instead of fees for the individual services they furnished. In addition, Permanente groups included a larger proportion of primary care physicians on their rosters than specialists, which contrasted with the relative distribution of generalists and specialists throughout the United States that we saw in Chapter 5. The combination of these characteristics meant that the groups, as groups, had both a financial incentive to use restraint in the services provided to their patients and, because all physicians worked only as members of a Permanente group practice, the means to accomplish that goal. They also had a powerful interest in creating clinical processes that facilitated coordination of care and maximized quality and in building administrative structures to facilitate achievement of those results.

That financial interest came from the fact that their *gross* income was determined independently of services provided, based only on the number and characteristics of the people who enrolled with them. In turn, the group's *net* income was the amount left over after they delivered services. Because it was organized as a partnership of physicians, some of the surplus, if there was any, was divided among the partners. Most of the group's expenditures were for salaries, space, equipment, and supplies. Further, as a not-for-profit organization, it did not have shareholders who expected either a distribution of profits or that their shares would increase in value. And as a not-for-profit organization controlled by physicians, its primary mission was to deliver good care to its patients. Finally, the group's leadership was able to influence service delivery to promote both quality and efficiency, since its financial well being depended on the extent to which they achieved both and because the physicians worked only as members of the group.

Another key feature was that patients who needed hospitalization were admitted to Kaiser-owned hospitals, which limited the supply of beds per thousand enrollees. The bed-to-population ratio outside the Kaiser system was much higher in those days, leading free-standing hospitals to look for ways to fill their much larger supply of beds. The importance of this dynamic was revealed in the late 1950s in the studies that led to formulation of "Roemer's Law," which asserted that under conditions of indemnity insurance, a built bed tended to be filled[7] (see Chapter 6). So even if Kaiser kept its beds filled at the same 78 percent rate that Roemer found in the community he studied, it had fewer beds to fill, so it could afford to hospitalize patients less often than other doctors and discharge sooner those who *were* admitted. Because both admission rates and average length of stay were lower, Kaiser spent less on hospital care for its patients than insurers in other parts of the health system did for theirs. That turned out to be a powerful factor leading to Kaiser's success in the California and Oregon markets where it flourished. (It should be noted, however, that as external forces, including technology, reduced the need for inpatient services, the fact that Kaiser owned those beds became something of an albatross. Where once they had fewer beds than the others to fill, later they came to have more than they needed.)

Ellwood and his colleagues believed that by aligning the incentives in this way so that everyone gained when care was organized efficiently and patients got only the care they needed, the prepaid group-practice mode of organization represented by Kaiser Permanente could lead the U.S. health care system both to strengthen its commitment to good-quality care and to save money in the bargain. Ellwood persuaded President Richard M. Nixon to introduce the HMO Act of 1973, which made federal funds available to groups that wanted to create Kaiser-style organizations, renamed Health Maintenance Organizations (HMOs).[8] A number of such organizations were formed in that period, some taking advantage of the available federal startup funds. But despite the Kaiser experience and the alignment of financial incentives, this incremental change in the system—stimulated by public policy—did not take hold. It turned out to be more difficult than anticipated to create such organizations that could be made financially viable in a system accustomed to indemnity insurance and fee-for-service medicine. Among other things, local efforts often met the resistance of physicians who did not like either the idea of being salaried or the presence of a new competitor in the community. Nonetheless, although it did not become the new model of organizing and paying for medical care, a number of the groups that began in that period succeeded for a time in delivering high-quality care for a well-satisfied clientele.

A key reason this model did not grow and that, instead, some of the plans that succeeded initially morphed into more conventional-looking arrangements was competition from traditional indemnity plans and from new forms of "managed care." Insurers competing in markets with these new HMOs turned some of their new features against them to undercut their appeal. For example, they argued that patients should not be "locked in" to seeing a limited group of physicians. In contrast, they emphasized the comprehensiveness of their own larger physician panels, which allowed patients who enrolled with them to "keep your own doctor." In addition, they signed up large numbers of physicians—pretty much anyone who practiced in the area—by promising to pay them fees for the services they provided instead of either salaries or capitation. Some medical societies were able to persuade their state legislatures to pass laws *requiring* HMOs to sign up "any willing provider." That enabled individual physicians to contract with several HMOs in a single market and permitted the HMOs to offer potential subscribers a large number of physicians.

As the competition played out, however, HMOs, now simply "managed care organizations," found themselves in a weakened position. On the one hand, they were obligated by the terms of their insurance contracts to provide comprehensive services to their subscribers for the premiums they collected. But by contracting with such large panels of physicians who also accepted patients from other insurers, and by paying on a fee-for-service basis, they lost the ability to influence utilization and improve the delivery of care in the ways that had enabled Kaiser Permanente to achieve the results that led Paul Ellwood to propose health maintenance organizations to Richard Nixon. So they resorted to administrative devices to keep expenditures down. Thus, among other things, they imposed prior authorization requirements and drug formularies, which doctors and patients alike hated, spawning the "managed care backlash" of the 1990s.[9] Ironically, despite the resentment they caused, these cost-containment measures were ineffective, and spending on care continued to escalate.

The result is that now we still have an unwieldy, fragmented, unreasonably expensive medical care system with dysfunctional incentives that patients and providers alike follow in rational pursuit of their perceived individual interests. It is this system that is the target of the growing calls for reform.

In this context, since the two primary goals of health care reform remain (1) to provide coverage for everyone and (2) to contain expenditures, the question is, Can these objectives be achieved with a strategy built on competition? First, we need to understand what competition is and the basis for its theoretical appeal.

The Promise of Competition

Competition, like other social processes, has no intrinsic value. Instead, it acquires whatever worth it does have only to the extent that it increases the probability that certain other things we value—such as economy, innovation, and quality—will occur. Those who propose a reform strategy based on competition assume that, indeed, it will produce those other good things. Is that assumption correct? What is competition?

Competition means, most simply, that two or more entities seek the business of the same people. Assuming, first, that they all want as much business as they can get (or at least more than they have now) and second, that the potential demand is finite, then to the extent that one gains, others will lose. The theory is that in such a market, therefore, each entity will design and present its products and services in ways that encourage buyers to select its offerings over those of its competitors. Further, it will be able to do that because it will be aware of the actions of competitors and will try to make its own products and services of higher quality, of lower cost, or both.

But competition is risky. If they fail, owners and managers may lose money and jobs, and in the extreme, the company may go out of business. So while some organizations may compete to see who can win the most customers and the highest profits, the leaders of others might decide to be less aggressive and settle for less than an outright win (that is, for less than customer or profit maximization). The situation is complicated still further by the fact that a firm may achieve high profits through means other than offering the best products and services at the lowest prices. If it turns out that people tend to select health insurance and health care services on the basis of factors other than price, as we learned in Chapter 6 they do, those companies that cut their prices to attract business may find that not only have they not maximized the number of clients, they may have earned less than they could have on those they did attract.

Given these circumstances, it would *not* be irrational for some companies to set limited goals as to the extent to which they want to grow. Indeed, some may set growth targets and be satisfied if they can attract that amount of business. (See Chapter 6 for a discussion of the target-income hypothesis.) This kind of behavior is especially likely in a sector of the economy in which demand is expanding because then *all* firms may continue to gain until total demand no longer increases. This is an important point because *unless an organization makes decisions that either anticipate or respond to decisions of the other firms in order to attract customers and keep them from going to those firms, then competition does not really exist.*

What types of decisions do (or would) rational leaders of health-sector organizations make in this context? And what factors influence the decisions rational consumers do or should make? These are the central questions. The answers will determine whether a competition-based strategy can succeed in achieving the goals of reform. We will return to these questions later in the chapter.

Since the health sector consists of at least two related but separate markets, we need to assess the potential of competition individually in each. One is the market for health insurance, and the other is the market for health care itself.

For those organizations that *are* competing, the essence of competition is to differentiate themselves from others on dimensions that are important to consumers. In the case of health *insurance* in the United States, the primary consumers are employers and employees. Regarding health *care,* they are the individuals seeking services to treat illness and injury as well as preventive services and management of chronic conditions. In the case of many specialty services, referring primary care physicians are also consumers, since they influence patient decisions as to which specialists to use.

Theoretically, competition might occur along many dimensions. In the market for health care services, for example, patients looking for a service might be attracted to providers that are conveniently located, have strong reputations for quality, or are inexpensive. Indeed, because the patient's concern is that his or her future health or even life may hang in the balance, it is not unreasonable to expect that financial considerations may not be paramount in some circumstances (see Chapter 5). Nevertheless, reformers offering plans that rely on competition tend to mean competition based on *price,* although some assume that quality will improve as well.[10] The general idea is that (1) competitors will lower their prices so they will be able to attract the amount of business they need to generate the profits they want, (2) they will keep costs down so they can charge lower prices without losing money, and (3) they will succeed because consumers will respond to lower prices. Many also believe that since consumers will spend less as a result, the system as a whole will spend less. If people really are attracted by lower prices, however, more are likely to use services than they would have otherwise, and therefore if demand increases enough, total spending may increase, as well.

With this introduction, we can get more specific about the utility of price competition among insurers and providers of care as a mechanism for reforming the health care system. Can a competition strategy achieve the access and expenditure-limiting goals articulated earlier?

Competition Among Insurers

We begin by assuming that the primary goal of health insurers is to increase the amount of their business and, in the case of for-profit companies, to maximize profit. It should be noted that companies organized on a not-for-profit basis (such as Blue Cross and Blue Shield) or as mutual insurance companies must behave like for-profit companies in many respects in order to attract and retain customers. As an example, witness the Kaiser Permanente–style HMOs that were forced to respond to competitors in the 1980s by broadening their physician list and giving up their ability to influence utilization decisions. Further, state regulations tend to require that all insurers maintain certain reserves to ensure they can pay the bills for services used by their policyholders.

In fact, as noted, the competition strategy depends on each firm's wanting more business in order to increase its income. Insurers attempt to achieve that objective in three steps: first, by selling policies that promise to pay some or all of the costs of covered services for subscribers; then, by investing the premium income before it is needed to pay for services; and finally, by paying out for services and their other expenses less than the total gross income from premiums and investments.

A key element of the strategy to accomplish that critical third step is to minimize two types of costs: (1) the cost of selling insurance policies[11] and (2) spending on the services that are provided.

LIMITING SELLING COSTS

Health insurers have two primary customer groups: employers, whom they try to induce to offer one or more of their policies to employees, and employees of the companies that offer their policies, whom they try to induce to choose one. Theoretically, they could try to sell to individuals, too, but the cost of doing so is high.

The primary method for limiting selling costs is to *segment the market* in order to sell primarily to large companies on behalf of their employees. The functions involved in selling include risk-determination and underwriting, targeted advertising and other marketing operations, and commissions. Expenditures and therefore premiums are much more expensive for small groups, ranging from 18 percent to 40 percent of insured claims.[12] The reasons are that administrative costs (for selling, setting rates, and other purposes) are higher and the risk of service use is less predictable in small groups. Selling costs are high because the number of small businesses that are potential customers is large, and the small number of employees in each firm limits the amount of premium income that can be generated from each sale. Even if the effort to close a sale to a small company were equal to or less than the effort needed for a large employer, those costs must be multiplied by the large number of small companies. Further, the contribution to insurer revenues from each sale will be smaller because the number of potential subscribers is smaller.

LIMITING SPENDING ON SERVICES

Because employing companies want to maximize *their* profits too, they find low premium prices appealing. So at least one precondition for a competition strategy is met: consumer (here, employer) interest in premium price as a potential decision criterion. In fact, about 20 percent of employers change insurers each year, in part because of the search for lower costs.[13] There are two main bases for setting premiums. *Community rating* means that everyone in the group (that is, the community) is charged the same premium. In essence, the insurer estimates the total expected expenditures plus an amount for its profit and divides by the expected number of subscribers. Premiums do not vary by an individual's health or need for services. Under *experience rating,* on the other hand, prices for each subgroup of the larger community are determined by the expected utilization expenditures of that subgroup (for example, the particular company's employees). If the insured group includes a large proportion of young, healthy, professional adults, their expected utilization is relatively low, so their experience-rated premium also will be fairly low. A firm that is able to offer coverage for those low rates will have a leg up on competitors that use community rating over a more diverse subscriber group. If, instead, the group includes many high-risk people who may use a lot of services, their experience-rated premium will be much higher. Think of the difference between a Silicon Valley high-tech startup firm and rust-belt manufacturers such as the automobile companies in Michigan.

If the experience-rated group consists of the employees of a small retail store or other small employer, the rates may be high for another reason: the health care risk in small groups is notoriously unstable because a single member who happens to develop cancer or is hit by a drunk driver will have a huge impact on the experience of the group as a whole. In fact, some insurers offer high premium rates in the hope of discouraging such firms or their employees from signing up.

An insurer can gain a competitive advantage by offering an employer low prices to the extent that it both limits service costs and, targeting firms with young, healthy employees, bases its charges on the favorable service utilization (that is, experience) expected from the group being insured. It can achieve this advantage in three principal ways: (1) by selling to groups in which higher-risk employees are such a small proportion of total covered lives that their impact will be limited; (2) by excluding from coverage high-risk people (for example, those with preexisting conditions); and (3) in those firms that offer policies from multiple carriers, by offering memberships in health clubs or other incidental inducements that are likely to appeal disproportionately to healthy young adults.

The primary mechanism for limiting insurers' spending is *market segmentation,* which enables insurers to charge different rates to different groups by dividing the population into preferred and nonpreferred patients (see Chapter 6). Preferred patients tend to work for large employers, which reduces insurers' selling costs, and to be young and healthy enough that insurers can expect to pay out relatively little in expenditures for services. Nonpreferred clients, by contrast, work for small firms or for firms that do not offer coverage (that is, people who are in the insurance market as members of small groups or as individuals) or are older and have preexisting conditions. Because all of those groups can be expected to need and use more services, they are charged higher premiums, partly in the hope that many will decide to buy their coverage from others.[14] The sad fact is that, like the Texas woman and her family introduced in Chapter 1, many are priced out of the private market altogether.

Second, following market segmentation, the insurer can limit the terms of the policy: by excluding dependents; by limiting the benefit package; by including cost-sharing for the services subscribers use; or by encouraging their employer clients to charge individual subscribers part of the premium price.[15]

Third, it can impose cost-limiting administrative mechanisms requiring prior approval of some services and making it difficult for providers to collect fees for services already rendered.

It is in this realm of the insurers' cost-limiting efforts that we find cause for concern. Suppose insurers succeed, using the methods indicated, in limiting their costs of selling and their outlays for services. Limiting spending on services is not, in and of itself, a bad thing—especially since, as we saw in Chapter 6, providers sometimes furnish services of marginal value in order to increase their income.[16] But what many would like to see is mechanisms that encourage appropriate care and efficiency and discourage unnecessary care and waste. The hard part is to design such approaches or strategies that do not also discourage some good care and encourage some unneeded services. What will happen to the goals identified at the outset? Can a competition-based approach to reform produce universal coverage, access for all to needed care, and limited spending? I believe the answer will always be "no." Here is why.

IMPLICATIONS OF INSURERS' COST-LIMITING STRATEGIES FOR HEALTH CARE REFORM

To begin, not all Americans work for large employers. Some work for small companies with under twenty employees, which in 2004 made up 86 percent of all firms;[17] some are self-employed; and some do not work at all because they are retired, they are children or other dependents of workers, or for other reasons. Therefore, to the extent insurers succeed in segmenting the market and limiting their costs as described, some of those who do not work for large employers will be excluded from coverage altogether.

It is important to recognize that people not working for large employers who do, nonetheless, obtain coverage will not benefit from lower prices even if those in larger, younger groups do. The reason that costs for these groups are higher than for employees of large companies has nothing to do with the efficiency of their providers of care or their own willingness to exercise restraint in using services. Rather, it is due to the progressively higher costs of selling and serving such customers and the actuarially greater risk that they will need and use services, as explained in the following.

First, the per-subscriber selling cost is higher for small companies than for large ones.[18] Insurers need to call on fifty firms with twenty employees each to have even a chance to equal the yield of a single successful sale to a firm with a thousand employees. Even if they use insurance brokers to act as middlemen, their costs will be higher than those for large employers. The higher selling costs contribute to the higher prices insurers charge to small firms.

Second, because the risk of utilization can be expressed only as a probability, not a certainty, even people in low-risk, low-premium groups face some chance that they will need expensive services. We all know young people who have developed cancers against all odds or have been in various types of serious accidents. Moreover, the financial consequences of using expensive services are much greater for the insurer if the patient happens to be part of a small group than of a large group. The $50,000 cost of a hospitalization and surgery will be a larger share of the premium income generated by a small group than of that from a large group.

Third, private insurers face the large risk of failure among small businesses, which, when it occurs, results in nonpayment of premiums. Thorpe estimates that as many as 35 percent of small firms fail each year and that "the average lifespan of small firms with insurance is less than 28 months."[19]

The result of all this is that because many small employers don't make enough profit to be able to pay higher premiums in the first place, their employees are less likely to be offered health insurance at all. And when it is offered, not only are the premiums likely to be higher, but the firms are likely to try to keep their own costs down by offering coverage that is less comprehensive in its scope, excluding the employees' families from coverage, and requiring the employees to pay a substantial part of the premium cost.[20]

In addition, administrative costs for individuals—whether self-employed or unemployed—are the highest of all,[21] and individuals have the least predictable risk of the need for services. For both reasons, they tend to face the highest premiums.

Therefore, some members of all three groups (employees of small businesses, self-employed people, and the unemployed) will not participate in the private insurance market. Many will end up without any coverage since most of them will not be eligible for public-sector safety-net programs that could fill in. We already have seen the effects of this scenario in the present health care system, which relies primarily on employers for health insurance and currently produces more than 46 million uninsured Americans.

The inescapable *first conclusion,* then, is that a health insurance system that depends on private insurers to compete on price to provide coverage *will always* produce large numbers of uninsured people and thus will fail to achieve universal coverage, a key goal of reform. Ironically, the probability that this result will occur is higher in a market in which insurance companies are most efficient and profitable. If we are wedded to both universal coverage as a goal and price competition as a strategy, then it follows that since a competition strategy by itself cannot succeed, some sort of nonmarket (that is, public-sector) plan will need to be added to it to cover those who are left out.

That may be worth doing if the combination of competitive private insurance for large groups and a nonmarket, public-sector alternative for small groups and individuals would produce reliably good-quality care, lower per capita costs for the system as a whole, and lower total health care expenditures. Whether that, in fact, will be the case depends in part on pricing policies of the insurers of the large groups. Will their prices, multiplied by the large numbers of people they cover, be low enough (1) to provide such reliable, stable coverage that the people they enroll can count on them to be there when they need it and (2) to compensate for the higher prices that must be charged to the smaller groups and the payments made for those who will be covered by a nonmarket plan? Evidence from our present mixed system strongly suggests the answer is no. Indeed, I believe it must always be no.

PRICING IN A MIXED SYSTEM

In a competitive market in which insurers expect consumers to choose policies on the basis of price, each insurer will want, at a minimum, to set its prices lower than its competitors but high enough to cover its costs. To offer an employer low prices and still cover those costs, an insurer must limit its selling costs, which we have already discussed; limit spending on services, which we will discuss further shortly; satisfy itself with a lower rate of profit; or all three.

This point holds even for the self-insured employer as long as it offers workers a choice of plans, because the self-insurer too must pay its share of the costs for workers in the highest-cost plan it offers. However, it need not set the prices of other plans as close to the highest as a profit-maximizing independent insurer would. (See discussion of the Honeywell Case further on.) On the other hand, if employees pay part of the premium, the employer has an opportunity to profit from insurance, too. Unless a state regulates needed reserves for self-insured plans,[22] the premium for the self-insured company may be an amount on paper only, not a cash expense (as it would be for the firm that purchases coverage from an outside vendor.) Therefore, if employees pay some of the cost of coverage, the employer can reduce both its insurance costs and the wages paid to employees (and thus increase its profit) by raising the "premium" and the share charged to the employees. Indeed, we have already seen that employees pay the cost of insurance anyway through lower wages.[23]

Before any of those strategies even becomes relevant, however, the insurer must induce workers to choose its policies over those of its competitors (unless the employer offers employees no choice of plan).[24] Selling health insurance means selling to the employee as well as to the employer.

Employees who face choices among several policies want low prices, too. Insurers can reduce the prices employees are charged by offering fewer benefits, paying providers less, or increasing patient cost-sharing (even though the actual price the employee faces will also depend on the share of the premium paid by the employer). That may be the case theoretically, but in trying to implement it, the insurer runs into a big dose of reality. At any given price, employees are likely to want the most covered services, the least cost-sharing, and the freest choice among providers, and will tend to choose the plan with the most advantageous combination of characteristics. All of these features will exert upward pressure on prices.

How does an insurer offer subscribers a wide range of providers? Usually, a big part of the answer is by getting physicians and hospitals to agree to accept the company's payments (otherwise, in addition to traditional cost-sharing, the patient may face the cost of "balance billing"[25]). To encourage physicians to accept its covered patients, the insurer (1) pays physicians fees that are at worst nearly as high as those paid by the competition and (2) offers relatively less scrutiny of their utilization decisions. This is the case even though in recent years, as health care costs have climbed so much, more employers are agreeing to require approval by a PBM, for example, before agreeing to pay for doctor-ordered prescriptions. Nonetheless, both of these actions also put upward pressure on the insurer's costs. The alternative is collusion among insurers that conspire to divide the market by setting comparably low physician fees.

In addition, the indemnity insurer faces other obstacles to achieving low service costs. One is the fee-for-service payment method, which encourages providers—both physicians and hospitals—to furnish additional services, even those with little or no demonstrated utility, in order to earn additional fees. Another is the fact that physicians control most utilization. Patients go to physicians for their expertise, as we discovered earlier, and, other things being equal, are likely to follow their recommendations. Thus, if the insurer imposes a fee schedule with prices that are lower than a physician's charges, the doctor can often increase the volume of services he provides in order to earn more income. (See the discussion of the target-income hypothesis in Chapter 6.) To counteract this tendency, insurers with a large share of the market (and therefore more of area physicians' patients) may be able to impose prior authorization requirements and other burdens on physicians that can reduce—or at least delay—utilization. In that case, their weaker competitors may follow suit—even though not doing so would give them an advantage with physicians and patients—because they too need to keep down their expenditures for services used and have few tools for doing so.

Nonetheless, even setting low physician fees does not guarantee that the insurer will be able to keep down its expenditures for services. State Medicaid programs discovered this truth, much to their chagrin, decades ago, as we saw in Chapter 6.

Whatever the benefit package and range of providers who participate in an insurer's offerings, the most reliable method of containing expenditures is to limit the services actually used by its subscribers. An insurer can limit *service* expenditures indirectly, as noted earlier, by restricting its clientele to those who are likely to need few services or inexpensive ones. It can also attempt to limit the utilization of services directly, especially those that are particularly expensive.

LIMITING UTILIZATION DIRECTLY

Insurers serious about limiting utilization can impose additional barriers to the use of services. They include (1) a requirement that, to be covered, certain services must be preauthorized by an employee of the insurer; (2) the imposition of cost-sharing provisions (such as deductibles, coinsurance, or co-payments) that create countervailing financial incentives on consumers to the use of services; or (c) before agreeing to pay, review of utilization decisions for services already provided to determine whether they were truly "necessary." The last device sometimes results in "retroactive denials" of payment for services already rendered, which is anathema to physicians and reduces their willingness to accept payments from insurers that use it. In those cases, the provider may insist that the patient pay the entire bill and then submit a claim to the insurer for reimbursement for as much of those outlays as the insurer is willing to pay.

A big problem with all these devices is that they tend to undermine the very purpose of insurance: to guarantee payments for needed services by spreading the risk over many people for whom regular manageable payments are made in advance. To the extent that objective is achieved, individuals will be spared having to make utilization decisions on the basis of whether or not they think they can afford the service, especially at a time they are sick and emotionally stressed. Instead, they can afford to follow the physicians' expert recommendations.

The most reliable means for an insurer to control utilization without denying needed services may be to become a staff- or group-model HMO, as exemplified by the Kaiser Permanente model described earlier in this chapter.[26] Other forms of HMO and other types of managed care have not demonstrated dependable success in reducing unnecessary utilization. Indeed, even group- and staff-model HMOs present challenges to plan managers that many have not mastered, although they do tend to have more influence and leverage over physicians than managers of other types of HMOs. Because other forms of practice organization will continue to be part of the American health care landscape for many years, however, insurers will have a hard time using this mechanism to keep down utilization and therefore expenditures.

Beyond setting prices to cover their costs, the rational strategy for competing insurers will be to charge as much as they can while still generating the amount of business they want.[27] That being the case, the counterintuitive reality is that the price they set will be determined by the insurer with the *highest* costs. That company will set its prices to cover expected costs, and while its competitors will want to charge less so as to get business away from them, they will also want to charge as much as possible under that constraint. In *The Honeywell Case,*[28] Fred Foulkes showed that, in order to maximize profits, HMOs set prices that "snuggled under" the higher indemnity rates. Where firms engage in "shadow pricing" like this, the price differential between managed care and indemnity plans will be small enough that even the higher-priced carrier will be able to obtain enough business to remain viable.

Even if companies do tend to "snuggle under" the prices of indemnity plans, however, why wouldn't an aggressive insurer set its prices still lower in order to take business from them? Apart from the inherent risk of such a strategy, the primary answer is the difficulty in controlling spending on services. Even HMOs with strong reputations for quality and service have not been able *reliably* and consistently to manage the utilization behavior of their subscribers and clinicians. In a risk-averse economy, therefore, a prudent insurer may very well choose to settle for a smaller but secure share of the market at higher prices and proportionally higher profits.

Even if plans do not *minimize* prices, if a large employer is offered a saving of even a few percentage points, that may still be enough for the lower-priced carrier to take business away from a competitor. Employers would be attracted to the lower prices because their aggregate saving would be substantial. Indeed, in 2003, 56 percent of firms offering coverage shopped for a new plan. Of those firms, 29 percent reported using their present carrier for less than a year, and only 13 percent had their present carrier six years earlier.[29] Yet even though the change of carriers may result in sizeable aggregate savings for the employer, it may not induce many individual consumers, if offered a choice, to change their plans. That is especially the case if changing means having to give up their primary care physician and the annual saving would put only a few hundred dollars in their pockets, some of which would be taken back in taxes. On the other hand, to the extent that employers and their employees do make such changes, primary care physicians may be discouraged from extending themselves, knowing the patient may leave for another physician in a year or two.

Although the trend in the 1990s was toward increasing numbers of "managed care" arrangements,[30] they tended more and more to resemble fee-for-service indemnity plans and thus were less and less able to control service expenditures. As a result, the potential for system-wide savings based on restraint in utilization is quite limited. It is likely that the price differential between plans in such a market will be fairly narrow and thereby will limit still further the theoretical system-wide gains from price competition.

The *second conclusion,* therefore, is that a competition strategy will not minimize either prices or expenditures in the private insurance sector. These will continue to rise as, indeed, they have for more than forty years. Those higher prices will, in turn, cause increasing numbers of employers to refrain from offering health insurance and cause large numbers of employees to reject it when it is offered. As a result, it reinforces the tendency already described to undermine universal coverage, one of the central goals of reform.

SHOULD WE REFORM OUR MIXED SYSTEM?

Currently, we have a mixed system that includes (1) a competitive private insurance sector that covers those individuals who work for companies that pay some or all of the cost of coverage or who can pay for coverage in the individual market and (2) a public sector that plays a residual role providing coverage to many of those left out of the private market. And while many of those covered by the private system have had reasonably good coverage to date, many others are underinsured,[31] and growing numbers are losing the coverage they have relied on for years. At the same time, the present residual public-sector programs not only exclude millions of the rest, but increasingly emulate the declining private sector by providing inadequate benefits for some of those they cover.[32] Nonetheless, it might be worth expanding the residual, public-sector component if the entire mixed system would be stronger as a result. The question is, What are the benefits of our mixed system? Is it efficient? Is it inexpensive?[33] If not now, can it be so?

Per capita costs for those covered by the residual public-sector segment of the system will tend to be higher than those in the private-sector component of the reformed system because of adverse selection. The people left for the public sector to cover will be those who are unwanted by profit-seeking private insurers because they tend to use more services than the younger, healthier, more affluent clientele the insurers hope to enroll and cannot afford the insurer's higher premiums. In addition to workers in small firms, these tend to be older people, the chronically ill, and the poor. Regardless of the administrative efficiency of the public-sector program, those groups of people, because of their health, are likely to use more services and more expensive services over a longer period—and, therefore, incur greater expenditures—than those cared for in the private insurance market. Indeed, this is the reality today.

In fact, since that *must* be the case, the presence of a public sector to fill gaps left by private insurance makes it easier for private firms to justify limiting the extent to which they provide coverage for their own employees and, especially, for their employees' dependents. Moreover, if complex eligibility determination and maintenance procedures were adopted, or if eligibility had to be reestablished frequently (as it does in means-tested programs such as Medicaid), the public-sector agency would have substantial administrative costs. (State Medicaid administrative costs tend to be higher than those for Medicare, largely for that reason.)[34] In addition, depending on methods and rates of paying for services, providers also would incur higher administrative expenses just to determine the nature of their patients' coverage. This too is already the reality because of the great variety of insurance products in the private market as well as means-tested public sector programs, especially Medicaid.[35]

The current mixed public-private system, which produced the problems described in Chapters 2, 3, and 4, can be modified to reduce the impact of some of the worst characteristics.[36] But unless common prices were paid by all payers, any mixed system would always tend to produce *higher total expenditures,* for several reasons.

First, public payers burdened with adverse selection would need higher budgets to cover their higher service expenditures. If they received what they needed to pay charges, then per capita costs in the residual public sector program would be higher than the per capita costs of private insurance simply because of the health care needs of their clientele. If, on the other hand, their budgets were less than that amount, then governments would pay lower prices to providers of care, and providers, comparing patients on the basis of what private third-party payers offer, would hold publicly funded patients in less favor than private patients. For many years, physicians in many states have refused to serve Medicaid patients,[37] and now growing numbers are rejecting Medicare patients as well.[38]

When public budgets become tight, per capita payments that were higher than those in the private sector—even though justified by patients' health care needs—would be an inviting target for budget cutters. Government officials would reduce prices still further or fail to raise them to keep up with private-sector fees, and publicly funded patients would become even less desirable for providers to treat. In fact, they might not be able to get care until they are so sick they have to go to a hospital emergency department, which is required to treat them even if they cannot pay. In that case, not only would we fail to achieve one of the main goals of reform, but the public sector would pick up some of the hospital's uncompensated care, with the hospital eating the rest. As we saw in Chapter 6, this would further undermine the hospital's ability to maintain its facility, to modernize, and perhaps to maintain the quality with which it treats even paying patients.

Second, providers would raise charges—and perhaps increase service volume—to private patients in order to subsidize the care they furnish to publicly funded patients and the uninsured or to replace the income they gave up by refusing to care for Medicaid and Medicare patients because those programs' fees were too low. In addition, the uninsured and people covered by public programs would tend to seek care later during an episode of illness than is clinically optimal, especially since the present system generally discourages such individuals from attaching themselves to a regular source of care or a "medical home."[39] As a result, the costs of treatment would tend to be still higher than if the same people sought care earlier in their illness.

Third, we already saw that when competing insurers set prices, they would tend not to choose the lowest amount that covers costs and provides a reasonable profit. Instead, they would tend to "snuggle under" the higher prices set by an expensive industry leader. This is especially likely if demand in the market is still expanding, their competitors cannot serve all employers, and they can expect to find companies willing to pay higher amounts. So for this reason too, such a system will not minimize spending levels.

Finally, the number of people who are uninsured or who are covered by an expanded residual public-sector program will always be large. In fact, as already noted, the very presence of a residual component in a mixed system makes it possible for, and may even encourage, companies to limit coverage of employed people. The extent to which firms actually do either drop or curtail coverage will vary with economic conditions, as the current recession has amply demonstrated.

The *third conclusion,* therefore, is that both per capita costs of care and overall expenditures will be higher in a mixed system like the one we have than would be likely under a system that did not reward market segmentation. Indeed, we saw in Chapter 2 that U.S. spending is already much higher than that of any other country no matter what measure is used. In addition, the mixed system will always produce inequities because providers will view the patients of some payers more favorably than the patients of others.

Although private health insurance has done a lot of good for the people who are covered by it, our present system also contains elements that encourage both unnecessary expenditures and unnecessary utilization. Can the system be reformed to solidify the benefits of competitive private insurance without the runaway expenditures? The analysis presented to this point suggests the answer is no. But there is one more possibility to consider: that if *providers,* too, were to compete on the basis of price, they would become more efficient, thereby reducing the amounts insurers would need to pay.

Having examined how insurers compete, we turn next to see if we can expect lower overall expenditures on services when providers compete.

Competition Among Providers

Medical care providers have always competed for patients. Julie Salamon provides several examples in her book about Maimonides Medical Center in Brooklyn. In one, she writes that to avoid losing cancer patients to centers in Manhattan, the hospital developed a first-class cancer center at Maimonides to compete, even recruiting some of its staff from those same Manhattan centers.[40] Traditionally, however, providers have competed not on the basis of price but primarily on their reputations for quality. More accurately, since quality is such an elusive characteristic, hard to define and hard to measure, those reputations are based in part on certain elements of care that people associate with quality: hospitals buy and offer the latest technology (such as CT scanners and MRI machines); they offer board-certified physicians; they offer more nurses. People often choose primary care physicians on the recommendations of friends who are satisfied with their service. In the case of referral services and hospitalization, the patient's trusted primary care physician attests to the specialist's or hospital's reputation for quality. The price of the service rarely comes up. Providers also offer varying levels of convenience and amenities, which appeal to some patients. Most of these items add to costs.

Can price competition by care providers increase the chances that services will be appropriate, of good quality, and efficiently provided so that spending can be contained? The answer to that question begins with the reminder that every dollar in health care spending is the result of individual patient and provider decisions to use or provide services. National health care expenditures are the aggregate of those decisions. Therefore, if we want to contain those expenditures, we must find ways to influence people to make different utilization decisions than the ones they make under the present system (see Chapter 6).

What has price got to do with it? The answer is "not much," primarily because of insurance, which insulates patients from much of the cost of care. They are certainly influenced by out-of-pocket payments, as shown earlier, but coinsurance and tiered drug pricing are the only ones that actually vary with the price of the service.

Could the amounts paid to providers by insurers lead to greater efficiency among providers and lower costs overall? Theoretically, yes. Insurers could pay a fixed amount for a service and require the patient to pay the balance. Then the patient's payment would vary with the price, and he or she would have reason to look for providers with lower prices. To the extent that actually happened, then providers might respond by becoming more efficient in order to be able to lower their prices and succeed in the competition. Or they could lower their prices not by becoming more efficient but by cutting corners. (Comparing providers on their prices is valid only if the services—or results, if we can know them—are similar.)

Leaving aside the question of whether providers would become more efficient or cut corners to lower their costs, how reasonable is it to think that patients would—or more important, *should*—really behave this way? Would they shop around for lower prices? Consider a patient suspected of having cancer. If he were referred to an oncologist for tests to determine if he really has cancer, as his primary care doctor suspects, should he ask the price of the tests, and then shop around for a lower price? And then, if the diagnosis is confirmed, instead of getting treatment from that same oncologist, should he shop around again for lower chemotherapy prices? Suppose the treatment includes radiation, as well, and the patient finds a lower price for that service at a cancer center that is different from the chemotherapy provider. Is it really a good idea to divide the patient's care in that way? And suppose the chosen oncologist's hospital where the services are to be performed is more expensive than another facility. These are all costly items, so the patient's out-of-pocket payments under a plan in which the insurer pays a fixed amount could be substantial. Assuming the patient has enough money to use those services, is care that is so fragmented a good idea? Wouldn't it be better to have a system that encouraged a patient to find a doctor in whom he had confidence—justifiably—and then rely on him or her to make recommendations based on his or her professional experience? And do we really want a plan in which the patient's out-of-pocket costs are so substantial that he decides to get only some of the recommended treatment because that is all he can afford? The Orozcos' story in Chapter 2 shows that this is already happening because of cost-sharing—and the effects on both health and family income are potentially devastating.

We cannot know for sure how patients and providers would behave if insurers limited the rates they pay. Would patients shop around for lower prices? Some might, but many would forgo services as too expensive. Would providers become more efficient and furnish higher-quality care in order to attract price-sensitive customers? Maybe, but as long as they are paid fee-for-service, providers have already shown us they will certainly do either or both of two things: they will reduce the amount of resources expended on care (shorter visits, for example) and, to the extent possible, they will increase the number of services provided. In other words, they may reduce their costs (perhaps by lowering quality) but increase volume. If they do, the cost of individual services may go down, but expenditures will not.

Yet the cost of care is important. So we need to find another method for trying to keep it under control—one that does not undermine the quality of care.

WILL PROVIDERS BE MORE EFFICIENT?

Will price competition among providers produce greater efficiency in the delivery of services? Only if consumers choose providers on the basis of price. Yet as the previous discussion showed, having insurance reduces consumers' sensitivity to price as a rationing device even though cost-sharing does diminish the utilization-enhancing effects of insurance. One way to increase the effects of price competition among providers is to eliminate or greatly curtail insurance. But obviously we don't want to do that. Indeed, the main attraction of insurance is that it frees patients from having to consider financial issues during a serious illness.

The main argument against increasing the utilization-inhibiting impact of price, even for more common, less expensive services, is that doing so increases the financial barriers not just to useless services but also to beneficial ones. These include preventive care and the early treatment of illness, both of which may result in the avoidance of higher future expenditures. Moreover, the impact falls most heavily on those Americans with the least disposable income. Nonetheless, it may be possible to introduce features of insurance policies that achieve a better balance between two competing social purposes: removal of the financial barriers to useful service and promotion of utilization that is both beneficial and no more expensive than necessary to ensure that sufficient services are available.

Assuming that insurance provisions can be designed that induce consumers to consider price in making utilization decisions and choosing providers *without undermining appropriate utilization patterns,* then we need to ask a second question: What will providers do in order to be able to offer lower prices than their competitors? Will they charge lower prices for comparable services? Will they also reduce the amount of service provided for the price so that the lower price buys less service? Or will they increase the volume of services provided to compensate for the reduced income that results from lower prices? Remember that patients go to physicians primarily for information, so if the doctor recommends a service during the visit, the insured patient is likely to use it if she can afford the out-of-pocket payments. Competition may result in lower prices without improving efficiency because what patients buy is services (office visits, tests, x-rays, drugs, procedures), even though what they really seek is the diagnosis and treatment of illness. Therefore, if the services are insufficient to diagnose the illness accurately or to treat the illness successfully, the patient who chose the lower-priced provider may require more service—perhaps from another provider—thereby incurring higher costs.

The answer to the first question (Should patients choose services on the basis of price?) will usually be no. A patient has varying levels of discretion when it comes to deciding on the use of services. When he is taken unconscious to a hospital emergency department following an automobile accident, he has no discretion; in fact, others are making decisions for him. What choices are they making? Will they know what insurance he has? If not, will they select an inexpensive mix of services in case he does not have good coverage? Would we want someone to choose for us on that basis?

At the other end of the spectrum, a fifty-year-old woman sees a televised announcement from the American Cancer Society urging women in her age category to have annual mammograms because, as a group, they have a significant risk of breast cancer and early detection produces better survival rates. She would like to follow their advice, but preventive services are not covered by her policy, and because she feels healthy and it is hard to make ends meet as it is, the test feels like a luxury she can forego. What if she later has symptoms, visits her doctor, and discovers she has a malignancy in her breast—what choices should she and her physician make then? Should they shop around for the best deal? Should she be entitled to less than if she had had the mammogram?

Most health care decisions tend to fall between the two extremes of discretionary preventive services and unconsciousness. People have different propensities to seek care on the basis of a variety of factors, including their ability to tolerate pain; their confidence in the benefits of care; and their willingness to face the unknown or, alternatively, their need to deny it. Sometimes cost matters too, especially when the decision is whether or not to seek care at all. Once they have visited a doctor, however, most patients tend to follow his or her advice, and at that point, cost often is not much of a factor. The number of patients in that category may be falling, however, with more and more evidence of insured people not getting services they need because of the cost-sharing provisions.

Is that an unreasonable scenario? Even though they may have preferences based on conversations with friends or reading the popular press, as lay people most patients are subject to the influence of professional caregivers. Indeed, the physicians they consult not only have greater knowledge but also the legitimacy conferred by that knowledge to influence demand on the basis of a relationship of trust built up with their patients. On the other hand, the fact that physicians in our system usually benefit financially from providing the service (and not from denying it) undoubtedly colors their decisions, especially in cases in which the medical value of the service is unclear.

WHO SHOULD DECIDE: PATIENT OR PHYSICIAN?

It can be argued that price *should* be a factor, and that the system *should* be designed to encourage its use as a rationing device. But whose decision should the system attempt to influence? The patient's? If her physician recommends that she see a specialist, should a patient ask how much it will cost? If she is told the price, should she ask her physician for a less expensive choice? And what kind of an answer should she expect from her doctor, who may have selected the referral physician on the basis of assumptions about quality? Suppose the physician says he does not know what the specialist will charge. Should the patient refuse to call for an appointment until her physician determines the cost or finds a specialist in the patient's price range? Alternatively, should the patient ask the physician for several recommendations, call them herself, and choose the one she can afford? If so, what does she ask? Does it matter if the patient's condition not only is serious but also is painful? What assumptions should the patient make about the relative quality of two physicians who charge different prices? And, even more, about the impact that each will have on her illness?

When she calls the specialist, should the patient say, "I can afford $300"? Suppose that is enough for tests to confirm the diagnosis, but not enough to treat the patient's condition? What should she do then? Does such a commercialized system give the doctor license to refuse to do anything beyond providing the diagnosis that, without treatment, is tantamount to a death sentence, but with treatment, could lead to the patient's recovery and many productive years ahead? What will have been gained if this becomes the norm? Given that much medical care is expensive—especially when serious illness is involved—will we be creating a system in which only the rich will survive?

PHYSICIAN QUALITY

If a patient can overcome the financial dimension of the challenge, he might be able to come to a judgment about physician quality. Data are becoming available that purport to reflect physicians' actual records of service and to show the extent to which they provide quality care. So far, however, these sources—often on the Internet—tend to have serious limitations. For example, not all doctors or all patients are included in the datasets from which the conclusions are drawn; the original data sources from which the summaries are taken may have other difficulties, as well; and the measures of quality themselves may be unsatisfactory. Moreover, methodologically, it is very hard to attribute with much confidence many measures of quality to individual physicians.

Nonetheless, some are moving ahead, even varying patients' co-payments to encourage them to choose lower-cost or higher-quality physicians.[41] A recent example in Massachusetts illustrates the difficulties. In an effort to contain spending and promote quality care, the state's Group Insurance Commission (GIC), which is responsible for health insurance for state employees, adopted a plan in which individual physicians are placed in groups, called "tiers," according to scores on various quality measures, with the highest tier being Tier 1 (excellent), followed by Tier 2 (good), and Tier 3 (standard). Patients face variable co-payments—lowest if their physician is in Tier 1 and highest if in Tier 3. The assumption is that patients will choose doctors in Tier 1 in order to have the lowest co-payment. The strategy is intended to stimulate physicians to take actions that, in order to attract or retain more patients, will cause them to rise to that highest tier. The plan sounds reasonable, but it raises important implementation issues regarding, especially, measures of quality and the variable-co-pay strategy.

Measures of Quality.   First, of course, the measures must be valid indicators of quality. The GIC uses measures of physician quality developed by Resolution Health, Inc.[42] In a report dated August 24, 2007, each measure is described, and references to the medical literature are provided to support the measures. Assuming they are, indeed, valid measures, questions remain about their use in this way: (1) Since quality data are organized by diagnosis, it is possible that many individual physicians will not have enough patients with a given diagnosis to allow valid conclusions to be drawn about the physician's abilities. This is a particular issue for primary care physicians (PCPs) who see patients with a great variety of conditions, some of which should be referred to specialists. (2) The measures are based on services received, so what happens if a physician orders the right test or prescription, but the patient does not follow through (perhaps because he or she cannot afford the cost-sharing amounts)? (3) And what happens to a primary care physician's score if he refers a patient, appropriately, to a specialist? Are the services that should be provided or ordered by the specialist *after* the referral assigned to the PCP or to the specialist? How will the GIC know that a primary care physician referred a patient appropriately if the patient fails to follow through because of the cost? (4) It turns out that some physicians are high on some measures and low on others. How should that be handled? This problem will be exacerbated if, instead of an organization such as the Massachusetts GIC, the groupings are done by an individual insurer using only its own data. (5) Since there are two goals—lowering costs and improving quality—they may not point in the same direction. Because higher quality reflects the use of more services, scoring high on quality probably also means scoring low on cost containment, at least in the short run.

Variable Co-Pays.   Assuming all questions related to measurement can be answered satisfactorily, additional questions are raised by the variable co-pay strategy. The assumption is that patients want the best physician they can have and will change physicians if they know theirs does not measure up to others. Since we already know that patient utilization decisions are influenced by a variety of factors, that basic assumption may turn out to be wrong. Nonetheless, here are some relevant concerns. (1) The GIC program began in 2006. Is there any evidence yet that patients actually move from lower-tier to higher-tier physicians? (2) Since the number of patients with a given diagnosis that a typical physician would have can vary randomly as a result of patterns in the incidence of disease from one year to the next, especially for PCPs, it could take time (maybe years) for scores to change enough for that physician to move into a higher tier. If this is the case, the number of physicians in the higher tiers might not increase, and, in the short run, the state would spend more. (3) Another reason it will take a long time to see change is that the GIC's patients constitute a small minority of the typical physician's practice. As a result, the incentive may be too weak to encourage the physician to adopt new behaviors. (4) Some patients who want to migrate to a first-tier physician may not be able to do so if the only available first-tier physician does not have room in her practice. Yet those patients who stayed with their lower-tier physician would be charged higher co-payments without having a way to access services with lower co-payments. (5) The strategy fails to recognize that the treatment decision is made by both patient and physician and, further, that of the two, the physician is more knowledgeable about the patient's condition and the best course of treatment. Even though patients will now also know which tier their physicians are in, as we saw already, there are good reasons to doubt the validity of those assignments.

Bad Apples Versus System Problems. To the extent that tiering applies to individual physicians, especially when they practice alone, it implicitly assumes that poor quality results from what Berwick calls the "theory of the bad apples"—that is, the problems are the result of poorly trained or careless individuals.[43] The alternative explanation is that characteristics of the system lower quality by facilitating errors. Further, most observers believe the best chance for improvement occurs when an organization (even a multiphysician group practice) has responsibility for the care and is graded for quality. The reason is that an organization is more likely to have the data needed to identify the sources of revealed problems and to be able to respond by introducing changes that do not depend on singling out individuals as "bad physicians." As a result, placing *groups* in tiers is more likely to pay off than assigning individual physicians to them.

The conclusion is that the current system makes it very difficult to use incentives related to patient payment—whether prices or cost-sharing—fairly to improve quality or lower spending.

INFLUENCING THE PHYSICIAN

It should be obvious from the discussion to this point that whatever its appeal in the abstract, competition based on patient payment applied to actual patient medical care decisions can produce unwanted consequences.

Yet certainly the avoidance of waste and improvement of quality are legitimate goals. A better system would increase the probability that the physician's initial recommendations were optimal from both the patient's and health system perspectives—and that patient and physician would be able to act on them.

The fact is that a lay patient will not be in a good position to make a rational choice about care options with varying payment implications. He will not know how important the services are. He will not know whether he can choose some and forego others and, if so, which ones. He will not know whether other doctors will be less expensive and, if they are, whether they are as good as the one recommended by his physician, or at least competent. He will not know whether other less expensive services would be adequate substitutes. And he may not know whether the delay necessary to get answers to these questions will be harmful.

As an alternative to the scenario in which price determines *patients'* decisions, I believe it is more reasonable to expect *physicians* to include cost as one of the factors *they* consider when deciding what recommendation to make to a patient in the first place. After all, they are the experts, not the patient. But research has shown that different financial arrangements tend to produce different sets of responses by physicians. For example, as already noted, fee-for-service is associated with a greater tendency to both recommend and provide services. Physicians exhibit more restraint when they are salaried and even more when they—or the organization they work for—are prepaid on a capitation basis. All payment methods carry distinctive financial incentives that—even if not the primary consideration—may influence clinical decisions. And when financial incentives are at work, we can never be completely certain that decisions are being made on the basis of what is best for our health. Given that they are *always* present, which brand of poison is least noxious?

Fee-for-service? It encourages provision of services because each service earns the doctor a new fee. Is it better to receive a service than to have it withheld even though it may not do much good? Services are not always benign. Indeed, the risk of harm from medical care has a special name, iatrogenesis.

Capitation? This method discourages provision of services because net income is what remains after care is given. Should we assume that the greater restraint found under capitation is more nearly optimal than the decisions made under fee-for-service? Or will physicians tend to withhold beneficial services in order to maximize net income?

Salary? The physician's annual income is fixed and not directly affected by his care-giving decisions. So on the one hand, it does not encourage provision of more services, which increase expenditures. But on the other hand, if he decides not to provide a service, can we be sure that it really is unnecessary and that he is not just lazy?

Does a system that promotes price competition among providers work best for patients, the providers, and the society? It is hard to see that it does. Yet if included as part of a comprehensive reform strategy, price competition *will* probably attract competitors. One reason is that since, with universal coverage, the market will be expanding, the financial risk associated with entry is reduced. But for the reasons already indicated, we should not expect that price competition will save money for the system as a whole or result in the most effective care for us as patients.

The system is under real pressure, and we still need a way to provide coverage for all while limiting expenditures. I believe the most promising way to do that is to guarantee the same comprehensive coverage for everyone under conditions in which providers have a fixed amount of money to work with in providing services. Then the competition can be not on the basis of price but on those other elements of medical care that we value—responsiveness, quality, and innovation. If patients are insured, they can obtain needed care without worrying about bankruptcy. If providers are not competing on price, patients can choose on the basis of other factors associated with timely, appropriate, good-quality care as long as they have access to the information they need to make good choices. If the funds for services are limited and providers are paid using methods that do not reward waste, the system can be more efficient and less costly than at present.

Porter and Teisberg[44] also argue that competition can be a good thing in medical care, but based on the value to be obtained, not on price. The problem is that the conditions described in Chapters 5 and 6 that created the problems that need to be addressed militate against such a plan. For competition based on value to occur, a necessary though not sufficient condition is that price must be removed from the equation. That is one of the reform ideas I offer in the next chapter.

Conclusion

At the outset, I noted that for a proposed reform to have the effects we desired, it would need to induce key participants in the health care system to change the decisions that have produced the problems we want to solve. The people whose decisions are most central to that effort are employers, patients, and providers. Competition proposals assume that decisions made by insurers and the purchasers of health care coverage (primarily employers) will influence patients and providers to be more cost conscious in their decisions. From the evidence in this chapter, however, it appears that reforms based on competition will not in fact produce the hoped-for effects.[45] Instead, price competition will exclude some people from the market; result in higher, not lower overall expenditures; and fail to promote improved quality and safety. Among other reasons, firms lower their prices in order to make *more* money in a market in which they expect people to spend *more* in the aggregate, not less.

Thinking about it, we should not be surprised at this result. After all, what happens when people want to buy a new computer? First, they check out what is available. Often, they will be able to choose from a variety of products made by several manufacturers that have different features and are offered at different prices. Depending on the amount of money they have available and their reasons for wanting the product, they may reasonably choose one at the high end or at the low end or in the middle. Or they may decide that the one they can afford does not do what they want it to do and so exit the market, at least temporarily, without buying any. Faced with large numbers of such potential customers, what does a firm do when it wants to sell more of its computers? It tries to develop better products and to produce its products more efficiently. Then it lowers prices, hoping to attract more customers, sell more products, and make more profit. When they succeed, the market as a whole grows—especially if other firms do the same thing. When computer makers lower their prices, it is not to *reduce* the society's spending on computers, but to encourage more *potential* customers to become *actual* purchasers of their machines. If things work as expected, the market for computers grows.

In contrast to the market for computers and most other things, however, one of our goals for the health sector is to limit total aggregate spending on health care in the United States as a whole. While we cannot actually reduce *total spending,* we want to reduce the *rate of increase.* In a market in which everyone is making decisions independent of anyone else's, and patient decisions are mediated by the presence of insurance, it is hard to see how such a system can produce lower expenditures.

In the private health insurance market, moreover, insurers have a some-what different dilemma. Prices differ because policies differ—usually by varying the services that are covered and the cost-sharing arrangements. Health insurers want to sell policies, but their profit (or surplus in the case of not-for-profit organizations, such as Blue Cross and Blue Shield plans) is determined not simply by the number of policies they sell, but by the amount of money they pay out when policyholders use covered services. And that figure becomes known only several months after the year ends when they have all the bills for all the services their policyholders used that year, add them up, and deduct that amount from total revenues earned from the combination of selling policies and investing that money waiting for claims against it to be paid.

What can they do to increase the probability that the bottom line will be in the black? Because their revenues are determined when they sell the policies, but most of their costs represent payments for covered services used by subscribers, insurers need to keep those payments down. To do that, insurance company innovation has taken two main tacks: the surest approach is to segment the market to induce disproportionate numbers of healthy people to buy their policies and, even more important, to *dis*courage unhealthy ones from choosing them. The other is to introduce rules and procedures that make it harder both for subscribers to use services and for providers to furnish them.

That is not the same kind of innovation that produces better, faster, and cheaper computers. It may benefit the firm's shareholders, at least in the short run, but it does not provide enough benefit to the public to justify the struggle to preserve the system that produces it.

Markets tend to work when demand is elastic—that is, when people's purchase decisions are influenced by price. When the price is higher, fewer people buy. When it is low, more people do. Moreover, markets also work better when people can exit them—that is, when those who are dissatisfied with a product or service or its price can walk away and decide not to purchase. That is the dynamic that imposes discipline on the market. Sellers of goods or services will make adjustments in quality, efficiency, responsiveness, price, and other attributes in order to obtain their desired share of the market. But the market for health insurance is not like the market for computers or most other things we buy. Since an important goal, for reasons discussed earlier, is for everyone to have insurance so all Americans can have financial access to needed medical care, we cannot depend on market forces to solve the problems identified earlier.

Implicitly, competition proponents expect the contest for subscribers to reduce insurance prices and limit the funds available for services, thus creating incentives toward restraint in the provision and use of services. For reasons detailed earlier, that outcome at best is unlikely. What is more likely is that competition not only will fail to achieve its promised goals but will produce unacceptable secondary consequences as well.

This result should not be a surprise for reasons that the Nobel Prize–winning economist Kenneth Arrow explained forty-five years ago in a classic paper.[46] These derive, first, from the special characteristics of the medical-care market, which include the fact that demand for services is "irregular and unpredictable."[47]

Also, as patients, we usually do not know what the potential benefit of a particular service is or the role of care in recovery from illness or even, in some cases, whether recovery can occur at all. And since the patient "cannot test the product [or service] before consuming it," he must "trust" that the physician's behavior is governed by a concern for the patient's welfare, "which distinguishes medicine and other professions from business, where self-interest on the part of participants is the accepted norm."[48]

Because society benefits when ill people, using medical care, recover from illness (or avoid it through the use of preventive services), but not everyone can afford needed care, "the welfare case for insurance policies is overwhelming."[49] That is because the cost of insurance for a large risk pool that includes healthy people who will use few services as well as people at high risk for needing care is more manageable than the cost of the care being insured against. Although the incidence of illness in a population group can be measured, it is harder to know in advance the probability of using services since not all insurance loss (that is, spending on services) is due to illness. Some is for routine primary care and preventive services. So insuring against the financial cost of medical services used differs from other types of insurance because the events being insured against do not occur randomly and are not always expensive. Moreover, even in the case of care to cure an ailment, "the cost of medical care is not completely determined by the illness suffered by the individual but depends on the choice of a doctor and his willingness to use medical services." Indeed, the presence of medical insurance, including specific provisions of a particular insurance policy, "increases the demand for medical care" beyond what it would be in a market for other goods and services.[50] That is, because it lowers the financial barrier to patients considering the use of services and, under the fee-for-service payment method, it increases the probability that physicians will earn income, insurance lowers the threshold to utilization for both participants in the decision, patient and doctor alike. The fear is that services will be overused and spending will increase unnecessarily as the result of insurance. Arrow wrote that, "To some extent the professional relationship between physician and patient limits the normal hazard in various forms of medical insurance," but developments in the organization and delivery of services since he wrote his famous article have tended to weaken that relationship.[51]

So the medical care market does not work like other markets, and its peculiar characteristics reduce the extent to which we can expect that competition will work the way it does in other markets. The bottom line is that the problems need to be solved, and the market cannot do it. Therefore, the public sector must. Only government can change the rules that can remove the dysfunctional incentives we saw in Chapter 6. Moreover, the rule changes must be at the national level. Even though some states might be willing and able to do so, not all could or would. Unless they all adopted the same system, relying on the states would create new counterproductive incentives encouraging people to cross state lines to practice medicine, to buy coverage, and to seek care.

So if only the public sector is up to the task, what does it need to tackle? Earlier, I showed that the United States spends more per capita on health care than other countries and that the rate of spending is growing faster than elsewhere. That high spending in the health care sector has two main negative consequences. One is that it reduces the ability to spend on other public necessities, such as public education and infrastructure (roads, bridges, and so on) The other is that it means that some employers and millions of people cannot buy insurance. As a result, many Americans are denied access to the care they need delivered by the most appropriate professionals in the most appropriate settings.

Changing the health insurance system is a necessary step, but it is not sufficient to solve the health system's problems. Services must be reorganized into systems capable of keeping up with the latest clinical developments and coordinating the care patients need from multiple providers both when they have serious acute illness and, even more, when they are trying to cope with chronic conditions.

Similarly, the unreliable quality and safety that we saw can improve *throughout* the system, but only if the system itself changes. While individual medical care institutions or conscientious doctors or nurses can make improved quality part of their missions, they cannot by themselves stop the deterioration of the delivery system as a whole. The incentives that produced the problems can only be changed at the system level.

Competition will fail to solve the problems. In fact, because the United States already has the most market-oriented system in the world, the results it has produced should be seen as evidence *against* continuing to rely on the market. Not only has it not worked yet, but I have demonstrated that it cannot be fixed to work better. And even expanding the public sector to fill in gaps and correct defects in the present mixed private-public system will fail to contain expenditures, ensure access, or promote improved quality. For these reasons, competition should be rejected as the principal basis for a reform strategy.

If we eliminate price competition, then what is a suitable basis for reform? In the next chapter, I lay out six elements that must be included in any national-level reform plan that aims to solve the problems identified earlier.

Chapter 8

Elements of a Solution for Increasing Access to Health Care, Improving Quality of Care, and Containing Health Care Expenditures

IN THE FIRST PART of this book I tried to demonstrate that the U.S. health care system faces very large problems, which must be solved. Our continuing failure to do so has, among other things, undermined the capacity of the delivery subsystem to reliably provide good care even to those of us who continue to have good insurance. I have also shown that the primary causes for all the problems are the dysfunctional incentives that operate on all parties to the system—employers, insurers, individuals and families, providers of care, and even state and federal governments. As a result of those incentives, members of each group make decisions that, while they appear to be rational for the decision makers, at least in the short term, have created a system that is the most expensive in the world by far; leaves at least 16 percent of Americans uninsured and many more underinsured; produces health statistics that are mediocre at best and worse than those of many countries that spend a lot less; delivers care of unreliable quality and safety; and leaves Americans less satisfied with their health system than citizens of other countries. The driver of these suboptimal results is utilization—the extent to which individuals and families use services (or decide not to do so), which services they use, when during an episode of illness they use them, and who provides those services. Although calling this phenomenon "utilization" implies an action by the patient (the user of services), the reality is that it is a two-party decision, made by the potential patient and provider, and often paid for (and influenced) by a third-party insurer. Therefore the focus of attention cannot be only on the patient but must include provider and payer as well, and the forces that influence them.

A better system would allow everyone to share in the enormous potential offered by modern medicine and to do so with services that in each instance are the most appropriate given the patient's condition and are provided by the most appropriate professional, in the most appropriate setting, at the most appropriate time during the course of the illness. In addition, such a system would provide preventive services that are appropriate to the patient's age and health condition and care for chronic illness in ways that enable patients to function optimally given their underlying condition. While everyone should have a primary care physician (PCP) with whom he or she builds a strong therapeutic relationship, that physician should be part of a multidisciplinary team not only informed by professional education and experience but aided by a robust electronic information system. That care would be less expensive than much of the care used now and would produce better health outcomes, as well as perhaps even lower levels of aggregate spending. Moreover, the beneficiaries would include not only the individuals who got that good care but also the society and the national economy of which they are members.

In the next section, I offer ideas for reform that flow from both the goals described in Chapter 5 and the understanding of the origin of the problems presented in Chapter 6. The recommendations are designed to create a health care system that will serve us well in the future by overcoming the causes of those problems.

Before presenting these ideas, however, I want to make two additional points. First, although I believe that my ideas are both logical and reasonable (and can be politically feasible, as will be discussed in the final three chapters), I claim neither that they are a panacea, nor that they are the only reasonable changes to make. For one thing, I do not believe that a system can be created that is perfect on day one and remains perfect as the years pass. No matter how good it is at the outset, it will be populated by doctors, nurses, technicians, hospital managers, patients, and others who—just as their predecessors did—will act rationally given the conditions they find to produce what they think will be the best result for them. The aggregation of all of their individual decisions will produce patterns that, slowly over time, will change the new system and what it produces. Thus the best we can hope for is change that will solve today's problems for a number of years but which will eventually need adjustments as well. If we can make adjustments steadily as they become needed, we may be able to avoid the need for dramatic changes like those required now to fix problems caused by years of neglect.

Second, other thoughtful people have espoused similar visions of a better health care system and have proposed policy changes to help us get there. While they differ in various ways, their ideas also overlap with one another, as well as with my own. Among these others are proposals by Arnold Relman, the distinguished former editor of the *New England Journal of Medicine;*[1] Tom Daschle, the former majority leader in the U.S. Senate;[2] and Ezekiel

Emanuel, a physician ethicist at the National Institutes of Health.[3] Another such proposal, by the Commonwealth Fund's Commission on a High Performance Health System, is one of the most comprehensive and illustrates the problems, opportunities, and dilemmas facing those who would reform the U.S. health care system to achieve the goals I have described.[4]

In 2005, the Commonwealth Fund created the Commission, headed by James Mongan, a physician who is president and CEO of Partners Health-Care System in Boston; a former assistant surgeon general under President Jimmy Carter; and a former chief executive of the Truman Medical Center, Kansas City's large public hospital, and later of Massachusetts General Hospital, one of the nation's preeminent academic medical centers. "The Commission's 14 members, a distinguished group of experts and leaders representing every sector of health care, as well as the state and federal policy arena, the business sector, professional societies, and academia, are charged with promoting a high-performing health system that provides all Americans with affordable access to high-quality, safe care while maximizing efficiency in its delivery and administration."[5]

The Commission has written that the current system falls short in many of the ways I described in Chapters 2 through 4, and as a result, "comprehensive health reform and bold actions to change direction are necessary."[6] Its vision of the desired high-performance delivery system is summarized in the following bulleted points taken from its February 2009 report:

- "All patients have access to appropriate care, including after-hours care with multiple points of entry; care is patient-centered and responsive to patient needs.
- "All clinically relevant patient information is available to all providers at the point of care; electronic information systems enable information to flow with patients.
- "Care is well-coordinated among multiple providers, and transitions across care settings are well-managed.
- "All providers—including nurses and all members of health care teams—are accountable to their patients and each other and collaborate to deliver safe, effective, efficient care with excellent outcomes.
- "There is clear accountability for the total care of patients.
- "The health system is continually innovating and learning to improve outcomes, patient experiences, and the value of care."[7]

The desired system would be supported by affordable universal coverage so that everyone would have financial access to the care they need, incentives that are aligned to produce the desired outcomes (high-quality, efficient care), and a delivery system that emphasizes the teamwork and coordinated care that are required by both the complexity of medical care and the wide range of clinical conditions—including chronic illnesses—found in today's population.

To achieve this vision, the Commission would build on currently available public and private coverage in order to minimize the disruption of existing doctor-patient relationships where they exist as well as existing coverage arrangements that people want to maintain. Their approach has the additional advantage of being relatively easy for the present system to absorb.

The Commission would offer enhanced choice of competitive private insurance plans, presumably in part at least because such a plan would be easier for the Congress to enact, given the commitment of so many to markets and their dislike of a large public-sector role.

The Commission's proposals have other features, as well, also apparently motivated by a concern that the needed changes be realistically implementable and manageable as well as politically acceptable to the Congress.

There is no doubt that the Commission's plan, which shares the same goals and some of the same elements as the ideas I offer here, would represent a major improvement over our present health care system on many dimensions. Indeed, so would many other proposals, including the ones just cited. In fact, some of their ideas can be found among my recommendations in part because our analyses led us to the same conclusions.

Having said that, however, in my view, the ideas I offer, though not as detailed as the Commission's plan, flow more directly and fully from the analysis presented in the preceding seven chapters. To reform the system so that it reaches this potential, I believe we need changes that substitute functional incentives for the present dysfunctional ones and that will encourage everyone in the system to act in ways that promote patient health and reasonable spending levels by using care most appropriately. Fundamentally, *those changes must induce better decisions regarding utilization.* If they do, the rest should follow.

Essentials of the Plan

What I propose is not a fully detailed plan but a group of six key elements that I believe should be included in whatever plan is adopted. With them, we can solve the health care system's three most persistent challenges: *limited access,* the fact that many have inadequate or reduced access to needed care; *rising costs* that have been climbing dramatically for the past forty years; and growing evidence that *quality of care and safety* is a serious problem. It will also create conditions that will *stop the erosion of the delivery subsystem* and stimulate rational provider organizations and professionals to adopt innovations, including greater use of teams and coordinated care, that will increase the probability that care is safe and of good quality.

Further, as long as the plan that ultimately is adopted contains these six elements, the choices made on other dimensions can be determined by the relative strength of the various groups active in the political process that will be necessary to enact the reforms. More about that in the book's final chapters.

The six key reform elements are as follows:

1. Everyone must be insured, so all will have financial access to the services they need and providers can be compensated fairly for treating everyone.

2. Individuals and employers must pay a premium or tax earmarked for the purpose to a federal agency. Using the tax system is the simplest way to collect the money, and using progressive rates is the fairest way for individuals and businesses to pay for it.

3. The amounts that individuals and employers pay *into* the federally managed Health Insurance Fund (HIF) must be independent of health status. In that way a person at greater risk of needing services will not face a large financial obstacle to obtaining coverage. Rates will be set so that the HIF's total collections will be sufficient to pay for needed care for all. An important benefit would be that we will know what our health care spending will be at the start of the year instead of several months after it has ended. Initially, the total would be something approximating current levels of spending so that, at the outset, health care providers as a whole would not be harmed by reduced income. Depending on actual utilization patterns, however, some provider organizations and professionals would probably earn less immediately after the plan went into effect than they earned before. Others would earn more.

4. At the same time, however, payments *from* the national Health Insurance Fund to health insurers and health plans must be risk-adjusted. Insurers and plans should be paid more for people who have a high probability of needing services and therefore of costing them money. The goal is to be sure that the insurers and plans have no financial reason to decline to enroll anyone who applies. In turn, the insurers and health plans will negotiate payment arrangements with providers knowing their own income is fixed. More about this further on.

5. All health insurers and health care plans must be required to enroll anyone who wants to do so. This is known as "guaranteed issue." In the enrollment of clients, carriers must be prohibited from engaging in selection bias on any basis, especially health status. (Reform Element 4 will mean that insurers or health plans will not be at a financial disadvantage as a result of this one, Reform Element 5.) Otherwise, the current system of segmented markets, which both

creates many of the problems to be overcome and prevents their solution, will persist. While risk-based payment should create a level playing field, regulations will be needed to keep everyone from being tempted to find ways around the rules.

6. Finally, patient cost-sharing at the point of service must be limited because out-of-pocket payments depress the use of medically appropriate and quality-enhancing services as well as those that are unnecessary.

The combination of these elements is intended to produce the well-functioning health care system that is our goal and that was described in Chapter 5. They address the dysfunctional incentives identified in Chapter 6 and, building on our understanding of the dynamics that produced the problems to be overcome, would replace them with others that should produce the desired outcomes—some immediately and others, over time. Moreover, if we are serious about wanting to transform our health care system so that it approaches the Chapter 5 vision, then all six elements need to be adopted and implemented because all are needed to create—over time—the smoothly functioning, reliable health care system that is one of our fundamental objectives.

Nonetheless, these ideas, most of which are familiar to those who have been following the health care system for years, have not been universally embraced. For some, the large role contemplated for government is anathema, a nonstarter even before any rational defense can be offered. Indeed, some people may never be convinced because they do not trust government as a matter of principle or because they are committed to the wisdom of the market. But these ideas are put forth in recognition of two facts: one is that, for most of our history, the United States has been a remarkably non-ideological country. Indeed, the conviction that we would always find a way to solve whatever problem we faced was long considered one of the strengths that ensured our long-term survival as a nation. The second fact, which follows from the first, is that the most distinctive American approach to solving problems is pragmatism. We tend to assume there is a way to make things better and that, with careful observation, dispassionate analysis, and a good dose of American ingenuity, we can find it. In that spirit, I assume that most readers will reflect on the evidence and the arguments seriously, without preconceptions, and most will reach the reasonable conclusion that I have reached.

How the System Could Work

Although other scenarios may also be consistent with the six reform elements, here is one way the reformed system could work for a typical citizen. Let's call him Bill.

First and foremost, Bill would be entitled to comprehensive coverage. So would his wife and children, if he had them (Reform Element 1). *Bill would receive a voucher* (as Emanuel and Fuchs suggest[8]) or a Health Security card (as President Clinton famously held up during his speech to the joint session of the Congress on September 22, 1993). He would be eligible not because of his employment, as is usually the case now, but because he is a citizen (or legal noncitizen).

With his voucher, *Bill would choose a qualified health insurance policy or health plan,* from among the available choices. Since all plans would offer the same comprehensive set of services, he would never need to choose a less-than-optimal plan because that is the only one he could afford, and he would never arrive at a doctor's office or hospital wondering whether or not the service he needed was covered or whether he could afford its cost.

Plans designated as "qualified" by a federal agency would compete to be selected by Bill and others with vouchers. A plan would be certified if its benefit package included the services required and if the organization offering it had the capacity to function as an insurer or health plan should. Regional offices of the HIF or of a Health Security Board, like that proposed by both Senator Daschle and Dr. Emanuel, would distribute information about all eligible plans in the region to help people like Bill choose one. Bill's voucher or Health Security card would be all he needed to select one of the qualified insurance policies or health plans available in his area.

What would Bill need to pay for his voucher? His payments into the system would be based only on his ability to pay (Reform Element 2). It would be independent of his health status and would not vary with the particular policy or plan he chose. Cost-sharing would be minimal, if not completely eliminated (Reform Element 6.)

How would the amount of Bill's payment be determined? First, health system planners would calculate the amount of money the health system would need to pay for expected services in the coming year. For the first year following the plan's start date, they should set the amount needed to be similar to the final year prior to implementation or add a modest and therefore manageable increment. They would divide that total by the number of eligible citizens to arrive at the needed per capita contribution. Then they would adjust that amount to create different payment rates based on the expected distribution of family and business incomes (Reform Elements 2 and 3). Bill's payment would depend on where he fell in the income distribution. Similarly, if he worked, his employer's contribution would be based on the firm's income or perhaps a manageable percentage of payroll. In that way the system would have the money it needed to operate, and individuals and companies would pay into that fund according to their ability to do so.

Since Bill and other citizens would be able to choose any qualified insurer or health plan (Reform Element 5) using only their voucher for enrollment, insurers and plans would need to find nonprice ways to compete for subscribers. In other words, they would need to make themselves attractive to potential subscribers primarily on the basis of the quality of their care and their service. Being certified for the competition, all would be offering the same comprehensive set of necessary services (though perhaps different providers). Some might choose to differentiate themselves by offering—for extra fees—additional services or a less restricted panel of providers.

How will the Health Insurance Fund decide how much to pay the insurer or health plan that Bill chose? The HIF would make a risk-adjusted payment to the insurer or health plan Bill chose (Reform Element 4). In other words, the amount paid to the insurer or plan on Bill's behalf would be determined by his health-related characteristics, which enable HIF officials to estimate how much service he would need in the upcoming year.

How do insurers and health plans differ? An *insurer* would be obligated to pay providers for the services furnished to their subscribers. By contrast, a *health plan* would also *arrange* for those services in the manner of a managed care plan or health maintenance organization of the Kaiser Permanente type. Both types of organization would be required to accept anyone who wanted to subscribe (Reform Element 5), but because the payments they receive would be risk-adjusted, they would be protected if disproportionately large numbers of people expected to need a lot of services enrolled with them. Risk adjustment of payments means that insurers or plans are paid more for subscribers who, because of age and other health-related characteristics, have a higher probability of using services. Since the *probability* of using services is not the same as a certainty, however, some high-risk subscribers would turn out to use fewer services than predicted and some of those at lower risk would turn out to use a lot. The expectation is that risk adjustment of payments would mean that no insurer or plan would be at a financial disadvantage across the aggregate of its subscribers because of the health characteristics of the people who happened to enroll with it. If, in a particular instance that assumption did not hold, a system of reinsurance created for the purpose would protect that plan from the effects of adverse selection.

How Will Insurers and Providers Adjust to the Payment System?

Because their gross revenues would be determined only by the numbers and characteristics of the people who signed up with them and they would be expected to pay for all covered services needed by their subscribers, insurers and plans would need to find ways to limit their expenditures on care. But they would be prohibited from using some of the devices that have been common among insurers in recent years, such as discouraging high-risk people from signing up with them (Reform Element 5) or imposing high cost-sharing amounts to discourage use of services (Reform Element 6). Though not prohibited from doing so, they would probably not want to use those tactics, since neither patients nor doctors like them and they would be giving competitors that did not use them a promotional advantage in the quest for subscribers.

One result is that both insurers and health plans would have incentives to help their *providers* (whether contractors or employees) deliver the right care effectively and in a timely manner so that their patients would not get more seriously ill unnecessarily and services would not need to be redone. A strategy to accomplish that goal could include assisting providers in acquiring and using information technology to help them (1) choose the most appropriate care in particular cases; (2) order tests and drugs electronically; (3) communicate electronically with other providers as well as with patients; and (4) create electronic medical records for their patients, which could also be accessed by the patients' other providers. While none would be required to do these things, many insurers and health plans would find it to be in their interest. Some may go so far as to organize as prepaid group practices like the old Kaiser Permanente, Harvard Community Health Plan, or Group Health of Puget Sound.

Insurers would also have incentives to encourage their *subscribers* like Bill to recognize their health care needs and to seek care promptly from the most cost-effective provider, who would have electronic access to their patients' entire multiprovider medical record. An effective strategy for accomplishing the latter would be to encourage subscribers to choose a primary care provider or a medical home and then facilitate the development of good relationships between provider and patient. In that way, individuals would be less likely to delay seeking beneficial care and more likely to avoid the services of expensive hospital emergency rooms.

Health plans would have similar incentives, but they would also have advantages over health insurers. The primary one is that they could limit the pool of eligible providers—including doctors, hospitals, and others. By doing so, they could create an integrated delivery system and gain greater ability to affect providers' clinical practice in positive ways. Among other things, health plans would have increased reason to invest in information technology because any financial and other benefits would be retained within the integrated system. Yet none of these advantages would be *imposed* on them. Some would act quickly to maximize the benefits; others would take longer.

Insurers and health plans would receive the same risk-adjusted payments and would negotiate arrangements with providers. Further, since their revenues would depend on the number and characteristics of their subscribers and all would have the same coverage obligations, they would want to avoid fee-for-service because total payments to providers could expand as additional services were provided. Instead, they could experiment with various ways of bundling payments—for example, making primary care providers responsible for a fixed set of services and drawing on a separate fund for referral or hospital care. Alternatively, they might find increasing numbers of providers willing to sign on as employees in exchange for predictable incomes and a higher probability that they would have access to state-of-the-art information technology. The resulting plans could find ways to facilitate the development of care-giving teams instead of today's more common fragmentary care. They could also offer bonuses for desirable outcomes at the group or practice (not individual physician) level.

By using his voucher to sign on with one of these plans, Bill would acquire guaranteed access to primary care and other services he needed. Having insurance, he could sign up with a primary care physician, thus assuring himself of access to care early in illness episodes as well as to age- and condition-appropriate preventive services. Finally, cost-sharing, another utilization limiting device, would be either eliminated or kept to a minimum so as not to be a deterrent to appropriate care (Reform Element 6).

Other advantages of a health system with these features are that it would build on existing organizations and organizational processes without creating large new public-sector organizations. This is important because, as Thaler and Sunstein demonstrate persuasively, people tend to have a "status quo bias" and resist giving up what they already have.[9] People who are happy with their coverage would be able to retain it—as long as the benefit package meets the requirements and the organization has the capacity to carry out its functions—with more stable funding than in the current employment-based system. In addition, as just noted, insurers would have incentives to evolve into health plans, but would not be *required* to do so. For example, insurers might find it advantageous to contract with some physicians and hospitals, but not others. To the extent they did so, subscribers like Bill would have a limited group of presumably good providers to choose from. Further, he might find a particular insurer or plan attractive because it includes a favorite physician on its roster. Finally, for insurers that evolved into health plans, they and their providers would have time to learn to work together effectively in a resource-constrained environment.

A major advantage for Bill and others is that insurers and plans would compete not by reducing the scope of the benefit package (that would be prohibited) or by imposing burdensome cost-sharing amounts (that, too, would be prohibited), but on the basis of how well they served subscribers.

In the rest of this chapter, I will present arguments in favor of these six reform elements and will rebut arguments commonly made in opposition to them. Although as the process plays out I would fully expect compromises to result from the political negotiations, it is critically important that they not be of the type that adopts some of the six elements and not others, thinking half a loaf is better than none. On the other hand, negotiated compromises may emerge on a variety of implementation choices, including a timetable for phasing some in more slowly than others. The embrace of those selections may enable interest groups that otherwise might oppose the reform ideas to accept them. Finally, I will examine briefly issues related to Reform Element 4.

Let me make emphasize that I deliberately did not present a detailed blueprint with all the "i"s dotted and "t"s crossed in part to permit sufficient opportunity for interest groups to bargain in the political process. Each would attempt to minimize the extent to which it suffers short-term harm, but none would be able to undermine achievement of the key reform goals. More about that in the final part of the book.

Arguments in Favor of the Proposal

IT IS THE RIGHT THING TO DO

This must be the first reason.[10] Because medical care can make such a huge difference in our ability to carry on productive, fulfilling lives, it is not like a product we buy in a store or even like other services we purchase. It can cure illness, prevent illness, and make chronic conditions bearable so that people can continue to work and play. It also contributes to the economy by minimizing time lost from work due to illness, thus increasing the economy's output and productivity. But care is expensive, and insurance improves the accessibility of useful services by providing the means to pay for them. People should have access to services on the basis of health-related need, not the amount of their take-home pay or disposable income. How can we justify anything else? Finally, if any nation can afford universal coverage, surely the United States, the richest on earth, can. Yet today we are the only developed country without it.

PROVIDERS WILL INVEST IN QUALITY

Second, the quality and safety of care will improve because of the increased extent to which rational providers will invest in improving the quality of care they provide. Among other things, they will be more likely to organize into coordinated systems of care and to buy information technology to help them diagnose their patients' condition more accurately, identify and choose the most appropriate treatment, reduce errors, and improve efficiency.

The reason that quality will improve is simple. Individual health plans, managed care organizations, physicians, hospitals, and others must attract enough clients or patients to survive (or thrive) economically in competition with other such organizations. If everyone is insured, the potential effective demand for care will grow, thus increasing the opportunities for those providers to expand, if they wish to, and to stabilize their panels of patients. Yet, being unable to compete on price because payments from the federal Health Insurance Fund will be risk-adjusted and determined by their patients' health-related characteristics, their ability to attract members and patients will depend on (1) their reputations for delivering good care and (2) the manner in which they serve patients (for example, with easy-to-get appointments; limited waits in offices; and respectful interactions with practice staff, including clinicians). If information technology can help establish and strengthen the quality of care they provide, they will be more likely to invest in it than they are today.

The gross revenues for insurers and health plans will depend on the number and characteristics of patients enrolled and the risk-adjusted premiums or service fees they receive, respectively. How can they earn a surplus or profit under these conditions? By attracting more patients as a result of developing and promoting a reputation for quality of both care and service. And then, by being more efficient and spending less to provide that good care, especially by avoiding unnecessary services. They will be less likely to try to profit by cutting services to reduce costs (as many do now) because doing so would give competitors who do focus on service an advantage. The best route to both efficiency and high-quality, coordinated care is by creating or contracting with organized providers of care. To the extent that information technology (IT) can improve efficiency as well as quality, health plans and providers will have incentives to invest in it.

This scenario is in contrast to today's situation in which provider organizations must bear the cost of buying information systems even though it would provide little if any direct benefit to them. In today's system, if IT leads them to become more efficient, they will provide fewer services at lower prices and therefore probably earn less. Moreover, if that does happen, the biggest winners would be today's insurers, which would pay them less. To the extent the technology enabled them to improve service to patients, it is unlikely to result in more patients or higher fees. While patients would benefit from better care and physicians might get greater satisfaction knowing they were serving patients more effectively, the financial outlay is too great for most to afford for that type and level of benefit. Indeed, misaligned incentives is a key reason, though not the only one, that relatively few physician practices to date have adopted electronic medical records and other information technology.[11]

IT WILL COST LESS

Per capita health care costs in the future will be less than in our present system, which is the most expensive in the world. Those outlays will be reduced primarily by ending market segmentation and the extra costs to insurers, employers, and providers that result from it and by removing financial barriers to obtaining appropriate care from the most appropriate source at the most appropriate time in the course of an episode of illness. Thus the many people who now either have no insurance or who cannot afford the cost-sharing associated with their plans will have no financial reason to deny themselves needed care until they are so sick they must go to an expensive hospital emergency department.

The reformed system will also cost less because the poorest health risks no longer will need to be covered by special public-sector programs—Medicare, Medicaid and state-level plans—which tend to cost more largely because they have concentrations of people at high risk for needing expensive services.

The proposed plan will also save money by ending dysfunctional financial incentives for both patients and providers of care: for patients, to delay or avoid seeking care, and for providers, to (1) refuse to treat some patients because their coverage, if they have any, pays too little or (2) provide extra services of undetermined or marginal benefit to compensate for low payment rates. Yet because every payment method carries incentives on both seekers of care and those who provide the services, regulation will be needed to prevent new forms of dysfunctional behavior.

Whether the increase in aggregate spending can be brought under control as well will depend in part on the extent to which per capita expenditures actually fall. Certainly, more people will enter the system to use services because the currently uninsured will now have coverage, and that will add to costs. But some of them already use services, especially in expensive hospital emergency departments. Now they will be able to use less expensive services in a more planful way and, as a result, per capita spending should drop.

Finally, it has been estimated that "nearly 5 percent of GDP—or roughly $700 billion each year—goes to health care spending that cannot be shown to improve health outcomes."[12] Risk-based payments to insurers and health plans will change the incentives under which they and, presumably, the providers of care operate. Assuming they act in concert with those incentives, that excess utilization should be reduced. The funds thus saved should therefore be available to pay both for new entrants to the system and for care that the *under*insured currently forego. Whether the combination of lower per capita costs and less waste fully covers new utilization is a matter for conjecture at this point.

HEALTH STATUS RESULTS WILL IMPROVE

People who currently are without a regular source of care, especially a primary care physician in the community, will now be able to have one. Over time, they will begin to use services differently than they do now by, for example, getting immunizations and other preventive services and seeking care early in an illness. They will have no reason associated with the arrangements for care—coverage or cost—to delay seeking service, so more illness will be caught early and kept from developing into serious, debilitating conditions that not only require expensive services to treat but also result in time lost from work. Other issues besides insurance and cost may still inhibit the use of services by some, as we saw in Chapter 6, but they can be dealt with separately after the major coverage issues are resolved.

U.S. FIRMS WILL NOT BE BURDENED WITH HIGH HEALTH INSURANCE COSTS

Large firms that currently offer coverage will eliminate the high cost of health insurance premiums as a cost of business. And their share of the national HIF is likely to be less than the premiums they pay now. They will also eliminate the expenditures associated with designing cost-effective plans, negotiating with insurers, monitoring the care used by their workers, and developing methods for reducing the aggregate spending on services provided to their employees. Their international competitors bear none of these costs.

Small firms that do not now provide health insurance will face somewhat higher taxes than at present, but payment rates would be progressive, based on the company's ability to pay. Moreover, although they would represent a new expense for those that do not now provide coverage to their employees, the rates are still likely to be less than the premiums they would pay if they did provide coverage to their employees. Further, the portion of their current tax payments that support Medicaid and state programs for the uninsured will be eliminated. While the net taxes may be somewhat higher than currently, in exchange, the firms will benefit from a more stable workforce. Nonetheless, no matter how fairly the payment rates are set and whatever the benefits are to the society and to individual employees (including business owners), we can expect grumbling from those who would be asked to incur new costs to pay for health insurance.

IT WILL CONTRIBUTE TO RESTORATION OF THE DAMAGED SOCIAL FABRIC IN THE UNITED STATES

In addition to providing these measurable health-care-related and economic benefits, the new health insurance program will be something of value that all Americans will share, like Social Security and Medicare, and in which all will have a major stake. In that sense, it will strengthen the social fabric, which has been fraying in recent years. Moreover, the common interest in the program that all Americans will share will be the strongest protection against its erosion in the future if the economy struggles or, despite the plan's provisions, it turns out to cost more than forecast. This may not be the primary reason for adopting the proposed reforms, but it is potentially a substantial benefit to the society nonetheless.

Common Arguments Against Universal Coverage Proposals

IT IS TOO EXPENSIVE

Despite arguments to the contrary, the new system will cost less in per capita health care expenses. One important reason, as noted, is that all the expenses devoted to market segmentation—complex actuarial analyses, high promotion and selling expenses, designing a multiplicity of plans aimed to attract low-risk patients and discourage high-risk patients, and the abundance of insurer-specific forms and payment rules—will be eliminated. In addition, as described earlier, the money that now goes for services that produce no clinical benefit can be redirected to cover the currently uninsured. Another reason is that the total cost will be known in advance since it will be the product of the number and characteristics of covered people and the rates paid on their behalf—instead of the sum of the bills paid for services rendered to individuals during the year that can only be calculated after the year ends. Most important, the annual rate of increase in aggregate spending should drop with the substitution of new incentives for the old ones. The United States will continue to have the most expensive health care system for years to come, but the gap will narrow as the new program takes hold.

Opponents of a large federal role argue that expenditures will be kept low by competition because insurers will want to charge lower premiums and will need to innovate to attract customers. While that scenario may hold in other sectors, in health insurance, innovation tends to mean finding ways to discourage high-risk people from enrolling and to discourage those who do enroll from using services or clinicians from providing them. (This is market segmentation, as discussed in Chapter 7.) Common devices to that end include requiring more cost-sharing from patients, covering fewer services, paying lower rates to providers of services, and imposing more rules to access benefits. Because nonpreferred patients can be expected to need and use more services, they are charged higher premiums partly in the hope that many will buy their coverage from other carriers. The sad fact is that, like the Texas woman with diabetes and her family introduced in Chapter 1, many are priced out of the private market altogether.

IT IS "SOCIALIZED MEDICINE"

Since well before the days of Harry Truman, the AMA and other opponents of reform have railed against "socialized medicine." But national health insurance is *not* socialized medicine. It changes the way people pay for care, not their providers or the organization of services. Medical care would still be provided mostly by private doctors, who would probably have more control of treatment decisions than private insurers accord them now. What will be different is that universal coverage will be required by law and paid for by mandated payments into a fund dedicated to health care, and private insurers and health plans will be paid by the public-sector insurance system. Eventually, medical practices and other delivery organizations may find it advantageous to combine with others in response to the incentives in the new payment methods. The formation of those organizations would not be mandated, however. Instead, to the extent that scenario unfolded, it would result from an evolutionary process occurring over a number of years in response to incentives created by the financial arrangements. (See the discussion further on about Reform Element 4.)

GOVERNMENT WILL CONTROL MEDICAL CARE

Even if they acknowledge that the plan is not socialized medicine, many may argue that the federal government will control medical care because it will have control of the funds. To the contrary, if these elements are adopted, responsibility for medical care decisions will return to where it belongs, expert professional physicians interacting with their patients. Not only that, but to the extent those physicians are part of an integrated prepaid group practice, their clinical choices are more likely to be good ones because they will have the support of health care information systems and decision support systems as well as well-trained colleagues to consult. Ironically, British and Swedish physicians, who practice in systems with "deep government involvement in the financing of medical care," have more professional autonomy than many American physicians burdened by the intrusions of private insurance firms.[13]

GOVERNMENT CANNOT RUN ANYTHING EFFICIENTLY

Many opponents of a large role for the public sector act as if government is another word for inefficiency. The fact is, however, that Medicare, operated by the federal government for the elderly and the disabled, is much more efficient than any private insurance plan, as measured by the proportion of premium income devoted to health care services (see Chapter 2). Further, the practice of medicine in the United States could hardly be less efficient than it is under the current system, which contains few penalties for inefficiency and, to some degree, even rewards it.

Regardless of the evidence, however, opponents of a large federal role are likely to argue that competition will keep expenditures low because, to attract customers, insurers will want to charge lower premiums and therefore will need to innovate in order to do so. We saw in Chapter 7, however, that, whatever happens in other sectors of the economy, in health care, innovation tends to mean finding ways to discourage people from enrolling in insurance plans, from using services if enrolled, or providing services to those who have enrolled. The costly mechanism that accomplishes this result is, again, market segmentation, which results in more uninsured people, reduced access to care, and a large and costly residual role for the public sector.

IT IS UN-AMERICAN

Many would argue that capitalism and individualism *define* the "American way," and that therefore these health reform ideas are "un-American." This is another example in which the facts do not fit the rhetoric because, to the contrary, the plan does embrace competition, but on the basis of service, not price. Moreover, what is really un-American is to be satisfied with spending so much per capita yet have more uninsured people, worse health statistics, and more dissatisfied citizens than other countries that spend much less. What is really un-American is the stubborn insistence on failing to solve this perennial problem and instead watching the vaunted United States health care delivery system deteriorate. Finally, since the most characteristically American philosophy is pragmatism, what is really un-American is to continue to resist rational solutions to real problems just to protect the short-term economic or political interests of a few instead of serving the long-term interests of the public and the society.

The Real Reasons Some Oppose Systemic Reform

While the five arguments summarized in the previous section are commonly offered by opponents of comprehensive reform, especially when it involves a large role for government, the real reasons that some people oppose actions of the type being proposed here fall into three broad categories: ideology and short-term economic or political self-interest.

IDEOLOGY

Many people simply believe that the market is the most efficient way to organize economic activity, and it is hard to shake them of that conviction. The justification for private markets in any industry is that competition spurs innovation that will both improve products or services and keep prices down. In the computer industry, for example, a firm that earns a profit on each computer it sells will increase its aggregate profit by selling more computers. Innovating to add new features and functions will make its computers more attractive to the public compared to those offered by others. And additional innovation to make its production methods more efficient enables the company to charge less, thus making it possible for more people to buy them. The last computer my wife and I bought does more and cost less than the one it replaced.

In the case of health insurance and health care, however, as I showed in Chapter 7, the market is not the best venue. Competition simply cannot produce better health care less expensively. Even if that were not the case, however, one of the inevitable results of a competitive health insurance market would be that many would be without health insurance as, indeed, sadly is the situation now, thus negating one of our goals in wanting to reform the system. Kenneth Arrow showed many years ago in his classic paper about the welfare effects of medical care that it does not follow the rules of the typical market—nor should it.[14]

Many also tend to believe that people should be driven by incentives that promote desired outcomes. As already noted, however, the perverse incentives faced by insurers and providers of care have contributed mightily to the current situation. They lead many employers to drop coverage and others to introduce provisions that make it hard for their employees to afford it even though it is still offered. The result in both cases is that many individuals and families go without health insurance.

In addition, some believe that under a universal coverage plan, insurance would be *provided to* people—instead of being earned through their employment—and that, as a result, they will be more inclined to engage in unhealthy behaviors (eat too much, smoke, drink too much) because they will not bear the costs of dealing with the health-related consequences. That argument can be rejected on at least three grounds. First, the patient always bears the illness cost of illness. That is, when a person who increases his risk of a heart attack by eating too much greasy food actually has that heart attack, he is the one who falls ill and may die. Second, citizens will indeed be paying for their coverage. While it is true their payments will not take the form of insurance premiums shared with their employers, as is the case for most now, they will pay taxes earmarked for the Health Insurance Fund.

Finally, it is an argument not against health insurance offered by the public sector but against health insurance itself because of the risks associated with moral hazard. Indeed, to the contrary, it can be shown that appropriate use of medical care by individuals has value for the society as a whole that would outweigh any possible negative consequences.[15]

SHORT-TERM ECONOMIC SELF-INTEREST

Despite the problems that affect the U.S. health care system, the fact is that a number of groups benefit from the present system. Moreover, if one of the goals of a new system is to contain spending, some groups that gain income from the present system will earn less under the new one. (To obtain their support for reform, it may be possible, in a negotiation, to hold many of them harmless financially in the short run and focus on keeping down the level of future increases. That result may be part of the political price to be paid for enacting reform.)

As the years pass, some of these groups might actually benefit even more from the stability and other features of a reformed system. Nonetheless, because they tend to believe that result is uncertain and have learned how to cope with the present system, these groups—which include organizations of physicians, hospitals, and other providers of health services, as well as small businesses that do not now offer health insurance coverage to their employees or their employees' families—resist change.

A historical example of the phenomenon can be found in the story of Medicare.[16] The American Medical Association opposed its enactment with every resource it could muster, but in the years that followed its adoption and implementation, it can be argued that physicians were among its biggest beneficiaries.

While some of the interests that oppose systemic change might do well in a reformed system, others may not be able to maintain their current level of income. On the other hand, some may be able to negotiate different, compensatory benefits. These include health insurance companies that transform their risk-bearing health insurance business into organizations focused on delivering good care to subscribers, as well as other firms whose claims-processing capability or their capacity to analyze utilization data to monitor the reformed system's functioning could be useful to the new system's managers.

SHORT-TERM POLITICAL INTERESTS

Economic entities, such as insurance companies, small businesses, and medical practices, are not the only ones with interests. Political parties and those of their members who are elected officials also have them. While the part of their job of most concern to us here is their ability to vote on important pieces of legislation, representatives and senators get to do that only as long as they continue to be elected by their constituents. Further, their influence in the chamber to which they were elected, as well as the specific roles they perform (for example, each house's leadership and committee chairs who together control legislative activity are chosen by the majority party in each house), depend to a considerable degree on whether or not their party is in the majority. For these reasons, among the considerations they weigh in deciding how to vote on an issue are the political implications. These include, Will I be able to be reelected? Will the vote affect my party's chance to retain or regain the majority? Do I have a chance to be a committee chair? As a result, in some instances, representatives and senators will tend to vote for or against a particular bill on the basis of their assessment of the bill's political impact. We will have more to say about this issue in Chapters 10 and 11.

Summary of Arguments

The health care market is not like others: no other market has a goal to limit or even reduce overall spending. Further, although demand rises and spending increases, as in other sectors, methods that would limit spending in other markets—raising prices to reduce demand or exiting the market altogether—are inappropriate in the health care sector. And health insurance innovation tends to take the form of finding ways to exclude people from coverage and discourage the use of services, even beneficial ones.

Competition can be most useful here not when it is based on price, as in most markets, but when it is based on quality of care and of service—that is, on the value provided.[17] For this type of competition to produce desirable results, price must be constant because, when it is in play, it is the easiest—perhaps the only—characteristic of medical services that patients understand, and it tends to dominate their decision making.[18] If they compete on the value produced by medical care—for example, improved health, reduced time lost from work—providers scoring well on those measures will be rewarded with more patients, which will increase their revenues. And those that are most efficient will take more money home at the end of the day. Provisions in the proposal make it possible to achieve the goals of reform because they change the incentives for everyone.

Reform Element 4: Making Payments from the Health Insurance Fund

The fourth provision, that regarding payments from the federal Health Insurance Fund, may present the most difficult implementation challenges.

It is also likely to contribute much to the political debate on passage of the reform plan. Here is why.

Earlier, I argued that dysfunctional incentives are largely responsible for the fix we find ourselves in. And some of those incentives derive from the way we pay providers. By giving them fees for each of the services they provide, we encourage them to provide more services—even when the value of these services for the patient's health is uncertain. That, in turn, increases expenditures without necessarily providing health-related benefit to patients or the society. And we have already seen the harmful effects on just about everyone that result from high expenditures. Since we want to limit unnecessary expenditures without discouraging people from getting care they need, a key challenge is to find a method of paying providers—physicians, hospitals, and others—that aligns the incentives so that all point in the same direction: providing appropriate care to patients without rewarding the provision of unnecessary services while at the same time removing financial barriers to patients' seeking that beneficial care.[19]

CAPITATION PAYMENTS AND INTEGRATED CARE ORGANIZATIONS

The most rational arrangement would be to pay health plans a capitation amount—risk adjusted—for each patient they enroll.[20] The plans, in turn, would assume responsibility for delivering care to the patients they enroll and would organize resources to that end. One element of that organization may be to pay physicians a salary—perhaps augmented by a modest bonus based on the plan's (not the individual physician's) year-end results, thus providing an additional incentive to do well. Those plans that deliver good care—defined not only as the right services delivered competently, but also those services delivered responsively, courteously, and with caring—would attract a lot of patients and retain them year after year. Those providing that care most efficiently would have the highest net income at the end of the year. Multispecialty prepaid group practices (PGPs), such as the original Kaiser Permanente or Harvard Community Health Plan, work best when physicians work under the auspices of only one such plan at a time instead of being able to supplement the income earned from a lower-paying or more heavily managed plan by also treating patients of other third parties.

Such an arrangement would have substantial advantages, which everyone—especially doctors and their patients—can appreciate. One is that physicians and other professionals would be free to make clinical decisions about the services to provide to individual patients based only on what they believe is best for their patients. In making those choices, they would be aided by health information technology and embedded decision-support systems. They would not need to worry whether their patients would be able to afford out-of-pocket expenses associated with particular recommendations, which affect patient compliance with physician recommendations, because all costs would be included, with the possible exception of small co-payments. In the course of doing an unpublished study at the Harvard Community Health Plan in the late 1980s, a colleague and I heard from physicians over and over again how much they appreciated being able to make clinical decisions under these conditions. Similarly, the physicians would not be influenced in their recommendations by considerations related to their own financial well-being. They would earn no more and no less as a result of their decisions, with the possible exception of modest annual bonuses based on the entire practice's performance.

The health plan or PGP would receive risk-adjusted payments from the fund based on the number and health-related characteristics of the people they enrolled. At least half of the physicians would be in primary care specialties, including general internal medicine, family practice, and pediatrics. The PGP would devise a budget that would include salaries paid to each of the physicians (presumably negotiated with physician representatives) and other staff, the cost of space, equipment, supplies, and other expenses, including services provided in hospitals and other facilities. Some might decide to set aside money for modest bonuses based on *the group's* year-end performance.

Among other things, the PGP would have an information system that would allow staff to track services provided to patients. Covering staff who fill in when a patient's regular physician was off would have access to the information system as well. It would include a decision-support component that would provide the latest information for a physician to consult about the diagnosis and treatment of symptoms or diagnoses he or she has not often seen. In turn, this would increase the probability that patients would get appropriate care. From the physician's perspective, the emphasis in using information technology would be on finding the most appropriate services for their patients, not just on improving efficiency and increasing the bottom line. Moreover, practicing in the same building with colleagues would facilitate consultations about difficult cases as well as occasional meetings to discuss issues related to the practice organization.

Given that the PGP's budgeted income would be reduced as patients received services during the year, it is possible that funds would be depleted more quickly than anticipated. If that happened, the group's leaders could analyze utilization data from the information system in order to understand the reasons for impending shortfalls and then convene a meeting of clinical staff to consider adjustments—within the practice—that would enable them to preserve remaining resources. One of the most important characteristics is that all care decisions would be made by the plan's physicians, and if they discovered they were using their annual resources faster than expected, they could analyze practice data and, as a group, come up with more effective patterns of care. Such an arrangement would be preferable to the current situation in which insurance companies, concerned about higher-than-desired outlays and reduced profits, impose restrictions on physician decision making externally and without taking into consideration idiosyncratic local conditions.[21]

Fuchs makes the case this way: "Both theory and experience show that integrated health care systems are usually the best way to deliver cost-effective care. The primary reason is the physician's central role in medical decision-making. Under any approach to care, it is the physician who admits patients to hospitals, orders tests and other procedures, and decides when to discharge. It is the physician who prescribes drugs and who refers patients to other physicians for consultation and treatment. . . . Only in an integrated system, however, do physicians have the incentive, the information, and the infrastructure needed to make those decisions in a cost-effective way."[22]

RELYING ON ALIGNED INCENTIVES INSTEAD OF MANDATES

For all its abstract appeal, however, to have included the PGP arrangement as a required reform element would have been a problem for several reasons. One is that today we have few organizations that can really deliver on the promise. Entities modeled after the Kaiser Permanente Health System were created with aligned incentives to accomplish these goals. Because they were paid capitation amounts, they had an incentive to invest in quality- and efficiency-management activities. Because doctors were salaried, they did not earn more income by providing more services. And because they worked only for the managed care organization (MCO), the MCO's leaders had the ability to engage the attention of the practicing physicians and the opportunity to develop methods for influencing clinicians' work in ways that emphasized both quality and efficiency. As a result, they were able, theoretically at least, to ensure that the services actually provided to patients were the right care at the right time during an illness episode, without additional services that cost the plan money but added little or no value for patients. If organization leaders and clinicians did their jobs well, patients would be more likely to get the benefits they wanted from their doctors, to achieve desired clinical outcomes, and to be highly satisfied.

Unfortunately, current conditions do not lend themselves to these arrangements, and few such organizations exist today. Moreover, the few that were organized years ago on the basis of these principles have evolved over time in response to pressure from competitors into entities that now are missing one or more key features. For example, most doctors do not like to be salaried, so now they are paid fee-for-service. Most don't like to be tied tightly to a single organization, so they tend to be free now to treat patients from other insurers as well. Like the rest of us, doctors tend to prefer the system they know, which has always rewarded them directly for the work they do. Patients too have been persuaded that they should have freer access to more of the delivery system than just to those providers that are part of a single MCO. As a result, these kinds of MCOs no longer exist to any great extent, if at all.

Another practical obstacle to Reform Element 4 is that risk-adjustment technology, though getting better, is not yet very good at predicting with a high degree of precision the future needs of individual patients for service. Thus to base payment rates from the federal HIF to the insurers and health plans on risk-adjustment techniques may produce too many misses. If the rates that are set as a result of those studies are too low, then patients are likely to get less than they need. Quality and outcomes will suffer. On the other hand, this reform element provides the strongest possible reason to speed up the risk-measurement improvement process by investing more resources in it.

As an alternative, we could pay capitation amounts to individual physician practices or small groups. Although many do exist, they do not have experience managing care either, and are not well organized for it. Further, they would face perverse incentives of a different type. An independent primary care practice that received capitation payments for patients who enrolled with them would be responsible for paying for specialty and hospital care, as well as for nonmedical services for chronically ill patients, out of the capitation funds. But then their financial incentive would be to make as few referrals as possible because paying for each one would reduce their net income. If instead the primary care practice were capitated only for primary care, and payments for specialty care, including hospitalization, were to come from money retained by the federal HIF, then it would have the opposite incentive, to refer more often than needed.

Even though the potential for financial gain or loss will not be physicians' primary consideration in making clinical decisions for their patients, it is bound to be a factor, however subtle. And without an infrastructure to support good decision making, clinical choices might be distorted in ways that are not best for patients.

In addition, patient panels in individual and small-group practices are likely to be too small to be able to absorb the financial risk associated with capitation. A single four-person family in a serious automobile accident or a handful of patients with cancer would put a major dent in such a practice's funds available for care—not because the physicians provided poor care or were inefficient, but just from the luck of the draw. To shoulder the risk, a clinical group needs to be quite large.

So for these reasons, we need to find creative ways of making payments from the federal fund that keep the principles underlying this reform element intact and, as a result, make it possible to achieve the goals of reform.

RISK–ADJUSTED CAPITATION

Given the difficulties described so far in this section, my suggestion is that the fund pay a risk-adjusted capitation amount to any insurer or health plan with which a patient enrolls. The insurers and health plans would then need to work out arrangements with physicians, hospitals, and other providers of care. It would be in their interest to create Kaiser Permanente–style MCOs because they would be obligated to take all comers and to cover a comprehensive set of services, and they would need to fulfill those obligations with an amount of money that, though risk-adjusted, would be fixed. Because of these conditions, they would put themselves under untenable fiscal pressure if they paid individual providers on a fee-for-service basis, as they do now. On the other hand, they would reach that determination themselves. It would not be imposed.

Payments might also be made to community-based physician group practices. For primary care practices that do not already have experience managing care, but are willing to accept the risk, the risk-adjusted payments to them could be divided into two parts. Some would be distributed to the practice for primary care, and some would be held back in a practice-specific fund for specialty and hospital care. Then the HIF administrators would provide monthly financial statements to the practices regarding the status of the referral fund, thus giving the practice the capacity to make clinical decisions taking their financial condition into account. These arrangements are similar to a prepaid managed care demonstration operated successfully for children by the Suffolk County, New York, Medicaid Program in the early 1980s.[23] Finally, seed money could be made available to help finance the creation of multispecialty group practices.

Even though payments from the fund would be risk-adjusted, this is not an ideal situation, for the reasons given. On the other hand, for the HIF to pay service fees directly to providers, the main alternative, would be to perpetuate the current dysfunctional incentives. It would provide coverage to all, but would do nothing either to contain expenditures or to improve quality.

I believe the likely scenario that would follow a plan with the reform elements I propose is that gradually, small community-based physician practices would recognize the value of joining with other such practices in organizations that can perform HMO functions of enrolling patients and managing care. *Forcing* the creation of entrepreneurially organized managed care organizations, however, by making payments *only* to such organizations, would be sure to incur the wrath of organized physicians, whose representatives, including the AMA, would oppose the reform and would form politically powerful coalitions with other groups that oppose it for different reasons. Moreover, since we do not now have enough such organizations, many of those whose creation would be stimulated by the new law would not have adequate infrastructure or management expertise at the outset. This proposal would, therefore, have the additional merit of creating the impetus for physicians or others to organize better ways of providing care under capitation payment.

Conclusion

These arguments may be persuasive for those who believe the problems are truly as serious as I have suggested and must be solved. They are unlikely to have much impact on those who are opposed on ideological grounds—government is the problem, not the solution, as Ronald Reagan used to say—or for whom short-term economic or political interest dominates their decision making.

People who have read this far might think that, however reasonable the plan sounds, it can never happen. Past reform efforts failed because proponents were unable to overcome the two main obstacles identified earlier. One is *the strength of vested interests.* Politically well-organized groups that benefit economically from the present health care system or fear the cost of universal coverage have, in the past, been able to hold back its adoption. Other opponents include those whose political interests led them to the same conclusion. The other critical obstacle is *ideology,* especially the commitment by many to a market-based approach to health insurance, or opposition to "central planning" or even just to a larger government role in health care. American pragmatism requires that rationality overcomes ideology, however, and there is plenty of evidence to support the view that this proposal is the most rational way to stave off the further deterioration of the American medical care system.

The interest groups that benefit from the present system will try to keep us focused on incremental adjustments that make us believe we are doing something of value without really changing much. Indeed, unchallenged, they will succeed. To change that outcome, a strategy is needed with three main parts. (1) Create a demand for universal coverage that *requires* a solution. Make the need for systemic reform inescapable and the need to solve the problems politically necessary. In the process, make the anti-reform ideology moot. (2) To help stimulate the public demand for reform, proponents must be aware of the importance of how the issues are framed. They must both present them in ways that will resonate with the public and, of equal importance, counter attempts by opponents to use other frames. (3) While holding firm on the six key elements of the proposal, put on the table for negotiation provisions related to implementation which could benefit interest groups that believe they would be hurt by the reform. For example, health insurers, which as a group strenuously opposed reform efforts in the early 1990s, could have a large role in the proposed program if they are willing to accept risk-adjusted payments for anyone who wants to enroll with them and to develop effective means for managing care to increase the chances that it is appropriate, delivered well, and efficient. Other insurers could act as fiscal intermediaries between the government and the providers or plans (as some do, now, with Medicare) or could perform the necessary monitoring function based on analysis of claims-like encounter data. Physicians will be concerned about payment levels and small businesses about their contribution to the federal HIF, both of which can be negotiated as well.

Let the political process work. In other words, to enact universal coverage with the six characteristics described here, the price may include satisfying in various other ways some of those who otherwise would oppose it. Although the six essential provisions must not be part of the negotiation, other elements can be. The political need is to eliminate some of the opposition and neutralize the rest so that elected representatives in the House and Senate will feel they can vote for it. A mobilized electorate can defeat powerful opposition, creating enough support to enable the Congress to pass a good bill and enough demand for a pragmatic president to sign it.

While some interest groups may be able to accept compromises that include a role in the new program or that reduce their costs, the reality is that the reform will produce winners and losers, at least in the short term. However much the society as a whole gains from the reform, some member groups will win more than others, and some will be worse off than they are now. But the strength of a capitalist economy is that many who "lose" in one competition find ways to reconstitute themselves and succeed in another.

If universal coverage with the six characteristics identified earlier can be adopted, the result will be a more rational health insurance system that will serve the public and society much better than the present one. Instead of acting simply like another interest group trying to keep a lid on its own spending, government can resume its proper place, serving the people by facilitating improvements for the benefit of the society as a whole. Then, the thirty-eight-year-old Texas woman with diabetes we met in Chapter 1 and others like her will be able to get the care they need, and the institutions that provide it not only will not go broke doing so, but also will have enough to invest in improvements. It may not be utopia, but certainly a worthy objective in the great pragmatic tradition of American democracy.

We turn next to an extended discussion of the political dimension of reforming the U.S. health care system.

Part Three

Politics!

Chapter 9

A Short History of Health Care Reform Efforts

THE HEALTH SYSTEM problems and what I believe is the logical solution to them should be clear from the discussion to this point. Yet even though it took two-thirds of the book to get this far, what we've covered is what Jonathan Oberlander, a political scientist at the University of North Carolina, calls the "easy part; designing an ideal plan or even a decent one that has *a compelling political strategy* to survive the legislative process is the difficult task. . . . Bad things indeed do happen to good health reform plans. Yet political calculations are too often a footnote in health care reform proposals"[1] (emphasis added). The fact is that, reasonable as it may sound given the analysis provided so far, legislation based on the reform elements offered here would meet stiff opposition if it were presented to the Congress, and without the right conditions and a well-conceived, well-executed political strategy, it might very well fail. As Lawrence Brown, political science professor at Columbia, reminds us, the health care system has proven to be remarkably resilient.[2] Not only has it refused to collapse as predicted by so many over the years, it has managed successfully to resist prior attempts at reform.

Many factors have contributed to the failure of past reform efforts. They include an antistatist "political culture" rooted in an "ambivalence toward government and . . . bias toward private solutions to public problems;"[3] the absence of a strong labor movement; race, especially during the period prior to the 1960s when Southern Democrats dominated the Congress; and the structure of government, which gives veto power to even small numbers of opponents because so many different bodies—especially the two houses of Congress—must agree to pass a major piece of legislation, but it takes only a few determined opponents to kill it.[4]

Nonetheless, the primary reason for the failure, I believe, is the fact that interest groups with a direct, economic stake in the outcome and which benefit from the status quo proved to be too powerful—not inevitably, but because they were better organized and more effective than their opposition. Because the nature of their continued existence, if not their very survival, depends on the legislation under consideration, they do what any threatened group would do—they fight back. Not only that, but because the stakes are so high for them and because they tend to have considerable resources at their disposal (in part because of the benefits they reap under the current system), they tend to go all out. They build coalitions with like-minded groups and spend lots of money to persuade Congress that the reform being considered should not pass. Although other groups—especially the general public—would improve their own condition under the proposed reforms, the issues tend to be less critical for them. After all, most people are healthy most of the time and interact with the health care system only intermittently. Also, in contrast to health care organizations—including insurers, pharmaceutical companies, device manufacturers, and providers of care, all of which have a direct economic stake in the outcome—the general public tend to be much harder to organize effectively.

That has been the main story in the past. One ray of hope for the present period is that recent developments have negatively affected many different groups. *Employers* are having so much trouble absorbing their share of the cost of offering coverage to their employees (estimated at about 75 percent of the $12,000 total on average[5]) that many are cutting back on the coverage if not eliminating it altogether. Those that do retain it find themselves at a competitive disadvantage in the global marketplace, since their international competitors do not bear those costs. Millions of *citizens* have lost coverage; millions with coverage and without it have had difficulty paying bills (many have even declared bankruptcy); and because of the cost, millions have denied themselves care they know they need.[6] And *providers*—both individual professionals and health care organizations—complain not only about low payments from third parties but also about the substantial administrative costs they incur just to cope with the multiplicity of insurers and coverage arrangements. The hassles faced by all these groups in their interactions with private insurers are very costly. Indeed, for many patients and providers, the sometimes Byzantine hoops they must pass through to have a chance to get even those inadequate benefits or payments are so discouraging and the outcomes so unpredictable that, finally, they just give up. As a result, proponents of reform have potential allies that may have been reluctant to join the effort in previous years. The case for change appears to be more compelling than it has been in the past, and a consensus is building that big changes are required.

Another potentially positive development is the 2008 national election. Democratic gains in the Senate may not be filibuster-proof, but they were substantial, as were gains in the House. They are even slightly better than those at the start of Bill Clinton's presidency in 1993. Further, Barack Obama's policy positions, though progressive, are not rigidly ideological, and he has deliberately avoided demonizing the opposition, which may ease the difficulty of putting together a winning coalition in favor of real reform. Finally, at this writing in the spring of 2009, it appears he may be more actively involved in the process and willing to use both his distinctive personal gifts and his popularity on what he has described as one of the critical goals of his presidency. Blumenthal and Morone identify these as critical ingredients to the successful passage of health care reform legislation.[7]

Regardless of these developments, however, whether the special interest groups constituting the U.S. health care system will once again be able to derail reform or the public-interest case for reform now is irresistible, the last chapter of the story will be determined by politics. No matter whether it is oriented toward improving market function or toward a large role for government guaranteeing coverage for all, any reform plan must pass the Congress and be signed by the president; and it will take a well-crafted and executed political strategy to create a different outcome this time. In these final chapters, I describe the challenges and present some ideas for a successful political strategy aimed at producing change.

A Different Orientation

During the most recent major reform attempt, the Clinton effort of 1992–94, Jay Rockefeller, the Democratic senator from West Virginia who has "well-established credentials as a crusader for universal health insurance," argued in a memo to candidate Bill Clinton in August 1992 that a direct approach would fail.[8] "Fear, he said, will dominate this debate much more than hope or altruism: 'Cost control is the reform Americans most need, want and are willing to pay for. . . . Peace of mind follows cost control. Voters fear losing coverage from loopholes, job changes, layoffs or catastrophic illness. Reform that makes insurance more affordable helps allay this fear, but voters want stronger safeguards.'"[9]

Yet part of the problem, as I argued earlier, is that real cost control cannot be achieved without universal coverage. So if Rockefeller's view still holds seventeen years after his memo to Bill Clinton, he would say the goal of reform should be to propose something that addresses the spending problem and will *make progress* toward universal coverage because that is all that can pass. Moreover, he called the argument that "Americans deserve or have the right to health care . . . a dead-end approach."[10] The reason is that among the voting public who are afraid of losing the coverage they have had, "fear, much more than compassion, drives support for universal guarantees of coverage."[11]

Although universal coverage is an important element of a comprehensive solution to the health care system problems we face today, the problems are much broader than simply the lack of access to needed care. As discussed in Chapters 2 through 4, the list also includes high and rising expenditures, uncertain quality and safety of care, a high degree of dissatisfaction among Americans, and a deteriorating delivery subsystem. Moreover, if all Americans were guaranteed comprehensive health care coverage—but nothing else were done—aggregate expenditures would surely rise. The reason is simply that many more people would have appropriate coverage and thus would be able to avail themselves of useful services early in an illness—as many would like to do now but cannot afford—instead of later in hospital emergency departments where care would be much more expensive. Further, in the process, universal coverage would provide support for existing health care organizations that now are threatened financially by the need to serve people who have no means of paying for their care. Chief among these are academic medical centers (whose emergency departments serve many uninsured), public hospitals, and other safety net facilities, like community health centers, which would be able to obtain payment for the work they did. But since now they often do not get paid for that care, expenditures would be likely to rise in the short run.[12]

For all these reasons, therefore, the plan must be broader than simply extending health care coverage to all Americans. Yet if Rockefeller is right, a more comprehensive proposal would not pass. Indeed, he, like many of those in the center of the Clinton effort, seemed to accept or reject proposals because of assumptions about what could pass the Congress rather than on the basis of an analysis of what would be needed to solve the problems. This conventional wisdom is based in part on widespread attitudes about the proper role of government in our society or on assumptions about the value of competition and the market.

Instead, I have taken a different approach. I started with an analysis of the problems and even considered the possibility that they are best solved by letting the parties work things out themselves in the tradition of incrementalism and a minimal role for government. Having reached the point, however, at which we have a good idea of what the problems are, where they come from, and what would solve them, in Chapter 8 I presented six elements of a solution *without considering the politics.* Yet I am not naïve. Politics is central to the discussion, progress rather than a solution may be the only achievable goal, and compromise is often required in order to accomplish anything. Indeed, in many legislative battles, the explicit goal is progress, not an outright solution to a problem. But this recognition leads to two additional questions.

First, at what point do you offer to compromise? Before presenting a plan? Do you propose only what you think can pass the Congress? Taking that approach does not *eliminate* the need for compromise. It just changes the place at which the opposition is engaged, and the resulting policy debates begin at a substantive point further from the ideal solution than necessary.

So instead of asking, "What will pass?" I ask a different question: "What needs to be done to get us as close as possible to a plan that will provide not only universal coverage, but also cost containment, more reliable quality, and a stronger delivery subsystem?" This approach does not deny the importance of politics. Indeed, it requires a healthy understanding of political dynamics to develop a strategy that would engage the opponents of reform about the persuasiveness of the public's issues instead of theirs.

That is the approach taken here, and what follows in Chapter 10 is the outline of a political strategy for a serious debate on the merits of the analysis and the plan offered in this volume. First, some history.

From the Progressives to Medicare[13]

The saga about the cause of national health insurance in the United States begins with the Progressive Party in the 1912 presidential election. With Theodore Roosevelt as its nominee, the Party included a plan for national health insurance in its platform. Moreover, that plan had much support among both organizations and the general public. Even the American Medical Association (AMA) was on board. But two things happened to derail the movement: the Progressives lost the election, and World War I intervened.

When national health insurance came back on the agenda after the war, things had changed. Among others, a particularly salient change was that the AMA itself had begun a transformation from a respected scientific society of professional physicians and scientists to an industry trade association for which the economic interests of its members, primarily community-based practitioners, seemed to be paramount. Moreover, its leaders took a particularly extreme, even strident, position on the role of health insurance (even when it was private) and, especially, on the role of government in providing insurance coverage.

The AMA extolled the sanctity of the "doctor-patient relationship," which, it said, included the notion that for medical care to have its maximum effect, patients had to pay for their care directly. The articulated rationale was that patients would be more serious about the care if they paid for it. A willingness to pay for care out of pocket was a measure of the value in which they held it. Moreover, the AMA argued that physician compensation must take the form of fees for the individual services they provided (as opposed to salaries from health care organizations, for example), and the doctors themselves needed to set those fees. Critics argued that a big reason physicians opposed private insurance was that another group, insurance companies, might set the prices to be paid for their services. In fact, insurers might even begin to intrude on other aspects of medical practice.

When the movement toward national health insurance picked up again in the 1920s and 1930s, it was bolstered by the first health services research in the United States. Besides measuring utilization rates and expenditures, the Committee on the Costs of Medical Care (CCMC) demonstrated that many Americans in the 1930s were unable to afford medical care that would benefit them. Nonetheless, the AMA continued to oppose it even though their statement of ethical principles had long ago included the idea that the doctor's primary allegiance was to his patients.[14] Its leaders used very strong language, even calling their own members who supported such plans—many of whom were distinguished academic physicians and researchers—"socialists" and "communists." Community-based physicians who had the temerity to support private or public health insurance were not simply called names, they suffered more direct economic harm. Membership in county medical societies was often a requirement for a physician to have admitting privileges to hospitals. Some physicians were denied membership in the local organization as punishment for either supporting insurance or, worse, being willing to work as a salaried employee of a health care organization, such as Group Health Association of Washington, D.C., one of the first prepaid group practices in the country (what we would now call a Health Maintenance Organization or HMO).

Leaders of the AMA fought these plans with every weapon they could think of. They even sacrificed the "sanctity of the doctor-patient relationship," which had been one of the cornerstones of their previous opposition to health insurance. AMA leaders encouraged their members "to issue warnings of political danger" to their patients, "people already feeling endangered by illness."[15] And those physicians whose patients included congressmen were encouraged to use their professional relationships to take the argument against public programs of health insurance to the seats of power.

The AMA's opposition was so effective that a provision that would have included health insurance in the original Social Security legislation was withdrawn by President Franklin Roosevelt, who feared that its opposition would jeopardize the entire bill. Later, legislation was introduced fourteen separate times from the late 1930s onward by Senator Robert F. Wagner Sr. of New York. After the first year, he was joined by Senator James E. Murray of Montana and Congressman John D. Dingell of Michigan in what became known as the Wagner-Murray-Dingell bill. None of the fourteen iterations ever made it out of congressional committees and onto the floor of either House even with President Harry Truman's enthusiastic support.

In the late 1940s and early 1950s, the group of leading proponents of national health insurance—veterans of the CCMC of the 1930s; the Social Security Board; and, later, the Department of Health, Education and Welfare (HEW)—went back to the drawing board and came up with a new strategy. Wilbur Cohen, who later became secretary of HEW under President Lyndon Johnson, is the name most often associated with this development.

Having failed so completely to make progress on national health insurance, Cohen, Oscar Ewing, and I. S. Falk turned to an incremental strategy focused on the elderly. As Marmor writes, they believed they needed to overcome four primary objections to the latest Truman plan: "(1) general medical insurance was a 'give-away' . . . which made no distinction between the deserving and undeserving poor; (2) it would substantially help too many well-off Americans who did not need financial assistance; (3) it would swell utilization of existing medical services beyond their capacity; and (4) it would produce excessive federal control of physicians, constituting a precedent for socialism in America. . . . [T]here was widespread fear, grounded in the bitter, hostile propaganda of the AMA, that physicians would refuse to provide services under a national health insurance program."[16]

The new, incremental proposals would provide coverage to the elderly for inpatient hospital services. Focusing on the elderly instead of the general population had several presumed advantages. First, given their age, they could be expected to need medical services. Second, because most are retired, they could be assumed to need help paying medical bills because they would have less income and would have lost any employer-based coverage they had had while working. Moreover, their pre-retirement lifetime of work meant they "deserved" help. Third, the focus on inpatient hospital care meant that services could be assumed to be both necessary (Who would want to be hospitalized if they didn't need to be?) and expensive. And finally, the plan to finance the coverage through Social Security was expected to attract additional support because, by the early 1950s, the program had achieved "widespread legitimacy . . . among all classes of Americans."[17]

Nonetheless, the story of the 1950s was much the same as that of the other efforts that had arisen since the 1930s. Although bills were introduced annually from 1952 to 1960, proposals still did not even get to the floor of the Congress. With the election of the Eisenhower administration in 1952, moreover, the executive branch was no longer supportive of the idea.

As the 1950s wore on, however, the perception increased that at least some among the elderly really did need help paying for care. In part this development resulted from discussion of the Medicare idea as introduced by Congressman Aime Forand, a Democratic member of the House Ways and

Means Committee. The focus centered on three related issues: Who needed help? What help did they need? How should the solution be administered and paid for? The Forand bill, which embodied the Medicare approach of Cohen and his colleagues, would have made all elderly Social Security beneficiaries eligible, but would have limited the benefits to hospital and surgical care. It would have used the Social Security mechanism to pay for and administer it.

Late in the decade, a more conservative approach emerged focusing on people who were not only elderly but also able and willing to document their poverty. It would have covered a broader range of services and been financed through the state-administered welfare program. These ideas were embodied in the Kerr-Mills Bill of 1960, which "conservative congressional leaders felt compelled to offer as a substitute for Medicare proposals."[18] Although it appeared to be more generous in the scope of covered services, the Medical Assistance for the Aged (MAA) program was to benefit only elderly welfare recipients instead of Social Security beneficiaries. The difference reflected a philosophical split. This was to be a means-tested program championed by those who thought public moneys should be used only for people who could *demonstrate* that they were in financial need (that is, welfare recipients) instead of the social insurance model, which *assumed* that people were in financial need because they were elderly and retired. The latter approach did not require that they demean themselves by proving they were impoverished. Moreover, the MAA program was structured as a federal grant-in-aid program to states willing to meet the goals and conditions articulated in the legislation. The federal government would reimburse those states between 50 percent and 80 percent of funds they spent to provide medical assistance to the elderly under the program's auspices. Poorer states would get a higher federal contribution. The success of the program would depend on the willingness of states to adopt enabling legislation and to create administrative structures to operate it. By 1963, "32 of the 50 states had programs in effect, and the provision of funds was widely disparate among the states." Only 4 of those states provided the full range of allowable benefits, however.[19]

After John F. Kennedy became president in 1961, activity continued with the goal of enacting a program of hospital insurance for elderly Social Security beneficiaries. This was now embodied in the King-Anderson bill, named for its sponsors, Senator Clinton Anderson of New Mexico and Representative Cecil King of California. Hearings were held, but despite President Kennedy's support and the support of the general public, not much legislative progress was made. The Congress was still controlled by mostly conservative Southern Democrats who opposed the legislation.

Then, in November 1963, President Kennedy was assassinated, and Lyndon Baines Johnson became president. Johnson lacked Kennedy's public persona and charisma, but he was a strong leader and skilled politician who, just a few years earlier, had been majority leader in the Senate, and he had become very good at persuading legislators.[20] Moreover, he took advantage of the public's grief at the loss of their charismatic young president and pushed the Kennedy agenda, in part as a legacy to the fallen leader. He would succeed at passing legislation that Kennedy, for all his gifts, had been unable to do. Chief among these was the King-Anderson bill.

The following year, in 1964, Johnson ran for election in his own right. As his opponent, Republicans nominated the widely respected but very conservative senator from Arizona, Barry Goldwater. Johnson won in a landslide with 61 percent of the popular vote, and Democrats won control of both houses of Congress with substantial margins. They had 66 of the 100 Senators and 295 members of the House (68 percent). Now the King-Anderson bill, still a limited program of hospital insurance for Social Security beneficiaries, looked as if it might actually pass.

The traditional story has Arkansas Democrat Wilbur Mills, the wily veteran chairman of the House Ways and Means committee, as the key figure in the drama. Seeing the handwriting on the wall, it was said, he wanted to get some of the credit for passing the bill that was beginning to appear inevitable, and as a fiscal conservative, he wanted to reduce the future pressure for a more comprehensive program of national health insurance for the entire population.

Recently released tapes and other materials, however, tell a somewhat different story. Even after the Democratic landslide in November 1964, Mills "did not see the passage of this still controversial expansion of federal health care authority as inevitable."[21] Mills himself gives Johnson credit, saying, "He had the greatest ability of any president to get things done."[22] In fact, Johnson had begun courting Mills as early as January 1964, only weeks after he assumed the presidency. And as now is clear from Blumenthal's and Morone's recent research, he was relentless, leaving nothing to chance.

The King-Anderson bill being considered after the 1964 election still included only hospital insurance for the elderly. Moreover, it still attracted opposition. Republicans, echoing the positions of the AMA—which not only remained opposed, but spent large sums to defeat it—argued that one reason King-Anderson should fail was that it left out too many people and too many services. Mills turned their logic against them, agreeing that, indeed, the bill should include more; and so he created what Marmor called the "three-layer cake" that eventually passed.[23] In fact, however, as is now apparent, Mills "floated the idea of a 'three-pronged' bill" in early June 1964, months before the fall election. His proposal "would include a Social Security cash benefit . . . , a hospital benefit . . ., and an expansion of Kerr-Mills (to cover health care for the poor). Johnson agreed and then upped the ante, . . . pushing for a bigger, more complete Medicare package, perhaps even physician coverage, while deferring to Mills on the details."[24]

Thus, when the bill finally passed the House, the King-Anderson plan for hospital insurance for Social Security beneficiaries had become part A of Medicare. A new social insurance program for physician services and other outpatient care became part B of Medicare. Both of these were embodied in Title XVIII of the Social Security Act. And the third element, which became known as Medicaid (Title XIX of the Social Security Act), essentially expanded the Kerr-Mills program of Medical Assistance for the Aged to all categories of welfare recipients, including families with dependent children and the disabled. Like MAA, Medicaid would provide federal funds to states that created programs meeting the criteria embodied in Title XIX. The federal government would reimburse the states from 50 percent to 83 percent of the funds they spent under the program.

Even with the favorable outcome in the House, Johnson knew passage was not a foregone conclusion in the Senate. The chairman of the Finance Committee, Harry Byrd of Virginia, was opposed and had the capacity to delay its consideration by his committee, which would give the opposition time to mobilize. So Johnson "ambushed" Byrd, calling him to the White House for an important, "sensitive" meeting. In reality, Johnson had arranged a press conference in which he embarrassed Byrd into agreeing not to delay action on the Medicare bill.[25]

Elsewhere, Brown has written that "the enactment of Medicare in 1965 coincided with several favorable political and economic conditions" and, while not the whole story, "it was 'surely no accident' that these circumstances were in place."[26] Among the factors he lists are the following:[27]

1. The United States "had a strong activist president working with a House and Senate that were controlled by his (Democratic) party and, more important, were ideologically sympathetic to his policy goals." Brown might have added that the president and key leaders in the Congress were skillful legislators who knew how to get legislation passed.

2. The economy was very strong and the federal budget was in surplus.

3. The mid-1960s was a period of "concern for social justice," which proponents used to address "a major 'functional' need . . . built on social insurance financing."

4. Strong nongovernmental allies, especially organized labor and organizations of the elderly, "lent formidable political muscle to the push to enact Medicare."

5. "Opposition to Medicare was grounded in a lethargic and 'reactionary' conservatism that was still reeling . . . from the electorate's repudiation of Barry Goldwater" in the 1964 presidential election.

6. "Health care costs were not so high that the mind boggled at spending more on health services."

7. "[M]ost analysts and activists assumed that one could finance care without having to 'manage' it too."

8. There was no pervasive "anti-governmental rhetoric."

9. Medicare was crafted by an experienced group who had "a sharp sense of the politically passable" and who knew that "the perfect could be the enemy of the good."

At any rate, the legislation passed the Congress in 1965, and President Johnson signed it into law at Harry Truman's presidential library in Independence, Missouri, with the former president looking on. It went into effect in 1966.

It is worth recalling that Medicare, albeit a more limited version than the law that ultimately passed in 1965, was part of a strategy developed by proponents of national health insurance for *all* Americans. Wilbur Cohen and his colleagues had anticipated that if this limited social insurance program for the elderly could pass—and if it succeeded as they expected it would—its popularity would make it possible to approach universal coverage over time by adding more services and more groups of eligibles. In the more than forty years since 1965, however, not much changed. Disabled people under age sixty-five and people with end-stage renal disease were added in the early 1970s. The latter were included partly as a response to the development of kidney dialysis as a dramatic new method to treat the condition. Prior to the first decade of the 21st century, when outpatient prescription drugs became a covered benefit, efforts to add new benefits or groups routinely failed.[28] The one exception over that period occurred in the late 1980s when coverage for "catastrophic" expenses was added; but then, soon after, it was repealed. Finally, a variety of policies were adopted over the years, in a series of efforts to contain spending, which, as we saw earlier in the book, grew prodigiously over most of this long period, far beyond the predictions of planners.

Marmor echoes Brown in saying that the story of Medicare's passage in 1965 was "atypical," and from the history since then, it appears that he was right. Although it added its own lessons as well, the tale of Bill Clinton's attempt to pass health care reform confirms the general narrative.

The Failure of the Clinton Plan

As we saw at the beginning of this chapter, President Bill Clinton was elected in 1992 having made health care reform a key plank in his campaign. Why did the Clinton plan fail in the 1990s?

Part of the answer is that President Clinton faced a large number of sub-stantial obstacles that, despite his expressed enthusiasm for reform, made the outcome far from certain no matter what he did. One was that he was a minority president. He won only 43 percent of the popular vote, which was split three ways between him; George H. W. Bush, the incumbent Republi-can president; and Ross Perot, a third-party candidate. And Clinton usually ran behind the members of Congress in districts where Democrats won.[29] So in contrast to Lyndon Johnson following the 1964 election, Clinton started out in a much weaker position from which to pursue health care reform even though it had been a major plank of his campaign.

Moreover, although Democrats won majorities in both houses of Con-gress, Clinton, the minority president, did not control them. Democrats held 56 of the 100 U.S. Senate seats and 258 of the 435 House seats (one, Representative Bernie Sanders of Vermont, was an Independent who tended to vote with Democrats). Although the party had 56 percent of Senators and 59.5 percent of Representatives (including Sanders), many were relatively conservative and, other things being equal, would not have been inclined to support major health care reform. Moreover, Democrats had the same num-ber of Senate seats following the 1992 elections as before them. And they actually had lost 9 House seats. In other words, the Democratic majorities were fragile and, in the House, actually shrinking.

Further, Clinton came into office following twelve years of administra-tions led by Ronald Reagan and George H. W. Bush. They left "a growing federal budget deficit and deepening popular distrust of the federal govern-ment" as well as a "determined anti-government insurgency . . . in the Republican party," which limited the prospects for bipartisan cooperation if indeed they existed at all.[30] Neither of these conditions supported an effort to create new spending and a new public-sector program, even one that promised self-regulation by competitive health plans and minimal growth of the federal bureaucracy.

Not only did the administration face these *structural* weaknesses, but as it unfolded, the *process* of developing and considering the plan worked against its ultimate passage as well. The Clinton administration might have been able to overcome the structural factors by designing and executing a strategy that included mobilizing public opinion in support of reform. On the other hand, Bill Clinton was a Washington novice who, though an acknowledged master of electoral politics, was "new kid on the block" when he took office in January 1993. Lyndon Johnson, a Washington insider and a master of the Senate, may have had a shot at overcoming these handicaps, but Bill Clinton could not do it.

Clinton first characterized his ambitious health care reform plan during the 1992 presidential campaign as "managed competition within a budget."[31]

These were terms that, while few really understood them, were intended to convey both a sense of fiscal responsibility and a nod to the iconic conservative principle of competition. Following the election, the plan was fleshed-out in great detail, largely behind closed doors, over many months by a task force chaired by the first lady, Hillary Clinton, and a very large group of experts providing technical support. The latter included more than six hundred men and women from government, academia, and elsewhere divided into thirty-four working groups. Although Skocpol argues that the process was not much different from the one used in 1934–35 to develop what became the Social Security Act,[32] Hacker writes that the "role of the working groups . . . quickly proved far too unwieldy to be an effective vehicle for policy formulation."[33] And former Senate Majority Leader Tom Daschle has written that, by using such a secretive process and not involving "committee chairmen and other congressional leaders who would determine the fate of reform,"[34] the Clinton team made their task in the Congress much more difficult. Similarly, by not working more effectively with representatives of key interest groups that may have been supportive, they lost the opportunity to build a strong, durable coalition committed to passage. Not only did those groups not get to work out their own concerns during the legislative process, they developed no sense of ownership of the plan which they might then have been willing to defend. It is not that the Clinton team ignored the Congress or interest groups entirely, but they appeared to treat them as secondary to the effort to develop a plan that could work. As Hacker put it, the "President and his advisers . . . misunderstood the politics. . . . The problem was the strategy itself."[35] And a big part of that strategy "was to remain true to the reform framework" of managed competition within a budget even though "the Congressional leaders whose advice and support Clinton sought were generally skeptical of the reform proposal Clinton advocated."[36] In addition, by focusing so much energy on the details of the proposal and taking so long to craft it, Clinton lost much of the momentum and goodwill that may have helped him maximize his chances for success.

The situation was complicated still further by the introduction in the Congress of competing proposals from the Democratic side of the aisle, an indication that the president did not control his own party. One, developed by Congressman Jim Cooper of Tennessee, was referred to as "Clinton lite" because it relied on market competition and encouraged insured people to enroll in managed care organizations but without providing universal coverage or requiring that employers contribute to their employees' health insurance. Another, introduced by Representative Jim McDermott of Washington, a physician, and Senator Paul Wellstone of Minnesota, had ninety cosponsors. It proposed a Canadian-style single-payer plan that guaranteed coverage of all Americans. While the single-payer advocates were willing to vote for the Clinton plan as a compromise, they and their grass-roots supporters persisted well into the spring of 1994 in the mistaken belief they could negotiate changes in the Health Security legislation when the reality was "they were part of a tenuous and inadequate coalition for universal coverage."[37] Together, these Democratic proposals—and especially their proponents' persistence in supporting them—showed that the Democratic president did not have the full support even of his own party's members of Congress.

Even so, enthusiasm for reform ran high both at the start of the administration in January 1993 and again following President Clinton's energizing speech before a joint session of the Congress on September 22 of that year. For those who had followed the issue from the days of the presidential campaign, the "overall thrust" of the Health Security proposal unveiled that September could not have been a surprise.[38] Indeed, a sense of inevitability had begun to build. In the summer and fall of 1993, a group of Republican senators, including the Minority Leader, Robert Dole of Kansas, put forward a proposal with many of the same objectives as that of the president, including a prohibition against insurers denying coverage on the basis of preexisting conditions, a guaranteed level of coverage for all buying insurance policies, and encouragement of individuals and businesses to join purchasing cooperatives to maximize their market power. They proposed an individual mandate instead of an employer mandate. Even Republicans in the House appeared poised to support some type of reform.[39] There were differences, to be sure, but there seemed to be enough common ground that compromises could be worked out.

Yet as the administration concentrated on passing its first budget and on the controversial North American Free Trade Alliance (NAFTA), time passed without action on the health care front. Not only did many lose interest, but in some cases, potentially supportive groups lost enthusiasm as a result of being on opposite sides of other issues. One example was the AFL-CIO, whose president, Lane Kirkland, told Clinton officials that his union had $5 million to spend and could use it either to support health care or fight NAFTA.[40] The president pushed NAFTA, which was ready for action while the health care plan was still under development, and the AFL-CIO fought it. When it came time for the health care bill, the unions had much less money, and much of their enthusiasm for the project had evaporated.[41] Organized consumer groups that would have supported the plan did much the same thing.[42] So when the president needed their help to combat the efforts of the special interests, they had little money or energy left to offer. Finally, as the complicated bill's content became known, individual provisions attracted opponents.

After the president's successful September speech to the joint session of the Congress and a dazzling performance by the first lady testifying before five congressional committees a week later, much of the energy—and with it, momentum—disappeared. Among other things, the president himself became preoccupied with foreign crises in Somalia, Haiti, and Russia and withdrew from the health care stage. All but one of the public events scheduled for October to promote the bill were cancelled. In the meantime, Congressional Republicans organized to derail the bill.

Opposition to the president's bill was led by two Republican congressmen, Newt Gingrich and Dick Armey, whose primary goal was to gain control of the Congress following the next year's elections. They were aided by the Project for the Republican Future, which, chaired by William Kristol, was launched in November 1993 with the goal of creating a "new Republicanism" that challenged the "very premises and purposes" of government policies. They saw passage of the Clinton plan as "a serious *political* threat to the Republican party."[43] In that context, Kristol advised that the debate "should *not* be about how to reform the U.S. health financing system in the direction of universal coverage. Instead, Republicans should use the debate as an occasion to embarrass Democrats and ensure a political turnaround that would enable conservatives to replace the 'welfare state' with 'free-market initiatives.'" Faced with the possibility of compromise in the summer of 1994, even after the Clinton plan had been taken off the table, Kristol wrote, "*Sight unseen, Republicans should oppose it*"[44] (emphasis added).

In carrying out this approach to governing, Republicans were joined by a number of other groups, some motivated by conservative ideological principles, such as the Christian Coalition, and others by their own economic interests, especially the Health Insurance Association of America (HIAA) and National Federation of Independent Business (NFIB), the organization of small businesses.

Skocpol describes an example that illustrates their uncompromising determination to derail the Clinton plan.[45] In February 1994, a representative of the U.S. Chamber of Commerce was scheduled to testify before the House Ways and Means Committee in support of a compromise with the president's Health Security bill. The Chamber's leadership had worked with the Clinton Task Force, which included some provisions the Chamber wanted in the original proposal, and it was understood that additional movement toward the Chamber's positions might occur as the bill worked its way through the Congress. The planned testimony included support for the idea that "employers should provide and help pay for insurance on a phased-in basis." As is often the case, the testimony was circulated to the committee in advance.

Before the Chamber's representative appeared, conservative Republicans, who had learned of the planned testimony, "arranged for Chamber officials to be bombarded by local business members angry about the national leadership's acceptance of modest employer mandates." The pressure was so intense that not only was the testimony rewritten, but also by the end of the month, the Chamber responded "by officially repudiating its earlier support for both universal coverage and employer mandates." The dynamics at work here included the fact that the Chamber of Commerce, whose members numbered large multinational companies as well as small and medium-sized ones, was in a competition for members at the local level with the NFIB. So when it was subjected to "cross lobbying" by the NFIB and to "reverse lobbying" by Republican members of Congress, it capitulated.

The irony is that a Democratic president proposed a plan that embodied conservative principles partly in an effort to gain support from Republicans and moderate or conservative Democrats. Yet, as noted, the Republicans at least had no intention of compromising. Their goal was not to "perfect" a bill by inserting provisions that were in concert with their convictions; it was simply to embarrass the president in furtherance of their overriding objective to win the next election.

But the story is more complicated because the arena in which its demise became assured was the competition between the Clinton administration and the interests arrayed against reform. Some of those were groups whose primary concerns were economic, while others' were mostly political. And as that competition played out, the role of public opinion, a potentially important resource for both sides, tended to come down against reform. The "White House developed a plan for bypassing Washington elites and taking the proposal directly to the public. . . . [But while the proposal had] many elements that were popular with the public, such as universal coverage, strict insurance regulations, controls on premiums, and modest new taxes . . ., very little intellectual energy had been devoted to the development of straightforward ways to explain the approach."[46]

Moreover, at least $100 million was spent by organizations to influence the outcome, and opponents outspent supporters by a more-than-2-to-1 ratio.[47] The lion's share of the money, an estimated $60 million, was spent on advertising, more than half of it by just two opposition groups. The Pharmaceutical Research and Manufacturers Association (PhRMA) spent $20 million and the HIAA spent $14 million, amounts that dwarfed those committed by advocates of reform.[48] In contrast, the leading supporter of reform legislation, a collection of consumer groups called the Health Care Reform Project, spent $4 million, only a fifth of the amount used by PhRMA and less than a third of the HIAA's outlays.

Why did these groups spend so much? "[T]he amount of money spent on most policy advertising pales in comparison" to the much larger amounts spent in recent presidential elections, but health care reform differed in two key ways from other policy arenas.[49] For one thing, the financial stakes were enormous. After all, health care is one of the largest U.S. industries, as measured both by the amount of spending and the numbers of organizations and individuals involved in it. Moreover, it has been growing for many years. The stakes for the small and medium-sized insurance firms represented by the HIAA were nothing less than their very survival, which Association officials cited as "the primary reason for their spending."[50] In addition to their advertising, the HIAA investment generated more than 450,000 phone calls, visits, and letters to congressional representatives.[51]

The second reason the health care reform battle drew so much money was "the extraordinary amount of news coverage" generated by a health reform proposal under which "almost every aspect of the health care system would change."[52] Ironically, "only 42 percent gave the media excellent or good ratings for coverage of health care reform. Forty-eight percent said news coverage of health care was only fair or poor."[53] One reason was that "the news media . . . [were not] capable of thoughtfully analyzing the problems in American medical care or explaining the merits and demerits of competing reform approaches. . . . Very little coverage explored the effects of reform on the public or explained the policy options before Congress."[54] This may explain in part why "few persons thought they knew much about health care reform . . . [and t]here was widespread ignorance about crucial features of the debate."[55]

The Health Security Act was so large and complicated that one administration official later described it as "such a big, fat, ugly bill" that it became "an easy target . . . the size of Philadelphia."[56] Not surprisingly, the public had concerns, including that it would cost too much and that government would take over the health care system. And many of those who had insurance they liked were afraid they would lose it.

Given the plan's complexity and the need to build understanding and support among the general public, it might be expected that targeted ads could make an important contribution to the effort. Yet in this case, surveys showed there "was no significant relationship between seeing ads and believing the Clinton program would increase taxes, create another large and inefficient government bureaucracy, cost too much, limit choice of doctors or hospitals, or pay for legal abortions" in spite of the fact that "many of the opposition advertisements emphasized these very themes."[57] Indeed, confirming Senator Rockefeller's advice to candidate Bill Clinton, ads by the opposition played on the public's fears as well as on the plan's complexity to create and amplify doubts about it. The Harry and Louise ads, which got so much attention in the media, are a case in point. This was a series of television spots featuring a couple talking at their kitchen table about one or another aspect of the plan. Each segment ended with one of them saying, "There must be a better way." Yet as one study put it, they "had a negligible impact on the public" primarily because the ads ran in only a few markets and were not repeated enough to have been seen by large numbers of voters during the health care reform campaign.[58]

Nonetheless, the money spent on those ads or the rest of the effort to influence decision makers was not wasted. The reason is that they targeted the media and key decision makers themselves at least as much as the general public. And they worked because "reporters, key members of Congress, and White House officials took the 'Harry and Louise' commercials seriously and *believed* they were decisive in changing the national political debate on health care"[59] (emphasis added).

One reason the ads were thought to be important was that they were so visible—not as ads, but as the subject of media stories, some of them stimulated inadvertently by "the White House's furious reaction to them."[60] For a time, they were almost ubiquitous even though, as paid commercials, they ran only a limited number of times in a few markets.

Another was that, to the extent that people paid attention to them, they and other ads tended to be accepted at face value. There were almost no independent assessments of their accuracy to correct errors.[61] Nor was the Clinton administration itself effective at responding to the negative arguments being made against their plan.

Indeed, for their part, the Clinton team left open to the opposition the first several months following the September 22 speech. In addition, in preparing and presenting their Health Security plan, they failed to make allies among the media and, with the bill's length and complexity, even provoked ridicule and opposition among them. At the same time, they tended to demonize the opposition, especially the insurance companies and pharmaceutical manufacturers, which reduced the potential interest of those groups in negotiating compromises on the points of most interest to them.

Finally, their strategy unwittingly discouraged the kind of substantive debate that might have produced consensus about both the need for reform and the nature of the reform needed as well as an effective outpouring of public support to counteract the opposition of the special interests. Lisa Disch, a political scientist at the University of Minnesota, writes that the "initial phases of the health care policy process sent a message that health reform was a technical and administrative problem to be solved by policy experts, not open to political debate."[62] The creation of the large group of experts, with subgroups working on specific elements of what turned out to be more than 1,300 pages of draft legislation, symbolized that approach. One result was that the "press retaliated against being shut out by caricaturing the task force as 'stealthy' for its secrecy and needlessly complex." It "not only drew ridicule" for these "technocratic excesses," but, perhaps more important, failed to build a foundation of public understanding or support for what became the president's plan.[63] It is now generally agreed "that the administration's withdrawal from the public during the task force period was a 'tactical mistake'"[64] that gave both grassroots opposition and the House Republicans many months to mobilize against reform.

By the time the administration was ready to engage the public in the spring of 1994, "the various public events from this phase, from the town meetings to the bus caravans, conformed to a . . . model of democracy that makes leadership a matter of packaging policy for a media-consuming public and blurs the boundaries between campaigning and governing."[65] Among other things, "by presenting health reform as an all-inclusive social problem, the administration paradoxically compromised inclusivity by obscuring group-specific social differences." It implied that the "'broken system' affects all Americans, all across society, and in the same way."[66] As a result, some groups were alienated by the impression that the president's plan did not address their particular needs.

Another result of the administration's approach was that a variety of ideas with support among people sympathetic to the need for reform—potential allies in the quest for passage—did not receive serious consideration, at least not in public. For example, the single-payer idea "was consistently positioned by the administration as a radical fringe threat to free enterprise, even though it had ninety-three sponsors in the House and was evaluated by the Congressional Budget Office as being likely to reduce annual medical spending by $114 billion per year."[67]

Disch also suggests that by the time the scene shifted to the Congress, the administration had lost the support even of its own party. She writes that in July 1994, Democratic leaders in the Congress decided to "underscore the distance between the reform proposals in Congress and the proposal designed by Clinton's task force, and thereby dissociate the health initiative from an increasingly unpopular president."[68] Moreover, this strategy was validated by voter opposition to the Clinton plan, which had increased to 49 percent.

The complexity of a bill that ran to 1,342 pages contributed to this result. One reason was that it was hard for reporters, who were having trouble understanding it themselves, to communicate its key provisions to the public in terms they could understand and form opinions about. It turns out that there are at least two kinds of reporters: one group follows various issues and becomes expert in a particular sector of the economy or other topic, and the other concentrates on the political controversies. By the spring of 1994, it was this latter group that was carrying the ball primarily, and as political reporters, they tended to emphasize the elements of conflict between the partisans. Not being expert on the subject matter and knowing that conflict attracts attention, they highlighted the differences without being able to help the public sort through them as a kind of "honest broker."[69]

For their part, as we saw above, "Republicans used health care strategically to weaken the Democrats, discredit Clinton, and thereby position themselves to win control of the Congress and the presidency. . . . Republicans generally met every Democratic proposal for reform, no matter how diluted, with the charge that it amounted to socialized medicine."[70] In the end, they won. Reform lost.

Outpatient Prescription Drugs—Medicare Part D

The absence of coverage for outpatient prescription drugs was recognized in the mid-1960s, soon after Medicare was implemented, as a hole that needed to be filled. Over the years, policy advocates and public officials made a number of attempts to fill in that gap, "seldom . . . as an independent issue."[71] The first occurred when President Johnson appointed a Task Force on Prescription Drugs in 1967, but even though it recommended adding drug coverage when it reported in 1969, by that time Richard Nixon had been elected president and that "window of opportunity" closed. In 1988, late in Ronald Reagan's term as president, the Medicare Catastrophic Coverage Act (MCCA) which included prescription drug coverage, was passed; but the law was repealed a year later. President Clinton's proposal for comprehensive health reform created another opportunity because it would have been difficult to sustain a Medicare program without prescription drug coverage if the population under age sixty-five had it as part of the Clinton plan. That effort failed, too, of course.

The issue surfaced again in the late 1990s when the problem had become more acute for many seniors as a result of several changing conditions. For one, many Medicare HMOs had responded to reductions in federal capitation payments by "reducing or eliminating coverage for prescription drugs and other supplemental benefits."[72] In addition, employer-sponsored coverage for retirees, a mainstay of many large firms, was eroding. Also, almost one-fourth of Medicare beneficiaries had no prescription drug coverage at all—even as the cost of prescription drugs was rising. It was becoming an issue for the non-elderly as well, because between 1998 and 2002 "per capita spending on prescription drugs rose at an annual rate of 13 percent."[73] So for all these reasons, prescription drug coverage took on a new sense of urgency for Medicare beneficiaries (and others) just as "the unexpected emergence of federal budget surpluses," beginning in 1998, appeared to make Medicare coverage of prescription drugs financially feasible.[74]

The three "streams" of the agenda-setting process—problems, policies, and politics—identified by University of Michigan political scientist John Kingdon—converged in 2003.[75] "[M]embers of both parties in Congress bowed to political realities and public dissatisfaction with managed care and developed what is primarily a package of new subsidies for prescription drug assistance."[76] Republicans now controlled the White House and both houses of Congress and saw an opportunity to take over a traditional Democratic issue. They had "sufficient political capacity and will" to take it on, and "President Bush made Medicare reform one of his administration's highest domestic priorities."[77] The ideas from recent failed proposals were available to build new policy, and "sensing that the limited bipartisan cooperation in the Senate prevented a filibuster, President Bush invested his political capital to win over skeptical allies and enact legislation as soon as possible."[78]

Finally, Oliver and colleagues write that because the Budget Enforcement Act of 1990, which required any new legislation to be self-funding, had expired in 2002, political support was easier to obtain. At the same time, the willingness to spend new federal revenues made it less likely that the public would rise up to force repeal, as it did with the MCCA in the late 1980s.

Eventually, outpatient drug coverage became irresistible even to the conservative Republican administration of George W. Bush. Although the plan that was put into place has made prescription drugs affordable to many elderly, it is widely considered to be "one of the least sensible innovations in the history of federal health policy."[79] Among other things, the law prohibits Medicare officials from negotiating with drug companies over the prices to be paid for the drugs used by program beneficiaries. Further, it *requires* beneficiaries to sign up with private insurers to obtain their prescription drugs, a departure for Medicare. The program pays 75 percent of the first $2,250 that a beneficiary spends on outpatient drugs. But then, until the person's spending level reaches $5,100, it pays nothing more. That is, the beneficiary must pay the next $2,850 of prescription drug costs out of pocket. After that, the so-called "donut hole," the program kicks in again, picking up 95 percent of the remaining costs.

In addition to the design features just described, a number of widely publicized implementation problems occurred. A partial list includes "mishandling of dual eligibles' switch to Medicare drug coverage; . . . rampant confusion among seniors facing a dizzying choice of, on average, more than forty different Medicare drug plans; the lack of consistently reliable and comprehensive information to guide such choices . . .; administrative headaches for pharmacists and physicians . . .; failure to enroll millions of low-income Medicare beneficiaries eligible for additional federal subsidies to help them pay premiums and cost-sharing for their prescription drug coverage."[80]

Oberlander asks the obvious question: "Why did the MMA become law when it was so widely viewed as bad public policy?"[81] Fundamentally, "its enactment served a range of political interests. First, . . . [it] represented an important political opportunity for Republicans to take ownership of a Democratic issue."[82] On the other hand, its timing before the 2004 elections increased the political risk for Republicans if they were unable to enact a new law. In this connection, offering the new benefit through private plans instead of traditional Medicare made supporting the bill "more palatable to congressional Republicans."[83] For their part, although most Democrats ultimately opposed the MMA, they faced their own risks, especially if, after blocking the bill, they were "unable to explain to the public why no legislation was better than flawed legislation."[84] After all, the new law would help many Medicare beneficiaries, and the political calculation was that, having put a new program in place, it could be improved in the future.

During Medicare's life to that time, the key policy issues year after year tended to be how to control the program's escalating costs. As that preoccupation grew, the influence of interest groups declined and that of the federal regulatory apparatus increased. But Oberlander tells us that pattern was "nowhere to be seen in the MMA. The MMA instead resembles a classic case of interest-group politics, and it is hard to find a group or parochial interest that did not benefit from the bill."[85] These included not only the AARP, as representative of the elderly who needed help with the cost of prescription drugs, but also pharmaceutical companies, the biotechnology industry, managed care plans and private insurers, small businesses, employers, physicians, hospitals, and even residents of rural areas whose access to care improved as their providers were awarded higher payments.

Among the most important lessons from this episode as we look forward to the next one are the following: as a legacy of the presidential campaign of 2000 in which it was a major issue, the public kept the issue alive and, with the help of groups such as the AARP, was demanding action. With Republican majorities in both houses of Congress, President George W. Bush and his Republican colleagues saw an opportunity to take ownership of an important domestic policy issue away from his Democratic opponents. Moreover, the president's active participation in the legislative process played an important role.[86] At the same time, however, ideology—and interest group politics—constrained the substance and is responsible for the peculiar form the final law took.

Lessons for the Future

This brief history teaches us several things that will be useful to reformers.

First, proposals for change—especially dramatic, comprehensive change to a status quo—always provoke determined opposition from interest groups that benefit from the current system and want to protect those benefits. This is true even though, as the number of special interests has multiplied, the ability of any particular one to dictate the outcome of the legislative process is diminished.[87]

Second, that opposition usually wins for several reasons:

1. Their interests are particularly salient to them. Depending on the nature of the reform, they expect to lose a lot of money if not their very existence if the proposed law passes. At the very least, they recognize that to succeed under a new order, they will need to transform themselves, which also tends to cost a lot. For these reasons, the proposal focuses their attention and leads them to take action to oppose the bill, or if passage seems a realistic possibility, to try to influence its content. Most of these interest groups are permanently organized to influence public policy—legislation as well as regulations—that affect them, their competitors, or both. As a result, they have a head start in organizing effectively to fight reform and tend to be able to finance their oppositional activities with a substantial war chest.

2. These interests are aided by a governmental structure that makes it much harder to pass laws than to stop them. That is especially the case when the stakes are high, and when the potential legislation has multiple provisions, each of which may have its own group of opponents.

3. Leaders of Congress, who control both the legislative agenda and the committee structure, are often conservative opponents of a large government role in whatever sector of the economy is under consideration. This is the case because leaders tend to be senior members of Congress or the Senate whose constituents have returned them to Washington many times and who, over long years in Washington, have built strong relationships with colleagues who, though in the same party, may have divergent views on key policy issues. These congressional leaders tend to have developed a perhaps exaggerated respect for both stability in established public- and private-sector relationships and the difficulty of passing legislation that, by embracing large changes, would disrupt them. This is particularly true in the House, where elections are held every two years and because congressional districts tend to be smaller and more homogeneous than the entire states in which senators run. Moreover, in the Senate the rules give political minorities added power. Chief among these is the ability to filibuster, through which determined senators are able to keep controversial issues from even coming to the floor for a vote. Because it takes sixty votes to end a filibuster, simple majorities usually are not enough to pass controversial pieces of legislation. The

power of reform opponents in the Congress is particularly strong when the issue is contentious, the vote is likely to be close, and the opposition party is focused on denying the majority a victory in the next election.

4. It is much harder to mobilize the general public than the special interests. This is especially true on an issue such as health care. People tend to be healthy most of the time and to interact with the health care system only intermittently. Moreover, those who think they have good insurance are hard to engage in the cause of change because so many are afraid of losing what they already have. They are also wary of change that, even if it sounds good, is untested and may not work as proponents expect. The public's interest in health care tends to be diffused, whereas the interests of health care professionals and the organizations that employ them tend to be quite concentrated.

Third, when reform has succeeded, as when Medicare passed, special circumstances often apply—although even then, success is far from a forgone conclusion.

For all these reasons, the political challenge is much the same today as it was through most of the period before the passage of Medicare. The differences between then and now are in some of the details, not the underlying political dynamics. Among them are the fact that the AMA is no longer the most vocal or influential special interest group opposed to national health insurance. In 2009, it even supports the need for some type of reform. When President Bill Clinton proposed his reform plan in the early 1990s, the key opponents were the health insurance industry and the organization of small businesses. The insurance industry, which by then included publicly traded managed care organizations as well as traditional indemnity insurance companies, had grown enormously in the intervening years and would stand to lose a lot under some forms of national health insurance. And small businesses, many of which offered either no coverage to their employees or limited coverage, were concerned about the financial burden they would be expected to bear. Pharmaceutical companies and other groups opposed it as well, and supporters of the reforms were unable to overcome the combined influence of these groups with the Congress.

While the current period contains some reasons to be hopeful that a new reform effort might actually succeed, in the passage referred to at the start of this chapter, Brown points out that the current system has proven to be remarkably resistant to prior attempts at reform despite dire predictions of the consequences of failing to act.[88] He urges caution in the effort to move forward.

Conclusion

From the Progressive era to the present day, the story of attempts to reform the health care system have had a remarkable sameness to them—certainly in their result, but also largely in their politics, as well.

In the next chapter, I will draw on the history to outline some elements of a political strategy that might result in passage of health care reform. An important part of that strategy is the use of public opinion. Can it be an effective antidote to the opposition sure to be mounted by "special" interests? How can it be mobilized in the cause of saving the health care system? And what options are there for framing the issues to maximum effect? This means not only how to present the issues and the options in a positive light, but also how to respond to opponents who frame the issues differently.

Chapter 10

The Politics of Reform

ELEMENTS OF A STRATEGY TO BREAK THE LOGJAM

GIVEN THE SERIOUSNESS of the problems and despite the daunting political challenge of passing comprehensive reform legislation, we do want to move forward. So we need to focus on the political dimension to identify key elements of a game plan that can succeed in passing reform. It will have at least two requirements. One is the articulation of a persuasive case for reform. Indeed, the first eight chapters of this book are a contribution to that case. But as Hacker has persuasively shown in his book about the 1993–94 Clinton reform effort, a focus on the substance is not enough. The decisions are made by political actors, chiefly members of the House and Senate, so the second requirement is to craft and execute a detailed political strategy aimed at producing a bill for the president to sign. This chapter identifies key elements of such a strategy. Before beginning to outline it, however, we need to review the process for passing laws.

How Laws Are Passed

Every year, the Congress considers hundreds, if not thousands of ideas for new legislation. Some aim to modify existing laws; some to solve newly arisen problems. In addition, of course, representatives and senators are asked to approve a budget appropriating money to carry out the functions of government. Many, if not most, of the new laws they consider have budgetary implications as well. The topics may include modernizing the courts; improving public education; making it possible for bright students to attend college to develop their potential in the modern world economy; repairing old bridges and roadways and building new ones; facilitating trade between American firms and those in other countries; and regulating complex, arcane sectors of the modern economy, including the financial system, which has created new instruments and processes in recent years that few understand. And, of course, there are foreign affairs and defense. In this context, it is exceedingly difficult for even the most dedicated public servant to know enough to make informed decisions in each area.

Faced with the multiplicity of its responsibilities, the Congress long ago organized itself into committees so that subgroups of the members, as well as their staffs, can develop expertise in subsets of these wide-ranging subjects. Some have become expert on foreign affairs, others on banking, and still others on agriculture or trade.

Moreover, because a democratic form of government assumes that public officials are serving the needs of the populace, citizens bring problems to their attention and ask for help, sometimes proposing solutions that they hope the government will adopt. In this environment, "citizens" are not just individuals who live in communities, work in firms, and send children to schools. They also include economic entities—businesses and other organizations that earn money by providing goods and services to the people— which also contribute to the society and its economy.

These are the factions that James Madison discussed in 1787 with such prescience in *Federalist 10*.[1] Factions are groups of citizens "who are united and actuated by some common . . . interest . . . ,[which is opposed] to the rights of other citizens or to the permanent and aggregate interests of the community." Factions, he writes, are the inevitable result of differences in people and lead, also inevitably, to conflicts. As a result, the "regulation of these various and interfering interests forms the principal task of modern legislation. . . ." He also argues that the best chance for "controlling the effects of faction" is in a government of representatives who can serve as "proper guardians of the public weal." That is the kind of government we have, of course, and over a period of more than two hundred years, it has worked pretty well. Nonetheless, progress is slow; and one key reason is that, in the legislative process, factions have certain advantages over the general public. One is that their interests are concentrated, whereas those of the general citizenry are diffused. As a result, they are better able than ordinary citizens to organize effectively to protect or serve those interests. And finally, those groups usually have substantial resources, including money, to devote to the pursuit of their interests.

To communicate their concerns and recommendations to public officials, many such groups organize to represent their interests more effectively. They hire staff to do studies that define the nature and extent of the problems they encounter—in part to persuade decision makers that their problems are important for the society at large—and they hire other staff (lobbyists) to communicate their needs and proposals for relief to those same public officials. Indeed, given the range of difficult issues faced by the Congress as well as their complexity, these functions have become a necessity. When the issue is a proposal from another interest that affects their domain, they have an easier time even when the primary beneficiaries would be the general public. Machiavelli wrote almost five hundred years ago that creating a new system was one of the most difficult challenges humans face. "For the initiator has the enmity of the old institutions and merely lukewarm defenders in those who would gain by the new ones." One reason is "the general skepticism of mankind which does not really believe in an innovation until experience proves its value."[2]

It should also be remarked that the process is not simply an effort of the various interests to persuade decision makers by the power of their data and argument. Newspapers and other media are full of stories of abuses of these processes, tales of attempts by lobbyists to "persuade" officials of their point of view by providing a variety of tangible benefits, including junkets, meals, gifts of various kinds, even contributions to political campaigns and jobs for relatives.

To help decision makers sort out the validity of competing special interest arguments, the executive branch and the Congress have their own staffs, which also do studies and provide objective data to inform both public officials and members of the public at large. (Indeed, much of the information reported earlier in this book came from some of those government agencies.) Many executive branch agencies have developed deserved reputations over decades for providing reliable data that help to illuminate complex developments in a variety of sectors. In the Congress, the Congressional Budget Office (CBO) and the Government Accountability Office (GAO), headed by respected professionals, are expected to be nonpartisan and to do the same thing for members of the House and Senate.

In general, laws are passed after problems are identified and representatives inform themselves by taking testimony in hearings, which are usually open to the public, using the resources described in the previous paragraphs. When a proposal is up for consideration, it is not surprising to learn that the 100 senators and 435 representatives hold views that vary across a broad spectrum as Madison predicted—some are oriented toward supporting a substantial government role in many areas, while others tend to prefer a hands-off, more laissez-faire approach. So how do they reach the point at which a majority in both houses agree to vote for the same bill? If enough believe that some type of action must be taken, they negotiate to make the bill acceptable to those with a variety of views regarding the form that action should take. In the end, if they succeed, the result may be no one's first choice, but everyone is reasonably satisfied.

This, in outline, is the situation we face when we want to pass laws reforming the health care system. Having read this far in the book, you know how complicated the health care system is, how many factors interact to affect the utilization and other decisions that have brought us to this point, and how many different interest groups—besides the general public—have a stake in the outcome. Representatives and senators, most of whom are not expert on health care issues, nonetheless will be asked to make decisions that will affect how the system should function in the future. To help them make those choices, they will rely on the experts among their colleagues; on knowledge-able staff; on data provided by federal agencies, including both the CBO and GAO; and on information and arguments brought to their attention by rep-resentatives of various interest groups, including both individual citizens (for example, older people as represented by the AARP, or workers represented by unions) and corporations. And everything they read and hear will be filtered through their general views about the role of government—from a minimalist view on the right that extols the market to a position on the left that is com-fortable with a large role for government in service of the public interest.

As I suggested in Chapter 8, much of the opposition to substantial reform in the past has rested on the twin peaks of ideology that favors a limited role for government in American society and the power of special interests. To achieve an outcome that includes my six reform elements, a way must be found to overcome those two prongs of opposition.

The Legislative Process as a Competition Among Groups

The first thing to recognize is that, fundamentally, the legislative process is a competition among proponents and opponents of congressional action for the votes of enough representatives and senators to either pass a law or defeat it. To enact a controversial law, supporters must play terrific offense for sure, but they must be equally good at defense. The opposition is certain to invest much effort in building coalitions and engaging in a campaign against the bill, as Quadagno shows opponents of health care reform have done many times in the past.[3] But they can lose if conditions are favorable (or at least not impossible) and the advocates plan and implement a smart, winning strategy.

Groups with a stake in the legislative outcome can attempt to influ-ence the result by advertising, by grassroots mobilization of an organization's members using direct mail and telephone banks, and by hiring law firms and public relations agencies to engage in traditional lobbying with congressio-nal decision makers. Through these methods, supporters and opponents try to persuade congressional decision makers to vote for their position. Not surprisingly, the effort takes money.

Because those groups with the most direct, concentrated interest in the outcome will pull out all the stops to defeat reforms that will threaten their gains from the current system, part of a successful legislative strategy must include a determined effort to counter their formidable resources and determination. Public opinion in support of reform is a potentially powerful counterforce, though it can be difficult to mobilize.

The Role of Public Opinion in the Legislative Process

Today, the "medium of political expression" is public opinion, and the goal of policymakers is to find or "produce tangible evidence" that it is on their side.[4] They know they cannot succeed politically if the public are mobilized against them so they try to influence the people to support their positions. Or when they do not have strong views themselves, they want to avoid going against the strong views of constituents.

As the tools of molding public opinion and studying it developed during the twentieth century, it attracted increased scholarly attention. Some believe that public opinion as an expression of the public's own interest on an important policy matter is an illusion, that there is no such thing as independently defined public opinion in that sense. Instead, they argue, the public is subject to the manipulation of elites—politicians and private interests—in pursuit of their own goals.

Others think that those elites are unlikely to be able to manipulate public opinion because elites are rarely unified on a given issue and cannot instruct the public "on a clear direction to follow."[5] Instead, they tend to be divided and offer diverse messages on particular policy matters because, among them, their interests differ from one another. On health policy, for example, insurers and providers have different interests. And although they may overlap sometimes, allowing them to make common cause on specific issues, their primary concerns regarding the nature and terms of insurance coverage differ. As a result, they and other elites may try to persuade individual representatives and senators of their (different) points of view.

Nor, in this view, is the public a blank slate subject to easy manipulation by determined advocates. Even when their views on a particular policy proposal may not yet be fully formed, they do have some beliefs that are both relevant to the matter at hand and relatively stable. For example, Americans have consistently and by wide margins supported universal coverage and substantial, if nonspecific, health care reform over many years, as we saw in Chapter 3. At the same time, however, nothwithstanding the fact that they support particular programs such as Medicare that include a large role for government, Americans tend to be wary of "big government" and ambivalent toward a greatly expanded role for government in health care.[6]

To understand how public opinion might contribute to the passage of comprehensive health care reform—especially given these contradictory strains in

Americans' opinions—we first need to take a step back to consider how public opinion can be used to help pass legislation in general. What we want to know are two things: since the actual decisions are made in the Congress, where does public opinion even fit in? And how can the general public, which though large in numbers are diffuse and amorphous as a group (in fact, they are neither monolithic in their interest in the health care system, nor an organized group at all), affect the outcome of controversial legislation in which well-organized and well-financed special interests have big stakes? The answers are not obvious, because agents of special interests have the need and the resources to create opportunities to get their views heard by senators and representatives, whereas the views of an individual constituent (even if he or she gets to communicate with legislators directly) carry weight only when joined with the voices of many other individuals holding similar views. In contrast, with their easy access, lobbyists for special interests are able to use not only the power of their argument but other means as well to persuade members of Congress to vote for their position.

The Executive Branch, too, has ready access to the Congress and, similarly, can bring to bear the inherent logic of its argument. Moreover, since the president and the Congress are interested in a whole range of issues, not just health care reform, the president may be able to offer a variety of trade-offs to win a favorable vote. Although it may not be done this crudely, a president might say to a representative or senator something like, "If you support me on this bill, I will support you on the legislation you want help with." Or he may arrange for a large federal project to benefit the congressman's district.

Nonetheless, public opinion is part of the equation as well, and it can be used either to support legislative proposals or to oppose them. The most direct method of communicating the public's views to legislators is for individual citizens, usually organized by an advocate from an organization such as the Children's Defense Fund or AARP or a labor union, to call or write or visit their congressional representatives. Sending a letter or an e-mail takes little time and can be done in the comfort of one's own home, and organizers make it even easier by providing draft letters and the names and addresses of the relevant legislators. Although it is said that thousands of identical letters carry less weight than ones that are actually written by the individuals who send them, news stories often report the large numbers of letters—identical or not—received by legislators on one side of an issue or the other. Doing so creates or adds to the impression of widespread support or opposition for a particular course of action. Phone calls in large numbers may have a similar effect. In-person visits to a congressional office either in Washington or in the district are more difficult to arrange, but they too can get the attention of the media if the numbers of participants are substantial and deliberate efforts to make them known are taken either by the group that organizes them or by the congressional office itself.

In addition, interest groups can target particular segments of the public by buying advertisements in media read or seen by those audiences or through public relations campaigns that include press releases and efforts to organize grassroots campaigns to encourage citizens to contact their congressional representatives directly. "The major strength of advertising is that the content and timing of ads is group controlled."[7] Public relations campaigns are more diffuse, but can have a wider reach. More recently, websites created for special purposes have been used to capture some of the strengths of both of these older methods. They allow control of content and can reach a wide audience, especially of people who regularly access the particular website because they are likely to be supportive. An example from the 2008 presidential campaign was the website fightthesmears.com, which the Obama team created to defend the candidate against opposition charges.[8]

Another critical audience for groups with a stake in the outcome of legislation is the news media. Complex issues, by definition, have multiple interdependent parts, and the relationships among them are not always obvious. We saw in Chapter 9 that reporters had trouble understanding the Clinton reform plan and therefore were unable to communicate its main provisions effectively to the public. Nonetheless, the ways in which issues and ideas are presented or "framed" by reporters can influence what their audience thinks. "Public policy making depends heavily on how options are framed and how particular proposals are covered."[9] I will discuss framing in more detail further on, but for now it is enough to recognize that grassroots campaigns can have a major impact through their influence on reporters for both print and electronic media outlets.[10] Reporters file stories that describe the issues, discuss the proposals, and indicate the degree of support or opposition of various groups. Given these conditions, it makes sense for interest groups—including ones representing ordinary citizens—to communicate directly with media representatives. Through press releases and other means they can present their views of what the problems are, the various solutions that have been offered, and the likely effects of each on different groups. Those efforts, in turn, can have a direct impact on how they are reported to both the wider public and congressional decision makers and thus on what those audiences think about the proposals. In the case of the Clinton plan, Hacker wrote that "Clinton's relationship with the Washington press corps was particularly strained."[11]

If we want to mobilize public opinion to help produce a different health care reform outcome next time, we need to pay attention to how the issues and competing proposals are presented. That is, how they are "framed." We turn to that topic next.

Framing

We know that Americans tend to believe in individual effort, the market, and a limited role for government. Yet the proposed reform elements I outlined in Chapter 8 are based in part on the notion that the market is a big part of the problem, not its solution, and that government must play a substantial role in the outcome for it to succeed. How in the world can we bridge the gap between those two opposing positions?

Ultimately, the decisions—even regarding whether or not to consider health care reform at all—are made by office holders. The tendency will be for elected public officials to make their choices on the basis of a combination of their own individual policy orientations and the influence exerted by those interest groups with the strongest, best-organized efforts to influence them. The insurers, small businesses, and others that are most persistent in trying to influence the outcome may try to get them to avoid substantial reform altogether. Public opinion can change that calculus. If the public is engaged in the issue and understands both the stakes and the dynamics that got us into the fix we are in, they may be able to change the policy balance. A recent example is the Medicare prescription drug bill. The public demanded action, and convinced a reluctant administration that it was in its political interest to comply. The unsatisfying form of the particular law that passed was determined by the power of those who held the minimalist ideology and the inability or unwillingness of those with different views to insist on eliminating some of the worst parts of the bill.

So the question is, How does public opinion get formed? How does it work to exert influence? How can we get it engaged in such a way as to overcome the power of special health-sector interest groups?

On most policy questions, competing groups vie over whose interpretation will prevail.[12] "[M]edia discourse dominates the larger issue culture" and the content of those media—including radio, television, and newspapers—is "the most important indicator of the general issue culture."[13] For that reason it is important to understand what the media actually communicate on complex policy issues such as health care reform.

At the core of what gives an issue meaning "is a central organizing idea or *frame* for making sense of relevant events, suggesting what is an issue."[14] Or as another scholar put it, "Media frames, largely unspoken and unacknowledged, organize the world both for journalists who report it and, in some important degree, for us who rely on their reports."[15] So if the media—as well as issue partisans—use frames to present complex choices, then we need to understand what a frame is and how it works before we can apply it to our primary interest in health policy.

Frames help to simplify complex issues so that people who are not experts but potentially at least have an interest in the topic can make enough sense of it to come to a conclusion about what the concerns are and how to resolve them. They work in part by using "condensing symbols—metaphors, exemplars, catchphrases, depictions, and visual images or icons," which may help to simplify the complexity but also may distort the choices and, in the process, influence the outcome in a specific direction.[16]

A framing effect "occurs when two logically equivalent . . . statements of a problem lead decision makers to choose different options."[17] Thaler and Sunstein illustrate this point with examples. In one, they suggest a doctor proposes an operation to treat your serious heart disease, and you ask what the odds of survival are. In one version, the doctor says, "Of one hundred patients who have this operation, ninety are alive after five years." In another, he says, "Of one hundred patients who have this operation, ten are dead after five years." The objective information is exactly the same, but more people are likely to choose to have the operation if it is presented in the first version than the second.[18]

"A framing effect is said to occur when, in the course of describing an issue or event, a speaker's emphasis on a subset of potentially relevant considerations causes individuals to focus on these considerations when constructing their opinions."[19] For example, in forming their attitudes toward the question of whether the Ku Klux Klan should be granted a permit for a rally, Druckman argues that people consciously choose on the basis of which consideration is more important to them: the right to free speech or the right to be safe in public.[20] And who wins depends on which of those two frames is used by the largest number of people.

Understanding frames is important because having that information opens the possibility that we can affect opinions deliberately by the way in which we present the possibilities. And indeed, studies show that people's choices *are* influenced by the frame that is used. For example, "when government spending for the poor is framed as enhancing the chance that poor people can get ahead, individuals tend to support increased spending. On the other hand, when it is framed as resulting in higher taxes, the probability grows that individuals will oppose increased spending."[21]

Frame effects are not the same as persuasion, which works by altering the *content* of one's beliefs. A discussant, *through his argument,* convinces a hearer to change his beliefs—for example, to believe that the economic impact of a new housing development will be positive or negative.[22] Framing effects, on the other hand, "work by altering 'the *importance* individuals attach to particular beliefs' (and this shift may or may not alter overall opinion"[23] (emphasis in original). So in the example given, the frame would determine whether or not the hearer thought that the economic impact of the new housing development was the most important consideration, not whether that economic impact would be positive or negative.

Early thinking about framing effects assumed that citizens were like "puppets, voting thumbs up or down depending on how issues are framed. . . ."[24] Druckman, more recently, conducted experiments which demonstrated that the credibility of the frame's source influenced whether or not it had an effect. Credibility of the source has two dimensions: the speaker's target audience must believe he (or she) has knowledge relevant to the decision and also that the speaker can be trusted to reveal what he or she knows.[25] Druckman showed that people will tend to accept a frame ascribed to a person with those characteristics and that, conversely, an audience will reject a frame presented by a person without them. In other words, frames do not always work. They can be overcome. There are limits to "*when* an elite *can* and *cannot* successfully engage in framing,"[26] and as a result, an "ideological faction" may not always prevail in defining the terms of a debate.[27] A further implication of his work is that different groups may accept the frame of different people. Thus Rush Limbaugh, the right-wing talk-show host, is accepted as an authority by some groups. People tune in to his daily radio programs because they tend to agree with his point of view. People who are turned off by what they consider his strident negativity, however, do not ascribe the two characteristics of credibility to him and are unlikely even to listen to him. Similarly, some people watch Fox News on cable television, but others who think its reporting is biased and cannot be trusted to present the news fairly or accurately do not even tune in. People on the other side of the political spectrum may watch Keith Olbermann or Rachel Maddow on MSNBC instead.

How These Ideas Apply to Health Policy

Are there frames that can increase the probability that the public will actively support health care reform? Are there other frames that will make passage of reform more difficult or even impossible?

The political scientist James Morone writes about the differences between American health care policy and that in other industrialized nations. "European health policy analysts regularly invoke a 'solidarity culture'—a staunch belief in sharing resources and concern for what might be called 'the people's health'."[28] In contrast, he writes, most people think of the American policy process as "the unabashed pursuit of self-interest. . . ."[29]

The implicit model behind this book is challenged by Morone's discussion of interest-group politics. What I have tried to do is present incontrovertible data about how the health care system works and the problems it has produced so that, instead of debating the problem and its causes, we can concentrate our efforts on debating the solution and how to achieve it. But

Morone writes that "[n]o matter how robust the scientific findings, political interests routinely mobilize and often delay or derail action. . . . In the political arena, your science is only as strong as your political coalition."[30] If he is right, then the task must be to build a winning coalition.

Putting together such a coalition requires not just a focus on the mutual self-interests of potential partners but also organizing principles or frames that legitimize the creation of such particular ad hoc coalitions. This is especially important because what we want to do is *pass* controversial health care reform legislation; it would be much less critical if our goal were simply to *stop* such an effort because, as I noted earlier, it is easier to derail reform legislation than to enact it. (Recall Machiavelli's insight from earlier in this chapter.)

But, Morone continues, "interest group politics is only the most obvious story."[31] "Americans also share an intermittent legacy of cooperation" and "a tendency to turn political differences into moral disputes . . . of virtue and vice, good and evil, us and them. . . ."[32]

Of Morone's other two traditions, the one built on community and cooperation has obvious relevance. He recalls that in the 1980s, some people became "uneasy about unabashed self-interest and untrammeled markets. What happens to the common good when everyone pushes only for number one?" An analogous statement found in various forms in several religious traditions is, "If I am not for me, who will be for me? If I am for myself alone, what am I?" Morone reports that historians have "documented rich networks of communal assistance."[33] Barn raisings are a particularly evocative example. In the health arena, the public health movement is another. Entire communities benefited from clean water, sanitary sewage disposal, and required immunizations even though all of those initiatives intruded on individual liberty.

Yet for all its benefits, "the communal alternative has always been the more fragile and intermittent approach, displacing individualism largely during crises and extraordinary circumstances."[34] One example was passage of social security legislation in the midst of the Great Depression when Franklin Roosevelt's argument that the "causes of poverty . . . are beyond the control of any individual" resonated at a time when large numbers of people who wanted to work had lost their jobs and could not find others, not because of their own limitations, but as a result of nationwide economic conditions. A plausible case can be made that, early in the twenty-first century we are at a similar watershed period in relation to the health care system for reasons detailed in earlier chapters. If so, then an argument can be made that the most important appeal is not to the self-interest of various groups but to the common interest that all Americans share in a robust, high-quality health care system. Nonetheless, to succeed, proponents of reform will need to withstand the challenges sure to be mounted by those who fear their economic self-interest will be harmed, at least in the short run.

The second of Morone's alternative frames, that of the tendency to turn political differences into moral disputes, also divides into two subgroups, this time what he calls the Puritan vision and the social gospel. They hinge on the question of who should be blamed for our troubles. The Puritans focus on individual behavior, on sinners who erode "our sense of common values and shared fate. The policy problem turns . . . to protecting us from them."[35] The sins that endanger us are alcohol and drug abuse, sexual practices, teen pregnancy, birth control, and abortion, among others. "In each case . . . [s]ome dangerous personal behavior . . . threatens the community." The policy problem therefore becomes how to protect the society from these dangerous people and their bad behavior.[36]

Morone contrasts that moral tradition with another that he calls the social gospel. "Social gospel thinking shifts the focus from individual sinners to an unjust system. The neo-Puritans blame individual misbehavior for society's troubles; the social gospel approach blames society—or socioeconomic pressures—for individual troubles."[37] Examples from our recent history are the Southern civil rights movement and the Great Society of the 1960s. Children cannot read or do math, not because they do not want to learn but because they did not have enough to eat or warm clothes to wear or a place to study at home or because the schools they went to had too few books and too many students in the class for them to learn. But the corrective public-sector programs created to overcome those societal handicaps were short-lived as successive administrations, beginning with Ronald Reagan, undid many of them.

"Proponents of the social gospel alternative reframe the problem away from sin and sinners. . . . [S]ocial gospel pushes for social justice; it promotes collective responsibility toward all members of the community."[38] This frame has a history in the United States and some notable successes even if, in recent decades, it has had the active support of only a minority of citizens. It may be significant in the present context, however, that Barack Obama's successful presidential campaign emphasized the values and interests Americans share instead of the differences that divide us.

Clearly, the case for reforming the health care system can be seen as part of the communitarian or social gospel traditions. To succeed, however, reformers will need to be more persuasive than opponents who, although they will be pursuing their own self-interests, are likely to make their case in terms that extol the market and individual freedom and to rail against the rigidities and inefficiencies of big government or socialized medicine.

The positive case for reform follows from the communitarian or social gospel traditions that Morone describes. It starts with an analysis that shows the health care system is not producing the results we want and that, given the causes, concludes that only systemic reform can change the outcomes. In addition to making the case *for* reform, moreover, it is critically important to answer the arguments of opposition groups firmly from the communitarian perspective.

Many statements typically made in opposition to reform are demonstrably false and merely perpetuate myths that can be discredited easily. For example, if the argument is made that the private insurance system is, by its very nature, more efficient and responsive than big government, call attention to the horrors of the present insurance system. Not only do insurers appear arbitrary in some of the decisions they make regarding individual patients, but the pursuit of profit by avoiding outlays for services used adds billions of dollars in administrative inefficiencies to the medical care system. Medical practices add staff whose only task is to respond to the insurers' demands and appeal the arbitrary rulings of insurance clerks. Not only do they add much to the spending that we want to reduce, but they contribute to errors that undermine good-quality care.

But it is not just that the private insurance sector is inefficient and arbitrary. The public sector can be quite efficient. Medicare spends less than 2 percent of its revenues on administration. If anything, that is too little and gives some functions, such as fraud control and research, inadequate attention.

Nor would the plan proposed in this book—or most other universal coverage plans—result in "socialized medicine." It would only guarantee that everyone has a way to pay for comprehensive insurance, which would provide them with financial access to *private* medical care services. When the argument is made that it takes away choice, the response should be that the only choice it takes away is the choice to go without health insurance or to buy inadequate insurance that, because it is inexpensive, fails to cover services people will need. Individuals would still have their choice of providers. And that is the one that matters most, after all.

If these arguments do not satisfy opponents, put them on the defensive by insisting that they *demonstrate* with data that private insurers provide better value than Medicare. Challenge them to defend these paradoxes:

1. The United States has the highest health care spending in the world by far even though 16 or 17 percent of Americans have no insurance.

2. Many medical innovations originated in the United States, but citizens of many other countries may have better access to them than the millions of Americans with no health insurance.

3. Millions of Americans who *do* have insurance cannot *afford* the care they need because of the high out-of-pocket costs required by their coverage.

4. The U.S. health care system is the most market-based of any in the world, yet competition has not driven out its notorious inefficiency or produced reliable quality of care.

5. Although studies have long shown that the quality of U.S. medical care is unreliable, system-wide quality measures have not improved over many years.

Useful Lessons for Enacting Health System Reform

Summing up, here are some useful lessons gleaned from what we have learned so far that may help get health system reform enacted:

- Create a public demand for reform that cannot be ignored so that members of Congress will feel compelled to act and the power of the minimalist, market-oriented ideology becomes moot.

- As part of that effort, pay particular attention to how the issues and proposed solutions are presented—that is, how they are "framed." This includes both the positive reasons to support the proposed reform and responses to arguments that will be raised on the other side.

- In the negotiation that will follow if senators and representatives are persuaded that they must act, be willing to respond to concerns of interest groups that believe they will be harmed by the proposals. This can include finding roles for some of the groups to play in implementing the plan that is adopted as well as addressing the rates that various other groups (such as small businesses) will be asked to pay.

What follows is more detailed guidance for the development of a political strategy that can result in the passage of comprehensive health care reform legislation. It is based on the review of previous reform efforts found in Chapter 9.

1. *Keep your eyes on the prize.* The only goal is to pass good reform legislation. And there is only one way to achieve it: to get majorities in both houses of Congress to vote for it (sixty in the Senate to avoid a filibuster). Everything needs to be oriented to accomplishing that single purpose.

The bill should include objectives and a framework for accomplishing them without the level of detail embodied in the 1,300 pages of President Clinton's Health Security Act. Leave most of the operational provisions to be negotiated between the executive branch, the Congress, and the interest groups that need to have a hand in the implementation and operation.[39] One important reason is that a complicated plan is harder to explain. It is also harder for the public to imagine how it will affect them. To keep a focus on those considerations, people who will be responsible for mobilizing public support should participate in policy design.[40]

Another reason is that the more details that are included, the more opportunities there are for representatives and senators—and the interest groups trying to influence them—to oppose the bill. Remember that it is easier to defeat a plan than to pass it. Opponents need only to get people to object to one provision (or maybe a few) that is (are) important enough to them to overwhelm all other considerations. Different people will object to different provisions, and if enough people object to enough provisions (even if they support others), the plan is doomed. In contrast, advocates need people to assent to all provisions—or at least to find that the ones they dislike are less important than those they support. It should be easier to gain support for a set of objectives and a general framework for achieving them if implementation issues are left to be worked out later.

In that subsequent negotiation process, the main criterion for choosing a particular implementation mechanism should be, "Does it achieve the goal stated in the legislation?" If it is possible to reach the goal in more than one way, but some groups have strong preferences for one path or another, then judicious choices may make it possible to build a supportive coalition among groups with different perspectives.

2. *Build the design of the program on well-understood and supported elements.* This will reduce the mystery surrounding the new program and the worry that too much will go wrong in its early days. Following are three examples. (1) Use payroll taxes or graduated income taxes to fund the program. Citizens know what they are, and the government and employers, as well as ordinary citizens, know how they can be collected. (2) Use the entitlement (embodied in a voucher or a Health Security card) to choose private insurance or a health plan that meets the law's requirements. This would simplify the government's role, avoiding government-purchased health care, and allow individuals to choose their own plan, including the possibility of keeping an existing one if it qualifies. (3) Use an existing federal agency for administration (such as the Medicare agency or the one that runs the Federal Employees Health Benefits Program). Expanding their functions would be simpler than creating completely new arrangements and new organizations.[41]

3. *A well-thought-out political strategy must be developed—and executed.* The strategy must include a clear understanding of the legislative process, including the roles of the leaders in the two houses of Congress, the roles and prerogatives of committee chairs, and the rules under which bills are considered and passed. The most obvious of these is the fact that Senate rules permit filibusters through which minorities of senators can keep a bill from even coming up for a vote. Because a filibuster can be overcome and debate closed off by a vote of sixty senators, it takes not a majority of fifty but sixty senators to pass controversial legislation. The exception to that rule is

budget bills, which require only a majority vote. This fact has led some to propose considering health care reform as an amendment to a budget bill. That strategy has both pros and cons.[42]

Part of the strategy is to orchestrate a process in which the members of Congress themselves can have input into or even create a bill aimed at accomplishing the purposes of reform. Moreover, make sure that the people in the Congress get credit for the achievement. This is the approach taken by Lyndon Johnson with Wilbur Mills to secure passage of Medicare and Medicaid. Johnson outlined his objectives, left it largely to Mills to put together the legislation that achieved them, and saw to it that Mills received credit for the accomplishment. He was so successful on this latter point that, over the intervening more-than-forty years, books were written telling that story even though we now know that Johnson was anything but a bystander during the process.[43]

Further, the effort to pass the bill must be led by senior people in the executive branch. The Clinton administration is reported to have developed such a strategy, but it got derailed—partly by other priorities such as NAFTA, the budget, and foreign crises and partly by the departure of senior leaders who could negotiate for the president with authority. Expect to make adjustments, because a president does not have complete control of events.

President Obama's team, at this writing, includes veteran public servants with a variety of prior roles related to health care. They include, among others, Katherine Sebelius, a former insurance commissioner and then governor of Kansas, as Secretary of Health and Human Services; Nancy-Ann DeParle, former head of the Health Care Financing Administration (HCFA), as director of the White House Office of Health Reform; and Peter Orszag, director of the Office of Management and Budget and former head of the Congressional Budget Office, who has made a serious study of health policy. While none had a leadership position in the House or Senate, all are knowledgeable, respected public officials. In fact, however, their greatest asset may turn out to be the commitment and engagement of President Obama. In any event, given findings from the Blumenthal and Morone study of the presidential role in past health care reform efforts, he must be heavily involved in ways that advance the strategy.[44]

The political strategy must include *obtaining and sustaining* firm commitments from supportive interest groups, which includes both financial contributions and an effort to organize or participate in a public persuasion campaign. If they try to hang back, as AARP did during the Clinton episode because of internal considerations stemming from past battles,[45] then pull out all the stops to court them. Failure to do so makes both negotiation with the Congress and the development of effective public support more difficult. To use a sports analogy, put points on the board early (gain commitments) and then, even as you try to add to the score, make them stand up by playing effective defense (expect opponents to try to soften those commitments). In the Clinton episode, some supporters or willing negotiators reversed course and became opponents partly in response to intense reverse- and cross-lobbying pressure.[46]

The analysis that informs the developing strategy should include a detailed examination of each stakeholder's interests because it may be possible to turn some potential opponents (physicians or hospitals and even small businesses) into supporters. The analysis must include a complete understanding of the groups' experiences under the current system because it will reveal potential concerns that can be addressed in the proposed legislation and that can be used to build a coalition of support. Here is an example from early in the Obama episode. In June 2009, the AMA announced its support for health care reform but its opposition to a public-sector plan to compete with private insurers. The latter position was somewhat surprising given the widespread physician complaints about the costly, infuriating hassles doctors face from private insurers in the current system. As already noted, many hire staff whose main job is to clarify details of their patients' coverage and to overcome insurers' reluctance to pay for services. In addition, in many cases doctors provide services that, after the fact, their patients' insurers refuse to pay for. And they treat many patients who fail to follow their recommendations because, even with insurance, they cannot afford the out-of-pocket costs.

Apparently the source of the AMA's opposition was the fact that when private insurers do pay, their rates are about 20 percent higher than those paid by Medicare, and the doctors fear that the public option would pay them at Medicare rates.[47] This scenario provides opportunities to refocus the doctors' attention, away from the 20 percent lower fees and toward not having to worry about whether they will be paid for their work at all. The fact is that doctors will probably do better if everyone is covered at Medicare's 80 percent than if some are higher, but others are uninsured. In addition, their administrative costs should be lower.

The analysis should also include an assessment of the competitive dynamics facing each organization—for example, the fact that the Chamber of Commerce was being challenged by the NFIB for the support of small businesses; that the AARP was weakened when the Medicare Catastrophic Coverage Act, which its leaders had supported, was repealed in the late 1980s; and that the insurance industry can be disaggregated into large national firms and others, which have somewhat different strategic interests. Understand which groups may be open to compromise, and which ones are likely to oppose reform under any circumstances.

Be aware of the role of lobbyists for critical interest groups and the influence they have on key representatives and senators. Some will oppose reform no matter what, but it may be possible to encourage others to support it.

A related point is to recognize that representatives and senators will make their decisions only partly (and perhaps a minor part) on the basis of the merits of the case. Lobbyists can gain considerable influence with some congressional representatives by contributing money to campaign funds as well as favorite charities, by providing jobs to family members and important constituents, and in other ways. These tactics can produce determined opposition to any bill or to particular provisions in a bill under consideration. Both can put passage of reform in jeopardy. Therefore the strategy needs to include counter pressure on or incentives for congressmen, first to pass a bill and second to pass one that comes as close as possible to achieving the articulated goals of the reform effort. The president needs to be the key actor in this part of the story.

One of the critical stakeholder groups is the Republican minority in the Congress which, as we saw earlier, had no interest in compromise on the Clinton Health Security Act. Look for ways to temper or constrain their natural tendency to oppose reform—primarily, by making it too costly to them politically (that is, with voters) to be obstructionists. This is critically important because it may not be possible to build a bipartisan coalition, which is necessary in the Senate to overcome a possible filibuster. Even if sixty senators were Democrats, unless all voted to stop a filibuster and allow the bill to come to a vote (in which a majority could pass it), Republican votes would be needed.[48]

4. *Despite their determined opposition, opponents should be treated neither as enemies nor as unscrupulous, predatory actors but as groups that respond rationally— as they see it—to the incentives they face in the current system.* The reason insurers and others do things we do not like in the health care system is because the current system allows—and even encourages—them to pursue their interests in those ways. There is no need to shy away from describing the dysfunctional and hurtful actions they take, but there is also no need to brand them as evil in doing so. Treating opponents with respect may help to leave open the door for compromise, at least with some.

5. *Anticipate ways in which opponents are likely to characterize the plan, as well as the types of arguments that they are likely to make, and prepare effective responses.* The opponents of reform are likely to invest large sums and much energy in a multipronged effort to persuade legislators because the stakes are very high for them: for some, the ability to continue their present way of doing business; for others, their very survival. Failure to anticipate and respond in this regard means losing control of the message, as Stan Greenberg, President

Clinton's pollster, warned at the start of the Clinton episode.[49] Effective answers must be developed to some common themes—such as opposition to "big government" or to "socialized medicine"—but also to the separate interests of insurers, pharmaceutical companies, providers of care, and small businesses, which may overlap but are not identical. Success may ultimately depend on the extent to which the general population can be mobilized to counter the actions of at least some of the special interests.

6. *In that context, assume a generally sympathetic public—but one whose support needs to be nurtured.* There is plenty of evidence from the Blendon surveys cited in Chapter 3, among others, that the general public wants secure, reliable health care coverage and even that they are willing to pay for it with some increase in taxes. Failure to build on their general affinity for the ideas of reform leaves the public vulnerable to actions of opponents. The Clinton plan experience in the early 1990s is but the latest example showing that opponents of reform—the special interests, conservative ideologues, and political partisans looking toward the next election—will use whatever tools they can find to persuade the public and the Congress, who must vote on it, to oppose comprehensive reform. The public had erroneous impressions about the content of the Health Security Act in part because many of the arguments used during the Clinton episode, though patently false, were inadequately answered. Reform managers must attempt to control the terms of the debate. Supporters of reform must hold the public's attention, interest, and respect. Repeated communication with the public is necessary but, in 1993 and 1994, was not forthcoming.[50]

Besides exerting his own behind-the-scenes influence, a president has a role that no one else is as well positioned to perform, and that is to use his "bully pulpit" to keep the public's focus on the problems to be solved and on the key principles to be included in a successful law. He needs also to articulate clear principles that need to be included in the bill. Part of his challenge is to give the public a vision of what reform can mean for them, how the new system would work, and, especially for those who already have employer-provided insurance, that they need not worry that they will be worse off. The Clinton plan failed in part because not only could the public not picture how his complex new program would work, but also those with good employer-provided coverage feared they would lose it. Finally, the president, above all others, must keep the focus—his own as well as those of his staff, the Congress, and the public at large—on the *goals* of reform and the *reasons* it is so important to achieve them.

7. *A key objective must be to persuade the public that the health system problems are so serious that they must be overcome, and the only way to do that is with legislation.*[51] Then, as noted, the public's support for reform must be actively courted throughout the campaign until the prize—legislation—is achieved.

Clinton started well. His September 22 speech got everyone excited. But neither he nor his team followed through—until spring 1994, when it was too late.[52] At the end of the Clinton episode, a majority of the public thought no action would be better than adopting any proposal then being considered. Among other things, Clinton did not discuss details of the plan, leaving people susceptible to the impact of negative stories promulgated by the opposition, including the Harry and Louise ads. People need a fairly clear idea of what their lives will be like under the reformed system. Provide enough details so people understand the plan well enough that they can support it.

Knowing they needed enough votes to pass the Congress and to withstand a potential filibuster in the Senate, the Clinton team sketched out "detailed strategies for political mobilization" in the spring and summer of 1993.[53] Assuming they contained adequate detail, the problem appears to be that they were not fully or consistently implemented. The result was that public support for the Health Security Act eroded, even though the public still favored its major provisions. A March 1994 survey by the *Wall Street Journal* and NBC News showed that although 45 percent opposed "the Clinton plan" and only 37 percent favored it, when respondents were asked about an unnamed plan with the main elements of the Health Security Act, 76 percent thought it had "either 'a great deal of appeal' or 'some appeal'." Moreover the survey showed that the other main proposals being considered by the Congress—including the Cooper plan, the single-payer plan, and others—had much less appeal.[54] So "the administration and its allies . . . had failed to get a coherent political message across" even though millions of citizens were potentially receptive.[55]

8. *Reformers need to pay attention to both the content of the program and methods for communicating to—and persuading—the public, the news media, and key decision makers.* The content follows from an analysis of health system problems, including an understanding of their *causes,* an explicit set of *goals,* and *policies* that would achieve the goals by overcoming the problems' causes. Then the effort to influence public opinion must be built on those three elements. If the connection between the problems and the proposal are clear, the plan will "make sense" to the public. As a result, it is more likely they can be energized to create the demand that reform *must* be enacted, which legislators will be much less able to ignore. The public are also more likely to be willing to try to influence legislators and, in that effort, will be able to interpret the reasons for reform more persuasively. That is, they will be much more effective in their role as influencers of legislative action. Further, if it becomes necessary to compromise in order to get a plan through the Congress, the logical relationships among the three elements will constrain what gets defined as reasonable compromise and therefore what gets adopted. (I will say more about this in Chapter 11.) This approach will also avoid what Hacker portrays as a critical

error of the Clinton episode. He writes that they were too wedded to their plan, which was so complicated and poorly explained that people could neither understand it well enough to urge their congressional representatives to support it nor resist opposition arguments.[56] Not only that, but the excruciating amount of detail in its 1,300 pages had two other negative effects. It had so many provisions that the number of groups opposed to one or more was quite large. In addition, the level of detail gave congressional leaders little opportunity to find compromises they could vote for.

9. Make use of varied *methods to communicate to the public and to decision makers.* Types of communication can include grassroots organizing leading to letter-writing, phone calls, and visits to legislators and their staffs; the use of databases of interested individuals, including contact information, that can inform and support the effort to contact legislators; preparation and distribution of materials for the media that lay out the problem analysis and the proposals that follow from it; the use of all available media, including the Internet; paid advertisements; extensive public relations efforts; and direct contact with legislators by both constituents and professional lobbyists. Most important of all is that the effort to mobilize the public must be determined, relentless, and persistent.

Conclusion

Although the problems are clear, the proposed reform elements are reasonable, and we understand a lot about what a successful political strategy would look like, particular provisions of any proposal may generate serious debate among reasonable people honestly committed to reform. As a result, success—actual passage of comprehensive reform—may require compromise. We will consider that possibility and what to do about it in the final chapter.

Chapter 11

Strategy and Compromise

THE CASE FOR HEALTH CARE reform rests on the contrast between a view about what the health care system should accomplish and what it actually produces. On the basis of that comparison, we can form several main goals: bringing the wonders of modern medicine to everyone, containing the cost of the most expensive medical care system in the world, reducing waste, and improving the quality and safety of care.

To achieve all of these goals requires transforming the system itself. A wise man once said that every system is exquisitely designed to produce exactly what it produces—even if it wasn't deliberately planned but simply evolved over time in response to unfolding forces. That being the case, we need to change the system itself in order to produce different outcomes. Moreover, only public policy can deal with system characteristics in a planful way.

A Political Strategy to Pass Health Care Reform

So what have we learned about a political strategy that can be effective enough to secure passage of health care reform? Here is an abbreviated outline of things to do.

1. Know what you want and why you want it. The underlying case for the particular proposal being put forth must be strong. We learned from Hacker and others that the actual proposal will not be enough by itself to secure passage, and if it is weak, it will be vulnerable to claims of inadequacy that will be hard to overcome. In earlier chapters, I not only described the problems to be addressed but also laid out my understanding of the factors that created them. As a result, the six elements put forth in Chapter 8 to be included in a plan to

change the outcomes are aimed at the root causes, and a clear connection can be made between those plan elements and the problems
for all to see.

2. Base the political strategy on knowledge that (1) the ultimate goal
   is to persuade members of Congress to vote for these reform ideas
   and (2) the primary task is to win a competition for their votes with
   forces arrayed against the proposal.

3. Then the strategy should include articulation of (1) a compelling brief
   that, indeed, the health system must be reformed, (2) a positive case
   that can influence decision makers to support the particular plan elements being presented, and (3) effective responses to the arguments
   that opponents are likely to offer. Keep opponents on the defensive.

4. The public can play a key role in the effort. A critical component of
   the strategy, therefore, must be to explain the plan well and to stimulate action by the public. A simple plan is easier to explain and to
   support with enthusiasm than a complicated one.

5. To execute the strategy will require money; organization; the active
   leadership of the president; and, as much as anything, fierce, unwav-
   ering determination and persistence.

These points follow from Chapters 9 and 10. The fact is, however, that
no matter how well advocates of reform are able to follow this outline, they
should not expect to get everything they want. Compromise is likely to be
needed. If the job is done right, decision makers will be willing to vote for
a good bill (because the public's demand for reform will be impossible to
resist), but they may not be willing to sign off on the original draft legislation
as presented, whether by the president or legislative leaders. Instead, they are
likely to want changes. So having arrived at the point at which passing a bill
appears to be a real possibility, the sixth point on this to-do list is this:

6. Be prepared to compromise—not on the fundamentals, but on
   implementation choices.

In previous chapters, I laid out what I believe is a cogent analysis of the
causes of the problems with the health care system and a set of reform elements that address both the problems and their sources and should therefore
be included in whatever bill passes. But even though I believe this plan offers
the best chance we have for solving those problems, I accept the possibility
put forth by former Senate Majority Leader Tom Daschle that it may be
better to make "worthy improvements" in the current system than to hold
out for perfection.[1] Part of the challenge for reform advocates is to differentiate between improvements that really are "worthy" and other changes that

leave untouched the dynamics that produced the problems in the first place. Compromise is justified only when it leads to real progress. In that spirit, therefore, in this final chapter, I discuss compromise.

Three Questions About Compromise

WITH WHOM?

The first question is, Compromise with whom? It should be apparent from Chapters 9 and 10 that not everyone will be interested in making the effort—even if publicly they say they are. Certainly, the Clinton episode suggests that Congressional Republicans—at least as represented by that period's incarnation—are not good candidates. And the experience in the early months of the Obama administration affirms that lesson. No House Republicans and only three Republican senators voted for the $787 billion stimulus plan for the economy despite President Obama's considerable efforts at bipartisanship. And no Republicans supported his first budget. Perhaps the partisan leadership in the stimulus debate represented by minority leader John Boehner, a key player in the Clinton debacle as well, will relax; and perhaps some moderate Republicans in the Senate, especially if they are up for reelection in states with greater diversity than a typical congressional district, will be willing to participate in a negotiation. Or maybe not.

Of course, a progressive Democratic president must also be concerned about some of the more conservative members of his own party. Yet presumably they would be willing at least to consider health care reform legislation proposed by a president of their own party. If the president is close enough to passing a bill that their help matters, the potential prize for being in the game rather than on the sidelines as the Republicans were in the stimulus debate is to contribute to—and get some of the credit for—solving a major societal problem by influencing the legislation that finally passes.

Morone reminds us that bipartisanship is a myth tantalizing those hoping for an era of good feeling in which all pitch in to do the country's business.[2] Even Social Security, the landmark program enacted in the 1930s under Franklin Roosevelt's leadership to ease the Great Depression's burden on families, passed with almost no Republican support. One of the few recent examples in which members of one party crossed the aisle to support major initiatives offered by the other was the Civil Rights legislation of the mid-1960s, which President Lyndon Johnson was able to get his former opposite number in the Senate, Everett Dirksen of Illinois, to support as a matter of moral principle.[3]

WHEN?

The second question about compromise is, When? Again, the Clinton health care reform attempt and the successful Obama stimulus package effort teach us a valuable lesson. In both cases, a president proposed legislation with elements designed to appeal to his opponents, and in both instances, he was rebuffed by people who did not want even to participate in a negotiation. Some may have taken that position out of a philosophical commitment to limited government even in difficult circumstances, but others appear to have been motivated primarily by the goal of partisan political gain. Whatever the reason, their objective was the same: neither Republican faction wanted to influence the legislation; both wanted to kill it.

The lesson is, don't weaken the bill in the hope of gaining across-the-aisle support. If you are willing to change some provisions—for example, to include competition among private insurers as the organizing principle—wait until you get a commitment from some on the other side to vote for a revised proposal. If you need their votes and they are willing to support a version of your bill, signal that you are open to revising it—assuming the resulting compromise allows you to make substantial progress toward achieving your goals if not actually reaching them. If you are going to lose anyway, keep the proposal intact and take it to the people. If it does not pass this time, maybe it will next. Morone cites James Madison in the *Federalist Papers* as saying that to defeat opposing interests, one should make his own case stronger. "In that way, our partisan debates are no shame. The clash and bluster may not sound pretty, but they are how we choose between great principles."[4]

ABOUT WHAT?

The third consideration concerns the substance of the bill itself. Here, the question is whether the price of compromise is too high. If we compromise in order actually to pass a bill, will that bill accomplish most of our goals? Does it allow substantial progress toward other goals without creating the seeds of its own destruction in a few years when the reform's costs escalate? In the effort to pass a bill, it will be important to keep one's eye on the ball. Protect what is essential, and reject proposals that will undermine the essence of the key design elements. At the same time, be open to negotiation on matters that are important to decision makers who, though reluctant, are nonetheless willing to support change and, by facilitating passage, will ensure real progress toward the ultimate goals.

In the pages that follow, I consider the six reform elements from Chapter 8 and the potential for compromise in each in the interest of legislative success. And then I examine other issues and consider suggestions for dealing with them, especially in terms of the trade-off between achieving the fundamental goals I laid out earlier and passing legislation that will lead to substantial progress in that regard.

Compromise and the Six Key Elements of Reform

REFORM ELEMENT 1: EVERYONE MUST HAVE FINANCIAL ACCESS TO THE SERVICES THEY NEED

As written, the provision assumes compulsory coverage in a single national insurance system. That insurance would cover virtually any potentially beneficial medical service and be administered by the federal government. Private professionals and organizations would provide the care; the government's Health Insurance Fund (HIF) would provide the funds to pay for it.

The principal reasons for Design Element 1 are that health is fundamental to so much of life; that medical care can do so much good for people and therefore for the society and economy as well; and that large and growing numbers of people lack financial access to it. For many Americans, these are reason enough to support this design. But another powerful one is the fact that it is an essential condition for achieving other systemic goals, including containing expenditure rates and encouraging investments to improve quality.

Many supporters of reform—including President Barack Obama—believe that a new system should build on the current one under which most people have private insurance obtained through their employment.[5] Staying with the devil they know would reduce the well-recognized fear of many citizens (that is, voters) that they will be forced to give up coverage they depend on in favor of a new, untested plan in which they lack confidence. They worry about this possibility even though they have many complaints about the present employment-based system: growing numbers of businesses are giving up health insurance altogether or raising premiums to the point they are unaffordable by workers; individuals are losing coverage when they change jobs; some services unexpectedly turn out not to be covered by their current plan; out-of-pocket costs are often so high that needed care is unaffordable, even for the insured; and having to appeal to insurance-company clerks for approval to get some services paid for is exasperating for doctors and patients alike and undermines quality of care.

In addition, many have an ideological commitment to the private sector and believe as a matter of faith that competing insurers will produce a more efficient, less expensive system than one operated by the central government. These ideas have enough appeal, even though I demonstrated in Chapter 7 that they do not survive careful analysis, that they represent opportunities for opponents of reform. They could become part of a successful antireform coalition if the opposition's expected public relations campaign raises enough doubt about the proposal to resonate with uncommitted legislators.

So the questions are, Is there room for a competitive private insurance sector? Can the system be voluntary? Is there a role for employers? Does the benefit package need to be comprehensive? If we can accomplish most of our goals with one or more of these provisions, then certainly we should be open to considering them.

Is There Room for Competition Among Private Insurers?   In fact, the ideas in Chapter 8 *do* include competition among private insurers, but they would compete not by offering different benefits or lower prices for their coverage, but on the providers who were included, the quality of care provided, and the responsiveness of their customer service.

Including private insurers would avoid the need to create a large federal organization to deal directly with providers. Insurers and health plans have experience doing that and could continue to do so. They have the ability to build on that experience to create the kinds of integrated health care delivery systems that can ensure that service improves, can increase coordination of care and teamwork among clinicians, and can deliver care more efficiently so that expenditures can be controlled without sacrificing quality. We can assume that participating insurers and health plans would evolve toward those kinds of organizations because that would be the most rational way to increase net income given the conditions they would then be facing. These conditions include the fact that everyone would have coverage, the benefit package would be comprehensive and the same for everyone, insurers would be prohibited from rejecting any applicant for coverage, and their revenues would be determined by the number and characteristics of the people who enrolled with them. To increase their net income under these circumstances, insurers and health plans would need to develop effective ways to enroll large numbers of subscribers and provide needed care at lower cost. For example, they might invest in information technology, facilitate the creation of clinical teams, and avoid duplicate or unnecessary services.

Including private insurers and health plans would also increase the possibility that people who wanted to do so could retain their current plans. Currently, insurers and health plans compete to offer coverage through employers, especially large ones. Their competition tends to be at the level of the employer and centers on the question of which insurer it should offer to its employees? Most employers that do offer coverage offer plans from only a single insurer.

When *workers* are given a choice, however, insurers tend to compete for individual customers by offering different amounts of services, different providers, and, especially, different prices. The theory is that competing insurers will try to win business by offering better value—usually defined as more services, more providers, or both—for less money.

Nonetheless, the reality for many Americans with insurance is that their costs rise each year, and their coverage erodes. Moreover, we also know that investor-owned insurers tend to focus primarily on profits and that they have few tools with which to ensure profits high enough to satisfy shareholders or even to differentiate themselves from one another. The most reliable methods at their disposal tend to undermine the value of insurance. The surest one is to discourage people who are likely to need services from buying the company's policies. A second-best method is to establish rules and administrative procedures that allow them to avoid paying for services (sometimes after they were already provided). Neither of these tactics results in better value for subscribers.

Despite this history, many argue that the key to success is a competitive system in which insurers and health plans compete for subscribers. Because everyone will be eligible for insurance, the potential market will be much larger than at present, and the opportunities for insurers will be huge—even if they made a smaller profit on the average subscriber. But including them in the new program will not be possible *unless* they are willing to follow a different set of rules.

The most important of those rules are that (1) an insurer may not reject anyone who applies, including those with prior conditions; (2) it cannot reject anyone who wants to renew for the coming year; (3) it must charge the same amount to all of an employer's workers; and (4) the policy must meet publicly set standards for services covered and cost-sharing.

With these rules, it may be possible to include arrangements that substantially increase the numbers of Americans with coverage, but without getting to 100 percent. Many people with limited means would try to get by without it, thus saving money for necessities instead of spending it on coverage they think they may not need. Therefore, an individual mandate requiring everyone to have insurance that meets the coverage standards would also be needed because a strictly voluntary plan will not achieve the stated goals of universal coverage, comprehensive benefits, cost containment, or improved quality.[6]

To make an individual mandate work will require public subsidies for those who will not be able to afford a private policy and an administrative structure to ensure that affordable policies are available to those who cannot participate in the wider competitive market. A model is available in the recent Massachusetts experience. Its Health Insurance Connector Authority performs the many functions needed to connect individuals with affordable coverage that meets "minimum creditable coverage (MCC) standards"[7] and to make that state's universal coverage program work.[8] This is not a perfect system, but it has dramatically reduced the numbers of uninsured in the state to an estimated 2.6 percent in summer 2008.[9]

The Connector offers plans with three tiers of coverage (gold, silver, and bronze). "Most policies cover the same comprehensive set of benefits, but cost sharing can differ. . . . Policies offered by competing insurers within each tier are supposed to be 'actuarially equivalent,'" but it turns out that coverage can vary considerably.[10] Pollitz and colleagues mapped simulated claims scenarios against ten supposedly equivalent Massachusetts policies. They found that plans could result in very different amounts of out-of-pocket expenses even if they were actuarially equivalent, covered essentially the same benefits, and were in the same tier. For example, patients in the bronze tier who developed breast cancer and used the recommended services could incur out-of-pocket expenditures ranging from \$7,641 to \$12,907. Patients with gold- or silver-tier plans would pay higher premiums, but have lower out-of-pocket outlays if they developed one of the conditions studied. And special plans for healthy young adults can result in still higher cost-sharing amounts for patients who were unlucky enough to come down with one of these conditions. The choice of plan is a gamble. How does a healthy person know what services will be needed in the coming year?

So choice is a big issue for Massachusetts residents using the Connector. The challenge is compounded by the fact that "currently it can be difficult to obtain information about coverage ahead of time," and by the "sheer number of ways in which health insurance policies can vary,"[11] which are not always easy to discern. Of course, that is a problem that is surmountable by a requirement that information about the ways in which policies differ be presented in a standardized form that facilitates comparisons in publications distributed to all participants in that market.

Some people may choose policies with lower premiums and higher out-of-pocket expenditures because they have limited income, are healthy, and do not expect to need much care. But if they happen to get sick or are in an accident, people who need subsidies to help pay for the premiums will also have trouble paying high cost-sharing amounts. To cope, they may decide to forego beneficial services in order to "save" money. The fact that, later, they may need to spend even more if the illness does not get better on its own is an example of a "penny-wise, pound-foolish decision." This problem occurs even with subsidies to help people to afford the premium. For the case against these kinds of mandates, see Emanuel.[12]

Regulations are needed to ensure both fairness and the achievement of the program's objectives. If insurers can reject applicants with prior conditions or can refuse to renew policies for high users of services, not only will we fail to achieve universal coverage, but those who are left out will be the most vulnerable, most expensive to care for among us. Similarly, if insurers are permitted to charge different premiums to different groups, then the person who buys that reduced coverage must hope he does not develop cancer or have an accident. And unless standards for covered services are set by a public body, insurers will be able to keep their charges competitive by either reducing covered services or imposing barriers to utilization instead of doing the hard work of investing in quality, efficiency, and productivity improvements.

It may be possible to reduce the administrative burden somewhat if the public sector offers coverage directly (that is, with the so-called "public option"). Hacker describes this as "the creation of a new public plan modeled after Medicare that would be available to Americans younger than 65 who lack employment-based coverage."[13] He offers three main reasons for this proposal. First, public insurance has done a better job of "reining in costs while providing inclusive, stable coverage with broad choice of providers."[14] Second, he argues that such a public plan would improve the quality and effectiveness of care by experimenting with delivery system reforms. Private plans would then piggyback on public plan investments by adopting the successful ones. He considers this a better option than regulation though, as we have seen, it would be foolish to abandon regulation, too, which is a necessary adjunct to a competitive, largely private insurance system. And finally the public plan "will create an important benchmark for inclusive quality coverage that private plans will need to compete [with] to match."[15] This proposal is attracting growing support, as the book goes to press, but it has also drawn critics as well.[16]

The bottom line is that competition among insurers—with or without a public option—can be consistent with the goals of reform. But we saw in Chapters 6 and 7 that insurers have only three ways to differentiate themselves from their competition: (1) availability—trying to enroll healthy people and to avoid those likely to need much care; (2) quality—what they cover and the terms of coverage, including their arrangements with providers; and (3) price. To keep prices low enough to be affordable, therefore, they can only make adjustments in availability and quality. But, except for changing their arrangements with providers to align incentives with the goals of reform—a difficult strategy but one that could pay dividends for all—limiting availability and quality would undermine the goals of reform. So for competition to work, regulation will be needed—perhaps through the Insurance Exchange—to avoid the temptation to reduce availability and quality. A strong public-sector plan competing with private insurers, as recommended by Hacker, could help as well.

Could the New System Be Voluntary?   A voluntary system in which individuals were encouraged but not required to purchase their own insurance would need subsidies from the public sector for those with modest incomes. Even so, however, it is likely that many struggling to make ends meet would forgo the subsidies and take the chance that they would not need care. One inescapable result would be perpetuation of the United States as the only developed country in the world with uninsured citizens. Subsidies and a program like that operating in Massachusetts (which includes an individual mandate) and the one proposed by presidential candidate Barack Obama would reduce the numbers of Americans without insurance, but would not *eliminate* uninsurance. A voluntary plan would also make it harder to contain costs or improve clinical outcomes since many would continue to avoid care early in an episode and be forced to go to hospital emergency departments when services were unavoidable. To sum up, a voluntary plan would require subsidies and regulation and would be limited to reducing the number of uninsured, not providing universal coverage.

Could the New System Continue to Be Based on Employment?   In the present system, most Americans with health insurance receive it through their employment, an approach with a number of well-recognized weaknesses that have been amply discussed in earlier chapters and elsewhere.[17] Nonetheless, a number of people, including President Obama, would build on it, in part because people who are satisfied with their current insurance would not be required to give it up and might therefore be willing to support reform.

Further, since it is the system people know, even those who decided not to retain their present coverage might find it less scary than a new federally operated program. If employers played the same role as they do now, however, we would carry forward the same disadvantages found in the present system: because an individual's coverage would be tied to his employer, family members might not be covered, and workers who changed jobs would need new coverage. Also, we should wonder where the constituency for this arrangement would come from since the trend is that employers are cutting back on their coverage. Nonetheless, if it would buy the needed congressional votes, it is worth asking if we could make progress toward achieving the goals of reform with an employment-based approach.

We already saw that most employers offering coverage make available only a single plan to their employees, and many offer no coverage at all. Therefore, for the new system to be based on employment would require inducing employers not only to offer coverage but to offer their employees more than one plan. That is likely to be a hard sell. Combining this employer role with competition at the individual level would be an even harder sell. A strategy based on increasing the numbers that offer multiple plans would increase employer costs, not lower them. Many would need to expand their Human Resources departments to be able to negotiate and manage insurance contracts with multiple insurers.

Nonetheless, Enthoven would combine employment-based insurance with a stimulus to promote competition among insurers. His plan is based explicitly on the recognition that "organized systems of medical care" are needed in order to achieve the additional goals of cost containment and quality enhancement. In Enthoven's plan, insurers would set premium rates (which would not vary by subscriber health status) and employers would contribute a fixed-dollar amount toward the premium. As a result, subscribers who chose efficient plans would save money (since their share of the premium is the difference between the premium and the invariant employer contribution).[18] Health plans would need to make their money by providing better value because traditional avenues to lower premiums—discouraging high-risk applicants from enrolling or reducing benefits—would be closed to them. As a result, Enthoven believes they might turn themselves into "organized systems of medical care" and invest in quality- and efficiency-enhancing tactics and technology to attract those employees.[19]

Following this route carries risks as well. The expectation is that insurers, faced with the incentives implied by these factors, will turn themselves into managed care organizations with the capacity and willingness to make quality-enhancing investments and to institute policies that build a team-oriented, coordinated approach to managing care. However, the risk is that, instead of doing those things, they will find new ways to discourage high-risk people from applying and to deny payments for services rendered—in other words, tactics that many insurers use in the present system. Only conscientious, well-funded, and adequately staffed regulation can protect the public against that risk. If it were in place, the numbers of Americans with insurance would increase, though not to 100 percent, and insurance subscribers would be protected from the dysfunctional tactics many insurers use now.

Even if the assumptions proved to be true, these provisions would leave out people who either do not work or whose employers do not offer coverage. The employers not offering coverage could be required to contribute to a fund that can be used to pay part of the cost of their insurance. For them, establishment of an Insurance Exchange that can aggregate such people into large risk groups and then make available at large-group rates policies that meet the standards required for employment-based coverage could substantially expand the numbers with insurance. The Massachusetts Health Connector is an example. Because many people who would benefit from this kind of arrangement, though employed, will have relatively low-wage jobs, it will be necessary to subsidize the fund to some degree with public money so that all who need to do so can participate. Qualified eligibles who do not work could continue to be covered by Medicare if they are elderly or disabled or by Medicaid if they are poor.

The possibility of including a continuing role for employers raises two additional questions. First, would employers want that role knowing the alternative is a publicly funded program of health insurance for all Americans? It would be more expensive for both the company and the country than a tax-funded public-sector program. Participating firms would need Human Resources staff to design or select insurance plans, negotiate with insurers, and monitor the resulting program. Yet they would still be unable to control their spending without cutting benefits or raising employees' share of the costs—which would not endear them to their employees who would know about the public-sector alternative. And for those companies with international competitors, it would leave them at a disadvantage that a public program would make avoidable.

Assuming some companies would choose to retain their own health insurance programs, the second question is, What would be the benefits of doing so? The most important are political. One is that employers, especially those not currently offering coverage, would not face a mandated premium charge, which would surely cause them to mobilize against the plan, as the NFIB did during the Clinton episode. The other is that by making it easier for individuals to retain their present coverage if they want to do so, proponents would avoid creating additional opposition among the general population as well.

The main downside of including employers in a voluntary plan as now—that is, without something like Enthoven's most recent ideas—is that it makes it harder to build a single national system, which we have seen is necessary in order to contain spending without damaging quality and service. It would also make more difficult the creation of integrated delivery organizations, which are necessary to develop the coordination and teamwork that today's illnesses and medical specialization require and to invest in the efficiencies that will allow us to contain medical care spending.

In summary, *with adequate regulation,* it could be possible to build on the present system and still accomplish some of the key goals of reform, especially expansion of the number of Americans with coverage. But since the only potential benefit of an employment-based plan is political, it should be used only if it helps ensure passage of the best bill we can get. And only if that bill is good enough to overcome the fact that it will be more expensive than the public system outlined, will leave many people uninsured, and will do nothing to promote *throughout the entire system* either efficiency or quality in the delivery of services. Ironically, the restrictions and regulation that would be needed might also reduce the numbers of insurers willing to participate.

Must the Benefit Package Be Comprehensive?   People who are particularly concerned about the cost of the reformed health care system might be tempted to recommend a more restricted benefit package. The limitations could take several forms: one would be to cap the annual covered amount of a particular kind of service. An example would be to limit covered physician visits to twenty-four, an average of two a month, or the number of covered inpatient hospital days to twenty-one. Another would be to limit the dollar value of particular services or of all services in the aggregate—say, $50,000 for inpatient hospital care or a total of $100,000 worth of all covered care over the course of a year. Among the problems with either of those approaches is that they are arbitrary and would fall most heavily on people who were sick and really needed services.[20]

For most people, these restrictions would probably be irrelevant because most people do not use that amount of care in a year. But for some, the amounts would be too little—not because these people are wasteful, but simply because of the nature of their medical problems. Moreover, not only will these kinds of limitations undermine the health-related goals of reform, they are unlikely to accomplish their supposed purpose of limiting health care expenditures. To understand why, consider this: What should a doctor or hospital do when a patient runs out of benefits during a hospitalization but still needs care? What should a hospital do with a patient brought to its emergency department by EMTs after falling on an icy street and being knocked unconscious? If that person has already used up his annual hospital benefits, there are at least three possible problems. One is that, being unconscious, he is unable to tell anyone that he has no more hospital benefits for the year. Another is that if he gets better, he may face a huge hospital bill. And third, if the hospital is able to determine, before beginning treatment, that his benefits for the year are gone, what is its obligation regarding his treatment?

A third way to limit benefits would be to increase the cost-sharing amounts. In fact, the several levels of coverage found in bills before the 2009 Congress, as well as in the Massachusetts health care reform plan, differ in the out-of-pocket costs they would require. If passed, the high cost-sharing amounts in the least expensive plans would certainly reduce the extent to which people used services, but as we saw in Chapter 6, some of the services they would do without would make them healthier and more productive. In other words, these provisions would reduce the number of *un*insured but increase the number of *under*insured and thus undermine one of the primary purposes of reform. So attempts to reduce the benefit package should be resisted.

REFORM ELEMENT 2: INDIVIDUALS AND EMPLOYERS
MUST PAY INTO A FEDERAL FUND

I proposed creating a dedicated federal Health Insurance Fund (HIF) to accept payments from individuals and employers. The money in that fund would then be used to pay insurers and health plans for the people they enroll.

Once the total amount required for the year is determined, rates that would generate enough revenue to populate the fund would be based on individual or family income so that those with little disposable income contribute to the fund amounts they can afford. By eliminating experience-based rates, those with preexisting conditions who are more likely to need services will not be charged higher rates that would put coverage beyond their means. Of course, that means that people with more income will need to pay more than those with less as they do now in our progressive income tax system. Because all will be covered, however, the amounts they pay into the HIF are likely to be less than their current insurance premiums. Moreover, using the tax collection system, which already has experience doing this, will be an efficient means for collecting the needed money.

Initially, the fund should have an amount adequate for health insurers and health plans to pay providers in the aggregate the amounts they earned in the last year prior to adoption of the new legislation or perhaps a modest additional percentage. In that way, providers would not be harmed, and another basis for their potential political opposition (that they would earn less) would be eliminated. We would also avoid erecting an unnecessary barrier to patients receiving the care they need.

HIF managers would determine the amount of future increases on the basis of what they estimate will be needed to continue to provide adequate levels of service. With a single fund from which all health care expenditures are drawn, as well as the other provisions already outlined, it would be possible not only to contain total spending but to stimulate the creation of the integrated delivery systems that so many believe are needed to modernize the delivery of services.

Do We Need to Pay into a Federal Fund?   Some people will object to paying anything that can be called a tax—even if it is earmarked for health insurance and replaces the higher premiums they now pay for their own coverage as well as the portion of their taxes that currently pays for Medicare and Medicaid. This position is not economically rational, and it should be possible to overcome it with a focused public relations campaign. It would be the height of folly to let this argument defeat health care reform that would benefit the entire country.

In addition, some groups will object to creating such a federal health insurance fund and the organization needed to manage it. Some of them will be ideologically opposed to a large organization at the national level. Others, especially insurers and providers, will object to limiting the money in the health care system at the same time that they are obligated not only to accept all comers but also to pay for or provide all the services included in the standard benefit package.

Is it possible to accomplish the essential goals without such a federal insurance fund? If the primary concern is about creating an entirely new organization, we can simply adapt and expand an existing federal organization that has already proven itself. The two obvious candidates are Medicare, which efficiently collects and pays out money for services used by elderly and disabled beneficiaries, and the Federal Employees Health Benefits Program (FEHBP), the organization that arranges for health insurance for federal employees, including members of Congress, just as we could use the IRS to collect health insurance premiums that the HIF would spend.

If instead the main issue is a federal tax earmarked for health insurance, then how would money get into the system? And what funds would be used to pay insurers and health plans? Retaining the employment-based system, as noted in the previous section, is an option. It currently provides coverage for about 60 percent of the non-institutionalized population, certainly a substantial figure. Moreover, retaining Medicare, Medicaid, and other current programs reduces the residual group that needs to be accounted for. Nonetheless, many millions of Americans are not connected to the workforce and do not qualify for public programs. For them, something like the Insurance Exchange, a new federal organization modeled on the Massachusetts Health Connector Authority, would need to be created. And again, we would be settling for reducing the numbers of uninsured instead of guaranteeing coverage for everyone.

We could expand the number of Americans with insurance by relying on individual employers, private insurers, and a new federal Insurance Exchange. Requiring insurers to use community rating or at least to charge the same rate for all of an employer's workers and their families who obtain coverage, as Enthoven suggests,[21] would avoid discrimination against those with pre-existing conditions. But, as noted earlier, premiums are likely to be higher than if we had a single national or even several regional risk groups, and it is likely that some would find the insurance too expensive to buy. Additional rules, like those described in the previous section, would also need to be in place for employment-based coverage to work without making things worse. And for those without employment-based coverage, the exchange would also need to require community rating by insurers offering policies. Reformers would need to insist on these conditions as part of the price for building on the employment-based private insurance system.

The bottom line is that a single federal fund provides advantages that alternatives cannot. But if we need to settle for less than full achievement of the goals established at the outset, the combination of an employment-based system and a federal Insurance Exchange could allow us to make considerable progress.

REFORM ELEMENT 3: PAYMENTS *INTO* THE FUND MUST
BE INDEPENDENT OF HEALTH STATUS

A key goal of reform is that everyone should have access to comprehensive health insurance. However it is provided, it must be paid for. The critical criterion for assessing a payment method is that it must not deter anyone from obtaining insurance. With that goal in mind, this reform element is essential to avoid a situation in which people who are expected to use more services are charged higher premiums, which are likely to cause many of them to reject the offered insurance.

The alternative is experience rating, a method insurers use to gain preferred customers and avoid others. They charge lower premiums for groups that are young and healthy in order to obtain their business. In due course, insurers earn higher profits because those groups use fewer services, and the insurers need to pay out less to providers. Some justify that approach as "fair" on the grounds that people should pay just for the care they use; those who are healthy and use few services should not be asked to pay more for their coverage because other people use more services. But, of course, that negates the insurance principle, which says that everyone at risk contributes to a pool of funds that can be used to pay for services needed by anyone in the pool. Even if they are healthy and do not expect to use many services, people are willing to make those payments so that—if they did become seriously ill or were in a serious accident—they would not need to worry about the cost of the services they would need or be forced to go without them.

Is There Another Basis for Setting the Payments That Won't Keep People from Obtaining Insurance?   One way or another, payments come from individuals and employers—as premiums or as taxes. The critical factor is to separate the amount of the payment by or for individuals from their health status and thus to avoid the situation in which payment is an obstacle to obtaining insurance, especially for those at higher risk for needing services. The best way to do that is for payments also to be independent of the choice of insurance policy.

Financing through the progressive income tax system is fair in three ways. First, the amounts people pay will be based on their ability to pay. If people have a bad year financially, their health insurance will not be jeopardized. Second, low-income people, who tend to need more services than well-to-do Americans, will more than likely receive medical services worth more than their tax payments. And so will well-to-do people who develop a serious illness. Finally, what anyone pays into the fund will have nothing to do either with his or her health status or with the care to which he or she is entitled.

Another approach, proposed by Emanuel and Fuchs, is to use a value-added tax (VAT) of about 10 percent on goods and services purchased and to dedicate the proceeds only to the health insurance program.[22] Some will consider this to be a regressive tax because people with limited income will be spending a larger proportion of it on the VAT than more well-to-do people even though most of what they purchase are necessities. Those with larger incomes, who can afford nonessential items as well, may spend more on the VAT in dollars, but it will be less of a strain on them than on their less-wealthy neighbors. Emanuel and Fuchs argue that to assess the VAT's true fairness, however, one must take into account, in addition to the tax itself, the benefits it funds and the costs and benefits of alternatives, including the cost of doing nothing at all. They point out that the VAT would improve on the present situation in which the rich get a substantially larger tax break than the middle class and others from the pretax treatment of contributions for health care coverage. Because under their plan people will pay the VAT in accordance with their consumption, lower-income people, who will buy less, will tend to receive more in health benefits than they would pay in the VAT.[23]

Both the progressive income–related tax and VAT approaches would feed a fund dedicated to paying for health insurance for all Americans. Regardless of the payment method, people would choose a health plan from among those that meet the conditions of guaranteed enrollment and renewal, a common comprehensive benefit package, and risk-adjusted payment on behalf of subscribers. Emanuel and Fuchs would provide everyone with a voucher that would entitle them to coverage. People then can use that voucher to select one of the competing health plans.

Other approaches, such as continuing the employment-based system, would, even with modifications, make payments not to a common fund, but to individual insurers that contract to provide coverage to that particular group of workers. In the present system, if two firms had the same number of employees and a similar wage distribution, the one with higher numbers of older workers would tend to face higher premiums than the one with younger workers. So even if the premium is the same for all workers in a single business, as Enthoven recommends, the share of the premium for those who work in the first company would be higher than for those working in the second one. As a result, it is likely that a larger number of workers in the first firm will find insurance to be beyond their means. If the reform includes an individual mandate to buy coverage and creates an Insurance Exchange, those workers will need to obtain their coverage from the exchange.

The goal is to keep the cost of insurance to the individual at affordable levels, especially for people with limited incomes and those at risk of being high users of services. The best way to do that is to separate the two functions of payment and eligibility for coverage. A progressive income tax and VAT both would do that. Retaining employer-based coverage and instituting an individual mandate and Insurance Exchange would not. Both would help to expand the numbers with coverage, but would not overcome the other problems that we are targeting. So again, if we need to settle for less than attacking the causes of the full list of problems, this can be a topic for negotiation, as well.

REFORM ELEMENT 4: PAYMENTS *FROM* THE FEDERAL FUND SHOULD BE RISK-BASED

Insurers and health plans would receive higher payments for people with preexisting conditions or other risk factors that predict they would use more services than those without them. It would then be up to the insurers and health plans to find ways to compensate providers using the resulting pool of funds at their disposal.

If there is no single Health Insurance Fund, as proposed, then it is hard to see how it would be possible to arrange for private insurers to receive risk-adjusted payments for all their subscribers at the same time that other goals are met. One issue would be, What body would do the risk-adjusting? And who would set the rates based on it? Insurers could be paid identical (community) rates for all of an employer's workers, as Enthoven recommends,[24] and if those rates were based on expected utilization in that group, the total should produce a fund sufficient to pay providers for the group's expected utilization. Even though some would be high users and others low users of services, all individuals would be charged the same amount. Again, however, legislation and regulation would be needed to make it work.

There are two potential problems, however. One is that individual employers generally have groups that are too small to produce stable aggregate utilization patterns from year to year. Therefore some insurers will do very well in some years and poorly in others, not as a result of their own efforts but because of the luck of the draw (that is, which ones have cancer patients or accident victims in a particular year). The other problem is that, whatever the premium is, the individual subscriber pays part of it (instead of contributing a share of the total risk pool based on his or her ability to pay), and it is likely that the employee's share will be higher than some will be able to afford. If subject to an individual mandate requiring everyone to have insurance, those people will need to use the Insurance Exchange to obtain their coverage, and the exchange could pay insurers on a risk-adjusted basis even if employers do not. But the exchange will probably need to pay higher rates than most employment-based groups, which are likely to be healthier than those needing coverage through the exchange. Also, even with lower premiums, insurers are likely to prefer the employment-based group over the exchange-covered group. The reason is that the latter's partially subsidized rates, even if risk-adjusted, are likely to be under pressure because the people covered by the exchange will tend to need more services. Thus, success for for-profit insurers dealing with the exchange is likely to be chancier.

Under these conditions, some insurers may find it advantageous to use their risk-adjusted capitation payments to create managed care arrangements on the Kaiser Permanente model. Then, although they would be at risk, they would have the tools to improve care, which indemnity insurers do not. While there are many benefits for insurers to be paid risk-adjusted rates, it is probably not a feasible option without a national health insurance fund. As a second-best substitute, community rating for large firms and for aggregates of small firms would reduce the extent to which people at higher risk of needing care will be charged higher premiums.

REFORM ELEMENT 5: ALL HEALTH CARE PLANS MUST ENROLL ALL APPLICANTS

This is a fundamental requirement of any reform. Without it, insurers and health plans would be able to continue to discriminate against those likely to be high users of services. They might find new ways to do it, but unless they are required to enroll all comers, their prior history suggests that they would discriminate.

Therefore, no matter what the reform, choice of coverage must reside with the individual, and no health plan or insurer can be allowed to reject any applicant or anyone wanting to renew for another year.

To ensure that this provision is followed will require regulation. It is naïve to expect that insurers and health plans would enroll all applicants if no one were watching.

REFORM ELEMENT 6: PATIENT COST-SHARING, IF ANY, MUST BE LIMITED

This is another essential. The evidence is incontrovertible that even fully insured people reduce their utilization when they face out-of-pocket cost-sharing (see Chapter 6). Some think that is okay because they assume that the services being foregone are unnecessary. The fact is, however, that too often patients cannot tell the difference between a service that will benefit them and one that is unnecessary. What they *can* tell, on the other hand, is that if they use it, they will need to make an out-of-pocket payment. While patient cost-sharing reduces utilization and the spending associated with it, it is a barrier to the use of *beneficial* services and therefore should be used sparingly, if at all. Besides, even though it exists in most private health insurance plans now, the evidence shows it is not effective at containing aggregate expenditures. Many other developed countries with various forms of national health insurance spend much less on health care than the United States without resorting to cost-sharing. The bottom line is that if one of our goals is to ensure that everyone has financial access to beneficial health care, it is counterproductive to use cost-sharing, especially since it does not even keep spending under control.

Compromise About Other Issues and Provisions

This is not an exhaustive list, but here are other provisions, some of which may lend themselves to negotiation in order to secure passage of comprehensive health care reform.

IMPLEMENTATION SCHEDULE

Because everyone will have comprehensive coverage if the design elements I propose are included in a reform plan, existing government programs such as Medicare, Medicaid, SCHIP, and even the Veterans Health Administration (VA) will become unnecessary. Phasing out Medicaid, even if it takes time, would be a particular benefit because although it has produced much good for many people over the years, its eligibles increasingly are relegated to hospital ERs and outpatient departments (OPDs), as fewer private physicians are willing to put up with the low fees and administrative burdens associated with care for Medicaid patients. This is an old story that has become progressively worse. On the other hand, it is not necessary to end these programs on the day that the new one begins, and some individuals may prefer to keep the plan they know until they are convinced the new one works. The old programs, therefore, could be phased out over a period of years—for example, by allowing those presently covered by them to continue, but adding no new eligibles. Emanuel estimates that following such a schedule would take no more than fifteen years to eliminate the existing programs.[25] In the case of the VA, given its special role and expertise regarding veterans and their particular needs, it could—over time—transform itself into a health plan, which veterans—and perhaps others with chronic conditions—would find attractive.

PROVIDER PAYMENTS

My proposal contemplates a federal Health Insurance Fund, which would make payments to health insurers and health plans when individuals choose them. Those payments would be risk-adjusted, since the insurers and plans would be required to enroll all applicants and without risk-adjustment, those with disproportionate numbers of high-risk subscribers would be at a disadvantage not of their own doing. That raises the question of payments from the insurers and health plans to the actual providers of service. I have been silent on that question. The problem is that, although a health plan that receives capitation payments and must pay for all services needed by its subscribers would benefit from being able to improve the quality and efficiency of care, few plans that can do those things currently exist. While the proposal might stimulate the formation of more such arrangements—which would resemble prepaid group practices of the original Kaiser Permanente model or what Enthoven calls "organized medical systems"[26]—it would be politically unwise to mandate them. Few currently exist, they would take time to develop and become operational, and requiring them would only stimulate unnecessary opposition to the program from doctors and others. If they evolved because health care leaders saw that they made sense, they would be a lot stronger and more likely to survive. Risk-adjusted payment would provide insurers with some protection against adverse selection and would give them time to develop into prepaid group practices or create other arrangements that align incentives with the goals of reform.

MAKING PAYMENTS TO INSURERS AND HEALTH PLANS

Payments from the Health Insurance Fund to health insurers and health plans could be made either directly by the federal government or by intermediaries, as in Medicare. If intermediaries were used, many of them would likely be health insurers, thus giving some of them another opportunity to make money and, in the process, lessening the sting of the reduced profits they would probably earn under the reformed system. To the extent using intermediaries had that effect, it might also reduce insurers' opposition to the legislation incorporating the reforms. Note, however, that insurers should not act as intermediaries in regions where they also offer insurance under the reform plan.

THE STANDARD BENEFIT PACKAGE

The proposal calls for comprehensive coverage that allows everyone to have financial access to the services they will need. The implication is that the benefit package is inclusive of virtually all useful services. Nonetheless, details will need to be worked out, especially regarding new services that have not yet been proven by research that compares them to existing services. (Most FDA studies compare new drugs to placebo to determine if they are safe and effective. They tend not to assess how the new drugs compare to existing treatments in terms of either effectiveness or cost.)

A reasonable place to start, as many—including President Obama—have suggested, is with the content of the Federal Employees Health Benefits Program (FEHBP).[27] How can senators and representatives reasonably deny other citizens the benefits that they enjoy, which include office and home visits, hospitalization, preventive screening tests, prescription drugs, some dental care, inpatient and outpatient mental health care, and physical and occupational therapy? Other issues concern how to ensure that cost-effective services are encouraged; how to add new services to the list; and how to bring data about the appropriateness, comparative effectiveness, and cost of particular services to the attention of physicians. All of these and other matters would take on new urgency in a national system in which everyone is covered and available funds are constrained.

One suggestion is to create a Federal Health Board modeled on the Federal Reserve Board, as Senator Tom Daschle has proposed.[28] Emanuel's National Health Board is similar.[29] Both would be composed of members appointed by the president and by the Senate who would serve long terms to ensure their independence. The board would define and adjust the standard benefit package; conduct research to determine risk adjustments needed for premiums paid to insurers and health plans; determine regional differences in payments based on cost of living; sponsor research on quality, outcomes, and performance of the health care system and needed for management purposes (following the adage that "you cannot manage what you do not measure"); and oversee twelve Regional Health Boards, whose principal responsibilities would relate to coverage and care issues in specific regions.[30]

RATES TO BE PAID BY SMALL BUSINESSES

Because many small businesses do not provide insurance to their employees, any payment they make for health insurance would constitute a new expenditure for them. As a result, they are likely to resist supporting the proposed reforms. (Indeed, their lobbying group, the National Federation of Independent Business [NFIB], was one of the most determined opponents of President Clinton's reform plan.) Here there is room for engagement and negotiation, however. While the portion of their current tax payments that support Medicare and Medicaid would end—if not immediately, then when the programs were phased out—payments to the Health Insurance Fund would be new. The actual amounts they should pay is a matter for negotiation. While it is certainly reasonable that they should contribute what they can, just as other groups will, the amounts should be fair. Probably the fairest approach is to base the amounts on income, but specifics can be negotiated. Another possibility is to base them on a percentage of payroll. In the long run, small businesses will benefit from universal coverage, just as others in the society will—a more stable workforce is one way—and it is reasonable to expect them to contribute to the effort.

RATES TO BE PAID BY INDIVIDUALS AND FAMILIES

Similar points can be made about individuals' contributions to the Health Insurance Fund. All citizens should expect to pay, but everyone's share should be fair. Assuming the tax system is used, progressive rates based on one's income and dependents is a reasonable approach. But starting at what income?

How many income levels or bands should be used? And what rates should be applied to each? Those with employment-based coverage would compare their current share of premiums and taxes for Medicare, Medicaid, and other public programs to their share for the new program. Indeed, advocates of the reform should do the calculations for them and make them known. In some cases, individuals might spend less under the new program; in others, the actual amount would probably be smaller than they imagined since the risk pool will be so much larger and more diverse. (Opponents of reform will try to scare them into thinking that they will pay much more.) For low-income workers at small businesses that did not provide coverage, any payment above current income tax rates will be a new expenditure, which they may have trouble making. These and related considerations need to be kept in mind as rates are set.

In sum, to the extent that the form that these and other provisions take results from negotiations during the political process, it may be possible for some interest groups that expect to be hurt by enactment of comprehensive health system reform legislation—at least in the short run—to reduce the extent of their injury and perhaps even develop additional profitable activities. Several ideas have been offered in this chapter. Undoubtedly there are others.

Conclusion

The health care reform ideas I offered in Chapter 8 are based on an analysis of health system problems and their causes. Addressing those causes provides us with the best chance of finally solving the complex health system problems we face. And although I hope this book can make a useful contribution to solving those problems, bringing health care reform to reality will not be easy.

Given that compromise will be necessary, is it worth giving up *universal* coverage in exchange for vastly increased numbers of insured Americans and reduced numbers of uninsured? In my view, only if that is all that can be accomplished. The primary reason is that more insured people will mean more utilization (good for those without regular sources of care, who rely now on hospital emergency departments), but that increased utilization will undoubtedly increase spending and require that we revisit reform again in relatively short order.

Is it worth giving up a single source of funds to pay for coverage, one that would provide the ability to align incentives so that it becomes rational for providers to invest in quality, in efficiency, and in service? Again, only if we cannot accomplish more. And again, the reason is that we will have done little to achieve our other goals of transforming the delivery system to produce more certain quality, greater efficiency, and more responsive service.

Senator Daschle wrote that one of the lessons he learned from many years in the House and Senate is that prior health care reform efforts faltered not so much because of ideological differences and disputes but because of narrow economic and political interests associated with the details of particular plans. One lesson from the experience of the 1990s is that it takes two to bargain, and proponents of reform should not compromise away what they consider to be important provisions without a commitment from the other side to support the resulting new bill.

Believing in the importance of reform and having been through the Clinton episode, as well as others, Senator Daschle recommends taking some of the most contentious policy issues, most of which are technical anyway, out of the political arena altogether. He would use the Federal Employees Health Benefits Program as the model for benefits choices and would assign the most controversial issues to a new Federal Health Board. That agency would be charged with setting rules for an expanded FEHBP, promoting high-value care that embraces both quality and cost, and aligning incentives to promote good-quality care.[31]

A considerable consensus that reform is necessary has been building among disparate groups—not just citizens struggling with their own health care, but providers, employers, unions, and others, including many political leaders. Many now agree that the health care system in the U.S. needs major changes in order for it not only to serve the people in the decades ahead, but also to maintain its place as a major source of innovation and excellence in the world. But having agreed to the need to do something is only the first step. Reaching consensus on what that something is will be as hard in the early part of the 21st century as it has been since the idea of universal coverage first surfaced in the United States, with Theodore Roosevelt and the Progressives in 1912.

In this book, I have presented an analysis of the problems, identified the major causes, and proposed rational solutions along with ideas to transform these recommendations into actual public policy. I have always been an optimist, and though I have no illusions about the difficulty of bringing this vision to reality, I believe there are enough practical people who recognize the stakes and know we need, finally, to realize Harry Truman's dream of making health care affordable and accessible to all Americans. With Ted Sorensen, I "have faith in the American people to do the right thing."[32]

Reference Matter

Chapter 1

1. Abraham Flexner, *Medical Education in the United States and Canada: A Report to the Carnegie Foundation for the Advancement of Teaching* (New York: Carnegie Foundation for the Advancement of Teaching, 1910).

2. See www.nobelprize.org; accessed on August 14, 2008.

3. Jerome Groopman, "Superbugs," *The New Yorker,* August 11 and 18, 2008, 46–55.

4. Alexander Fleming, "On the Antibacterial Action of Cultures of a Penicillium, with Special Reference to Their Use in the Isolation of *B. influenzæ,*" *British Journal of Experimental Pathology* 10 (1929): 226–236; Charles M. Grossman, "The First Use of Penicillin in the United States, *Annals of Internal Medicine* 149 (2008): 135–136; John S. Mailer Jr. and Barbara Mason, "Penicillin: Medicine's Wartime Wonder Drug and Its Production at Peoria, Illinois"; accessed on July 29, 2008, at lib.niu.edu.

5. Elizabeth Arias, "United States Life Tables, 2001," *National Vital Statistics Reports* 52 (February 18, 2004): Table 11.

6. Barbara Starfield, *Primary Care: Concept, Evaluation, and Policy* (New York: Oxford University Press, 1992), 17.

7. Starfield, *Primary Care,* 18.

8. Erik Eckholm, "To Lower Costs, Hospitals Try Free Basic Care for Uninsured," *The New York Times,* October 25, 2006.

9. Linda T. Kohn, Janet M. Corrigan, and Molla S. Donaldson, *To Err Is Human: Building a Safer Health System* (Washington, DC: Institute of Medicine, National Academy Press, 1999).

10. Stephen M. Davidson and Janelle Heineke, "Toward an Effective Strategy for the Diffusion and Use of Clinical Information Systems," *Journal of the American Medical Informatics Associativon* 14 (2007): 361–367.

11. Donald Berwick, *Escape Fire: Lessons for the Future of Health Care* (New York: The Commonwealth Fund, 2002).

12. Sheila Leatherman, Donald Berwick, Debra Iles, Lawrence S. Lewin, Frank Davidoff, Thomas Nolan, and Maureen Bisognano, "The Business Case for Quality: Case Studies and an Analysis," *Health Affairs* 22 (2003): 17–30.

13. Arnold Relman, *A Second Opinion: Rescuing America's Health Care* (New York: Public Affairs, 2007).

14. George Halvorson, *Health Care Reform Now! A Prescription for Change* (San Francisco: Jossey-Bass, 2007).

15. David M. Cutler, *Your Money or Your Life: Strong Medicine for America's Health Care System* (New York: Oxford University Press, 2004).

16. Jonathan Cohn, *Sick: The Untold Story of American's Health Care Crisis—and the People Who Pay the Price* (New York: HarperCollins, 2007).

17. Victor R. Fuchs, "Economics, Values, and Health Care Reform," *The American Economic Review* 86(1) (March 1996): 1–24.

18. Other economists, most notably Kenneth Arrow, argue that health care differs from typical markets in important ways. We will explore the characteristics of health care markets in Chapter 5.

Chapter 2

1. Howard H. Hiatt, "Protecting the Medical Commons: Who Is Responsible?" *New England Journal of Medicine* 293 (1975): 235–241.

2. Garrett Hardin, "The Tragedy of the Commons," *Science* 162 (1968): 1243–1248.

3. Hardin, "Tragedy of the Commons," 1244.

4. Hiatt, "Protecting the Medical Commons," 235. The observant reader may complain that the analogy is imperfect since the American economy continues to grow and, therefore, is not finite. On the other hand, as we will see, the health care sector has grown faster than the economy as a whole. As a result, it has been absorbing an increasing portion of the society's resources for many years. Some estimate that, unchecked, it will grow to 25 percent of the gross domestic product.

5. Michael E. Chernew, Richard A. Hirth, and David M. Cutler. "Increased Spending on Health Care: How Much Can the U.S. Afford?" *Health Affairs* 22 (2003): 15–25.

6. Aaron Catlin, Cathy Cowan, Micah Hartman, Stephen Heffler, and the National Health Expenditure Accounts Team. "National Health Spending in 2006: A Year of Change for Prescription Drugs," *Health Affairs* 27 (2008): 14–29.

7. Chernew, Hirth, and Cutler, "Increased Spending on Health Care."

8. Congressional Budget Office, *Technological Change and the Growth of Health Care Spending: A CBO Paper* (Washington, DC: Congressional Budget Office, January 2008). See pages 4–5 and Figure 5.

9. Chernew, Hirth, and Cutler, "Increased Spending on Health Care."

10. Bai Xu, "Taking Affordable Medical Service to Farmers," *China Daily: Weekend,* June 11–12, 2005, p. 3.

11. Jon R. Gabel, Roland McDevitt, Ryan Lore, Jeremy Pickreign, Heidi Whitmore, and Tina Ding. "Trends in Underinsurance and the Affordability of Employer Coverage, 2004—2007," *Health Affairs* Web Exclusive, June 2, 2009, w5-95–w6-06. Available at http://content.healthaffairs.org.

12. D. U. Himmelstein and S. Woolhandler, "Cost Without Benefit: Administrative Waste in U.S. Health Care," *New England Journal of Medicine* 314 (1986): 441–445

[Erratum, *New England Journal of Medicine* 315 (1986): 905]; Steffie Woolhandler, Terry Campbell, and David U. Himmelstein, "Costs of Health Care Administration in the United States and Canada," *New England Journal of Medicine* 349 (2003): 768–775. See also accompanying editorial: Henry J. Aaron, "The Costs of Health Care Administration in the United States and Canada—Questionable Answers to a Questionable Question," *New England Journal of Medicine* 349 (2003): 801–803; National Center for Health Statistics, *Health, United States: 2007* (Hyattsville, MD: National Center for Health Statistics, 2007), Table 141, 408–409.

13. Quoted in Malcolm Gladwell, "The Moral-Hazard Myth: The Bad Idea Behind Our Failed Health-Care System," *The New Yorker,* August 29, 2005, 44–49, at pages 46–47.

14. Although the decision of a physician to set up practice in a particular locale is a complex one, it is likely that, for most, the widespread presence of insurance in the area—or its absence—is a contributing factor.

15. K. N. Lohr, R. H. Brook, C. J. Kamberg, G. A. Goldberg, A. Leibowitz, J. Keesey, D. Reboussin, and J. P. Newhouse, "Use of Medical Care in the RAND Health Insurance Experiment: Diagnosis- and Service-Specific Analyses in a Randomized Controlled Trial, *Medical Care* 24 (1986): September Supplement, S1–S87.

16. Michael E. Chernew and Joseph P. Newhouse, "What Does the RAND Health Insurance Experiment Tell Us About the Impact of Cost Sharing on Health Care Outcomes?" *American Journal of Managed Care* 14 (2008): 412–414, at page 412.

17. Chernew and Newhouse, "What Does the RAND Health Insurance Experiment Tell Us," 413.

18. Chernew and Newhouse, "What Does the RAND Health Insurance Experiment Tell Us," 413.

19. Paul Fronstin, *Sources of Health Insurance and Characteristics of the Uninsured: Analysis of the March 2006 Current Population Survey,* Issue Brief No. 298 (Washington, DC: Employee Benefit Research Institute, October 2006), Figure 1, page 4.

20. Karen Davis and Diane Rowland, "Uninsured and Underserved: Inequalities in Health Care in the United States," *The Milbank Fund Quarterly: Health and Society,* 61 (1983): 149–176.

21. Paul Fronstin, *Sources of Health Insurance and Characteristics of the Uninsured,: Analysis of the March 2007 Current Population Survey,* Issue Brief No. 310 (Washington, DC: Employee Benefit Research Institute, October 2007), p. 11.

22. Jonathan Cohn, *Sick: The Untold Story of America's Health Care Crisis—and the People Who Pay the Price* (New York: HarperCollins, 2007).

23. Jon R. Gabel, Jeremy D. Pickreign, Heidi H. Whitmore, and Cathy Schoen, "Embraceable You: How Employers Influence Health Plan Enrollment, *Health Affairs* 20 (2001): 196–208.

24. Fronstin, *Analysis of the March 2007 Current Population Survey,* Issue Brief No. 310, Figure 20, p. 21; Kenneth E. Thorpe and Curtis S. Florence, "Why Are Workers Uninsured? Employer-Sponsored Health Insurance in 1997," *Health Affairs* 18 (1999): 213–218.

25. Fronstin, *Analysis of the March 2007 Current Population Survey,* Issue Brief No. 310, Figure 19, p.21.

26. The News Hour, *Even Insured Patients Struggle as Health Care Costs Rise.* Broadcast on January 5, 2009; transcript accessed on January 6, 2009, at www.pbs.org/news hour/bb/health/jan-june09/healthcare_01-05.html.

27. Gabel, McDevitt, Lore, Pickreign, Whitmore, and Ding, "Trends in Underinsurance and the Affordability of Employer Coverage, 2004—2007," w5-95–w6-06. Available at http://content.healthaffairs.org.

28. Reed Abelson and Milt Freudenheim, "Even the Insured Feel Strain of Health Costs," *New York Times,* May 4, 2008.

29. Ezekiel J. Emanuel and Victor R. Fuchs, "Who Really Pays for Health Care? The Myth of 'Shared Responsibility'," *Journal of the American Medical Association* 299 (2008): 1057–1059.

30. Kaiser Family Foundation and Health Research Educational Trust, *Employer Health Benefits: 2007 Summary of Findings.* Available at www.kff.org.

31. Kaiser Family Foundation and Health Research Educational Trust, *Employer Health Benefits.*

32. Fronstin, *Analysis of the March 2007 Current Population Survey,* Issue Brief No. 310, Figure 1, page 5.

33. Fronstin, *Analysis of the March 2007 Current Population Survey,* Issue Brief No. 310, Figure 1, page 5.

34. David Blumenthal, "Employer-Sponsored Insurance—Riding the Health Care Tiger," *New England Journal of Medicine* 355 (2006): 195–202.

35. Personal health care expenditures is national health expenditures without the amount spent on program expenditures and the net cost of private insurance, government public health activities, and investment in research and physical plant.

36. Centers for Medicare and Medicaid Services, Office of the Actuary, National Health Statistics Group, *National Health Expenditure Data,* Table 6; accessed on January 23, 2008, atwww.cms.hhs.gov/NationalHealthExpendData.

37. Gary Claxton, Jon Gabel, Isadora Gil, Jeremy Pickreign, Heidi Whitmore, Benjamin Finder, Bianca DiJulio, and Samantha Hawkins, "Health Benefits in 2006: Premium Increases Moderate, Enrollment in Consumer-Directed Health Plans Remains Modest," *Health Affairs* 25 (2006): w476–w485. It is irrelevant for our purposes that these figures are somewhat different from those cited earlier from other sources. Although the details vary because different studies use different methods, the general tendencies in the data are the same.

38. Jessica S. Banthin, Peter Cunningham, and Didem M. Bernard, "Financial Burden of Health Care, 2001—2004," *Health Affairs* 27 (2008): 188–195, p. 188.

39. Catherine Hoffman, Diane Rowland, and Elizabeth C. Hamel, *Medical Debt and Access to Health Care,* Kaiser Commission on Medicaid and the Uninsured, September 2005, p. 1.

40. Blumenthal, "Employer-Sponsored Insurance," 195–202.

41. Fronstin, *Analysis of the March 2007 Current Population Survey,* Issue Brief No. 310, page 5.

42. U.S. Census Bureau, *Statistical Abstract of the United States: Population Estimates of the States, April 1, 2000, to July 1, 2007;* Accessed on July 31, 2008, at www .census.gov/popest/states/.

43. Hoffman, Rowland, and Hamel, *Medical Debt and Access to Health Care.*

44. David U. Himmelstein, Elizabeth Warren, Deborah Thorne, and Steffie Wool-handler, "Illness and Injury as Contributors to Bankruptcy," *Health Affairs* Web Exclusive, February 2, 2005, w5-63–w5-73. Available at http://content.healthaffairs.org.

45. Himmelstein, Warren, Thorne, and Woolhandler, "Illness and Injury as Contributors to Bankruptcy," at page w5-66.

46. The paper presents data for nineteen different countries and, although U.S. rates are always among the highest, when all the data are presented, other countries have higher rates for a small number of conditions.

47. Gerard F. Anderson, Bianca K. Frogner, Roger A. Johns, and Uwe E. Reinhardt, "Health Care Spending and Use of Information Technology in OECD Countries," *Health Affairs* 25 (2006): 819–831, p. 822.

48. Anderson, Frogner, Johns, and Reinhardt, "Health Care Spending and Use of Information Technology in OECD Countries," 822.

49. Anderson, Frogner, Johns, and Reinhardt, "Health Care Spending and Use of Information Technology in OECD Countries," 822.

50. Anderson, Frogner, Johns, and Reinhardt, "Health Care Spending and Use of Information Technology in OECD Countries," 822.

Chapter 3

1. David M. Cutler, *Your Money or Your Life: Strong Medicine for America's Health Care System* (New York: Oxford University Press, 2004), xii. Cutler's finding that spending more has produced benefit *in the aggregate* does not mean that, within the United States, spending more to treat particular conditions or particular patients necessarily produces better outcomes.

2. Cutler, *Your Money or Your Life,* 7–8.

3. Cutler, *Your Money or Your Life,* xii.

4. Kevin Sack, "Study Finds Cancer Diagnosis Linked to Insurance," *New York Times,* February 18, 2008.

5. Jessica S. Banthin, Peter Cunningham, and Didem M. Bernard, "Financial Burden of Health Care, 2001—2004," *Health Affairs* 27 (2008): 188–195.

6. Catherine Hoffman, Diane Rowland, and Elizabeth C. Hamel, *Medical Debt and Access to Health Care,* Kaiser Commission on Medicaid and the Uninsured, September 2005, p. 12.

7. Hoffman, Rowland, and Hamel, *Medical Debt and Access to Health Care,* 2.

8. Banthin, Cunningham, and Bernard, "Financial Burden of Health Care, 2001–2004," 188.

9. Banthin, Cunningham, and Bernard, "Financial Burden of Health Care, 2001–2004," 190.

10. Banthin, Cunningham, and Bernard, "Financial Burden of Health Care, 2001–2004," 191.

11. Kaiser Family Foundation and Health Research and Educational Trust, *Employer Health Benefits: 2007 Summary of Findings.* Available at www.kff.org.

12. Paul Fronstin, *Sources of Health Insurance and Characteristics of the Uninsured: Analysis of the March 2006 Current Population Survey.* Issue Brief No. 298 (Washington, DC: Employee Benefit Research Institute, October 2006), page 8.

13. Gary Claxton, Jon Gabel, Isadora Gil, Jeremy Pickreign, Heidi Whitmore, Benjamin Finder, Bianca DiJulio, and Samantha Hawkins, "Health Benefits in 2006: Premium Increases Moderate, Enrollment in Consumer-Directed Health Plans Remains Modest," *Health Affairs* 25 (2006): w4-76–w4-85, at page w479.

14. Fronstin, *Analysis of the March 2006 Current Population Survey,* Issue Brief No. 298, page 8.

15. "World's Best Medical Care?" *The New York Times,* August 12, 2007.

16. Linda T. Kohn, Janet M. Corrigan, and Molla S. Donaldson (Eds.), *To Err Is Human: Building a Safer Health System* (Washington, DC: Institute of Medicine, National Academy Press, 2000.

17. Kohn, Corrigan, and Donaldson, *To Err Is Human,* p. 26.

18. Kohn, Corrigan, and Donaldson, *To Err Is Human.*

19. National Committee for Quality Assurance (NCQA), *The State of Health Care Quality 2006* (Washington, DC: National Committee for Quality Assurance, 2006), 8.

20. D. M. Eddy, "Performance Measurement: Problems and Solutions," *Health Affairs* 17 (1998): 7–25, at p. 8; E. A. McGlynn, "Six Challenges in Measuring the Quality of Health Care," *Health Affairs* 16 (1997): 7–21; David Blumenthal, "Quality of Care: What Is It?" *New England Journal of Medicine* 335 (1996): 891–894.

21. Eddy, "Performance Measurement," 8; McGlynn, "Six Challenges in Measuring the Quality of Health Care."

22. Avedis Donabedian, *Explorations in Quality Assessment and Monitoring. Volume 1: The Definition of Quality and Approaches to Its Assessment* (Ann Arbor, MI: Health Administration Press, 1980).

23. Lewis Thomas, from an article in the *New York Times Magazine,* quoted in the *Encyclopedia Britannica,* 2008; accessed August 28, 2008, at http://www.britannica.com/EBchecked/topic/592834/Lewis-Thomas.

24. In the absence of utilization data, Donabedian also suggested that inferences about quality could be drawn from evidence about structural properties of the care. Among those indicators are number of board-certified physicians, hospitals accredited by JCAHO, and nurse-to-patient ratios.

25. N. R. Kleinfeld, Ian Urbina, and Marc Santora. "Bad Blood," a four-part series on diabetes, *The New York Times,* January 9, 10, 11, 12, 2006.; See also Editorial: "Declare War on Diabetes," *The New York Times.* February 5, 2006.

26. Thomas Nolan and Donald M. Berwick, "All-or-None Measurement Raises the Bar on Performance," *Journal of the American Medical Association* 295 (2006): 1168–1170.

27. Stephen M. Davidson, Michael Shwartz, and Randall S. Stafford, "The Feasibility and Value of New Measures Showing Patterns of Quality for Patients with 3 Chronic Conditions," *Journal of Ambulatory Care Management* 31 (2008): 37–51.

28. J. Ma and R. S. Stafford, "Quality of U.S. Outpatient Care: Temporal Changes and Racial/Ethnic Disparities," *Archives of Internal Medicine* 165 (2005): 1354–1361.

29. Institute of Medicine, *Crossing the Quality Chasm: A New Health System for the 21st Century* (Washington, DC: National Academics Press, 2001).

30. Edward H. Wagner, Brian T. Austin, Connie Davis, Mike Hindmarsh, Judith Schaefer, and Amy Bonomi, "Improving Chronic Illness Care: Translating Evidence

into Action," *Health Affairs* 20 (2001): 64–78; Edward H. Wagner, Brian T. Austin, and Michael Von Korff, "Organizing Care for Patients with Chronic Illness," *The Milbank Quarterly* 74 (1996): 511–544.

31. D. M. Berwick, D. R. Calkins, C. J. McCannon, and A. D. Hackbarth, "The 100,000 Lives Campaign—Setting a Goal and a Deadline for Improving Health Care Quality," *Journal of the American Medical Association* 295 (2006): 324–327.

32. L. Liang, "The Gap Between Evidence and Practice," *Health Affairs* Web Exclusive, January 26, 2007, w1-19–w1-21. Available at http://content.healthaffairs.org.

33. Commonwealth Fund Commission on a High Performance Health System, *The Path to a High Performance U.S. Health System: A 2020 Vision and the Policies to Pave the Way* (New York: The Commonwealth Fund, February 2009).

34. William Rosenberg and Anna Donald, "Evidence-Based Medicine: An Approach to Clinical Problem-Solving, *British Medical Journal* 310 (1995): 1122–1126.

35. Frank Davidoff, Brian Haynes, David Sackett, and Richard Smith, "Evidence-Based Medicine," *British Medical Journal* 310 (1995): 1085–1086.

36. Liang, "The Gap Between Evidence and Practice," w1-19–w1-21.

37. L. L. Leape, D. M. Berwick, and D. W. Bates, "What Practices Will Most Improve Safety? Evidence-Based Medicine Meets Patient Safety," *Journal of the American Medical Association* 288 (2002): 501–507.

38. Robert J. Blendon, Minah Kim, and John M. Benson, "The Public Versus the World Health Organization on Health System Performance," *Health Affairs* 20(3) (2001): 10–20.

39. Blendon, Kim, and Benson, "The Public Versus the World Health Organization," 16.

40. Robert J. Blendon, Cathy Schoen, Catherine M. DesRoches, Robin Osborn, Kimberly L. Scoles, and Kinga Zapert, "Inequities in Health Care: A Five-Country Survey," *Health Affairs* 21(3) (2002): 182–191, p. 184.

41. Robert J. Blendon and John M. Benson, "Americans' Views on Health Policy: A Fifty-Year Historical Perspective," *Health Affairs* 20(2) (2001): 33–46, p. 36.

42. Blendon and Benson, "Americans' Views on Health Policy," 36.

Chapter 4

1. Arnold S. Relman, *A Second Opinion: Rescuing America's Health Care: A Plan for Universal Coverage Serving Patients Over Profit* (New York: The Century Foundation and Public Affairs, 2007). See especially Chapters 3 and 4.

2. Kenneth J. Arrow, "Uncertainty and the Welfare Economics of Medical Care," *The American Economic Review* 53 (1963): 941–973.

3. Relman, *A Second Opinion: Rescuing America's Health Care.*

4. Relman, *A Second Opinion: Rescuing America's Health Care,* 66.

5. Linda T. Kohn, Janet M. Corrigan, and Molla S. Donaldson, *To Err Is Human: Building a Safer Health System* (Washington, DC: Insitute of Medicine, National Academy Press, 1999). See also Institute of Medicine, *Crossing the Quality Chasm: A New Health System for the 21st Century* (Washington, DC: National Academy Press, 2001); J. Ma and R. S. Stafford, "Quality of U.S. Outpatient Care: Temporal Changes and Racial/Ethnic Disparities," *Archives of Internal Medicine* 165 (2005): 1354–1361; National

Committee for Quality Assurance (NCQA), *The State of Health Care Quality 2006* (Washington, DC: NCQA, 2006). Also available at www.ncqa.org.

6. S. M. Davidson and J. Heineke, "Toward an Effective Strategy for the Diffusion and Use of Clinical Information Systems, *Journal of the American Medical Informatics Association* 14 (2007): 361–3677. Adam Smith, *An Inquiry into the Nature and Causes of the Wealth of Nations* (New York: The Modern Library, 1937), 423.

8. Stephen M. Davidson, Joseph D. Restuccia, and the Boston University Health Care Management Program Group, "Competition and Quality Among Managed Care Plans in the USA," *International Journal for Quality in Health Care* 10 (1998): 411–419, p. 417.

9. See Organization for Economic Cooperation and Development, *OECD Health Data 2006.* Reprinted in The Henry J. Kaiser Family Foundation, *Snapshots: Health Care Costs,* January 2007.

10. See Organization for Economic Cooperation and Development, *OECD Health Data 2006.*

11. See www.ihi.org.

12. H. T. Tu and P. B. Ginsburg, *Losing Ground: Physician Income, 1995–2003,* Tracking Report No. 15 (Washington, DC, Center for Studying Health System Change, June 2006).

13. J. Goldsmith, "Hospitals and Physicians: Not a Pretty Picture," *Health Affairs* Web Exclusive, December 5, 2006, w72–w75. Available at http://content.health affairs.org.

14. Gina Kolata, "Lessons of Heart Disease, Learned and Ignored," *New York Times,* April 8, 2007, p. 1.

15. Kolata, "Lessons of Heart Disease."

16. Relman, *A Second Opinion,* 33–34.

17. American Hospital Association, *Adopting Technological Innovation in Hospitals: Who Pays and Who Benefits?* October 2006, p. 2.

18. Since 1983, Medicare payments for hospitalized patients have been based on patient characteristics, including especially diagnosis and severity, rather than on the services provided. All hospitals get a predetermined payment based on those characteristics, regardless of the services actually provided or the length of time the patient stays in the hospital. The intent is to give hospitals an incentive to provide only necessary services, thus avoiding suspected waste.

19. American Hospital Association, *Adopting Technological Innovation in Hospitals,* p. 3.

20. American Hospital Association, *Adopting Technological Innovation in Hospitals,* p. 1.

21. Steve Lohr, "Who Pays for Efficiency?" *The New York Times,* June 11, 2007; Special Section on the Business of Health.

22. Tu and Ginsburg, "Losing Ground."

23. When drug companies sponsor them, the programs may be free to physicians who attend. Doctors would still face travel expenses where necessary and other costs.

24. Goldsmith, "Hospitals and Physicians," w72.

25. Jonathan Cohn, *Sick: The Untold Story of America's Health Care Crisis—and the People Who Pay the Price* (New York: HarperCollins, 2007). See especially Chapter 7, Los Angeles.

26. Donald M. Berwick, *Escape Fire: Lessons for the Future of Health Care,* Nov. 1, 2002. Available at www.cmwf.org/publications. See pages 20–29.

27. Philip Musgrove, "Life and Death and Who's Going to Pay," *Health Affairs* 25 (2006): 1664–1667.

28. Beth Boehne, "Cash Before Chemo: Hospitals Get Tough," WSBT Television. Reported by Barbara Martinez in *The Wall Street Journal,* April 29, 2008; accessed on August 12, 2008, at http://www.wsbt.com/news/health/18353979.html.

29. Boehne, "Cash Before Chemo."

30. Boehne, "Cash Before Chemo."

31. Kohn, Corrigan, and Donaldson, *To Err Is Human.*

32. L. L. Leape and D. M. Berwick, "Five Years After *To Err Is Human:* What Have We Learned?" *Journal of the American Medical Association,* 293 (2005): 2384–2390.

33. Jay Himmelstein, "Bleeding-Edge Benefits," *Health Affairs* 25 (2006): 1656–1663.

34. Erik Eckholm, "In Turnabout, Infant Deaths Climb in South," *The New York Times,* April 22, 2007.

35. Reed Abelson, "Financial Ties Are Cited as Issue in Spine Study," *The New York Times,* January 30, 2008.

36. Reed Abelson, "Some Hospitals Call 911 to Save Their Patients," *The New York Times,* April 2, 2007.

37. Abelson, "Financial Ties Are Cited."

38. Gardiner Harris and Benedict Carey, "Researchers Fail to Reveal Full Drug Pay," *The New York Times,* June 8, 2008.

39. Robert Steinbrook, "Disclosure of Industry Payments to Physicians," *New England Journal of Medicine* 359 (2008): 559–561, p. 559.

40. Andrew Vickers, "Cancer Data? Sorry, Can't Have It," *The New York Times,* January 22, 2008.

41. Stephanie Saul, "Merck Wrote Drug Studies for Doctors," *The New York Times,* April 16, 2008.

42. Daniel Carlat, "Diagnosis: Conflict of Interest," *The New York Times,* June 13, 2007, op-ed page.

43. Richard H. Thaler and Cass R. Sunstein, *Nudge: Improving Decisions About Health, Wealth, and Happiness,* revised and expanded edition (New York: Penguin Books, 2009).

Chapter 5

1. Robert F. Hartley, *Management Mistakes and Successes,* 8th edition; Chapter 16: Harley Davidson: Success Through a Mystique, 221–234 (New York: John Wiley and Sons, 2005).

2. James C. Robinson, "The Commercial Health Insurance Industry in an Era of Eroding Employer Coverage," *Health Affairs* 25 (2006): 1475–1486; Walter A. Zelman, *The Changing Health Care Marketplace: Private Ventures, Public Interests* (San Francisco: Jossey-Bass, 1996); Stephen M. Shortell, Robin R. Gillies, David A. Anderson, Karen Morgan Erickson, and John B. Mitchell, *Remaking Health Care in America: The Evolution of Organized Delivery Systems,* second edition (San Francisco: Jossey-Bass, 2000); John D. Wilkerson, Kelly J. Devers, and Ruth S. Given (eds.),

Competitive Managed Care: The Emerging Health Care System (San Francisco: Jossey-Bass, 1997); Bradford H. Gray, *The Profit Motive and Patient Care: The Changing Accountability of Doctors and Hospitals* (Cambridge, MA: Harvard University Press, 1991).

3. Lucien L. Leape, "Unnecessary Surgery," in *Annual Review of Public Health 1992* (Palo Alto, CA: Annual Reviews, Inc., 1992), 363–383.

4. Neil J. MacKinnon and Ritu Kumar. "Prior Authorization Programs: A Critical Review of the Literature," *Journal of Managed Care Pharmacy* 7 (2001): 297–302; Walter E. Smalley, Marie R. Griffin, Randy L. Fought, Leo Sullivan, and Wayne A. Ray, "Effect of a Prior-Authorization Requirement on the Use of Nonsteroidal Antiinflammatory Drugs by Medicaid Patients," *New England Journal of Medicine* 332 (1995): 1612–1617; Stephen B. Soumerai, "Benefits and Risks of Increasing Restrictions on Access to Costly Drugs in Medicaid," *Health Affairs* 23 (2004): 135–146.

5. Paying a plan an annual fee for each person it enrolled is called *capitation,* based on the Latin word for head.

6. Lawrence D. Brown, *Politics and Health Care Organization: HMOs as Federal Policy* (Washington, DC: The Brookings Institution, 1983).

7. Anne R. Somers (ed.), *The Kaiser Permanente Medical Care Program: A Symposium* (New York: The Commonwealth Fund, 1971); John G. Smillie, *Can Physicians Manage the Quality and Costs of Health Care? The Story of the Permanente Medical Group* (New York: McGraw-Hill, 1991).

8. Anita J. Bhatia, Sheila Blackstock, Rachel Nelson, and Terry S. Ng, "Evolution of Quality Review Programs for Medicare: Quality Assurance to Quality Improvement," *Health Care Financing Review,* 22 (2000): 69–74.

9. Stephen M. Davidson, "Physician Participation in Medicaid: Background and Issues," *Journal of Health Policy, Politics, and Law* 6 (1982): 703–717; Janet B. Mitchell, "Physician Participation in Medicaid Revisited," *Medical Care* 29 (1991): 645–653.

10. For an example of this tendency carried to an extreme, see Atul Gawande, "The Cost Conundrum: What a Texas Town Can Teach Us About Health Care," *The New Yorker,* June 1, 2009.

11. Chris Hartman, "*By the Numbers: The Latest and Fullest Data on Income, Wealth, CEO Pay, Etc.*"; accessed on September 8, 2008, at www.demos.org/inequality.

12. Arthur M. Okun, *Equality and Efficiency: The Big Trade-Off* (Washington, DC: The Brookings Institution, 1975).

13. An extensive literature exists arguing that medical professionals, if not the society as a whole, have an ethical obligation to ensure that people receive care according to their health needs, irrespective of race, gender, employment, income, or other non-health factors. While consistent with that line of thought, the case I am making does not depend on it.

14. Stephen M. Davidson, *Medicaid Decisions: A Systematic Analysis of the Cost Problem,* (Cambridge, MA: Ballinger, 1980).

15. David C. Hsia, Medicare Quality Improvement: Bad Apples or Bad Systems? *Journal of the American Medical Association* 289 (2003): 354–356.

16. The Commonwealth Fund Commission on a High Performance Health System, *The Path to a High Performance Health System: A 2020 Vision and the Policies to Pave the Way* (New York: The Commonwealth Fund, February 19, 2009).

17. Kevin Sack, "Coming Soon: Health Care Debate, Part 2," *The New York Times,* March 2, 2008, News of the Week section.

18. Drew Altman, *Pulling It Together,* Kaiser Family Foundation, May 1, 2008.

19. Note that although for insurance to work a carrier needs to enroll lots of such people, it is more problematic that many insurers tend to discourage people at high risk from signing up.

20. Fred Foulkes, *The Honeywell Case* (Boston: Boston University School of Management, n.d.).

21. Bruce P. Kennedy, Ichiro Kawachi, Roberta Glass, and Deborah Prothrow-Stith, "Income Distribution, Socioeconomic Status, and Self-Rated Health in the United States: Multilevel Analysis," *British Medical Journal* 317 (1998): 917–921.

22. Ronald Andersen, Joanna Kravits, and Odin W. Anderson, *Equity in Health Services: Empirical Analyses in Social Policy* (Cambridge, MA: Ballinger, 1975).

23. Julie Salamon, *Hospital: Man, Woman, Birth, Death, Infinity, Plus Red Tape, Bad Behavior, Money, God, and Diversity on Steroids* (New York: Penguin Press, 2008), 2.

24. Neal A. Vanselow, "Primary Care and the Specialist," *Journal of the American Medical Association* 279 (1998): 1394–1395.

25. Walsh McDermott, "General Medical Care: Identification and Analysis of Alternative Approaches," *The Johns Hopkins Medical Journal* 135 (1974), 292–321, p. 300.

26. McDermott, "General Medical Care."

27. Roger A. Rosenblatt, L. Gary Hart, Laura-Mae Baldwin, Leighton Chan, and Ronald Schneeweiss, "The Generalist Role of Specialty Physicians: Is There a Hidden System of Primary Care?" *Journal of the American Medical Association* 279 (1998): 1364–1370.

28. Vanselow, "Primary Care and the Specialist," 1394–1395.

29. National Center for Health Statistics, *Health, United States, 2008* (Hyattsville, MD: NCHS, 2008), Table 94, pages 375–377.

30. Richard M. Scheffler, *Is There a Doctor in the House? Market Signals and Tomorrow's Supply of Doctors* (Stanford, CA: Stanford University Press, 2008).

31. Mark V. Pauly, "Is Medical Care Different?" In *Competition in the Health Care Sector: Past, Present, and Future,* Warren Greenberg (ed.) (Germantown, MD: Aspen Systems Corporation, 1978), 11–35.

Chapter 6

1. Richard H. Thaler and Cass R. Sunstein, *Nudge: Improving Decisions About Health, Wealth, and Happiness* (New York: Penguin Books, 2008, 2009).

2. Nathan Sinai, Odin W. Anderson, and Melvin L. Dollar, *Health Insurance in the United States* (New York: The Commonwealth Fund, 1946), 7.

3. Paul Starr, *The Social Transformation of American Medicine* (New York: Basic Books, 1982), 294.

4. Starr, *The Social Transformation of American Medicine,* 294.

5. Sylvia A. Law, *Blue Cross: What Went Wrong?* (New Haven, CT: Yale University Press, 1974), 6.

6. Law, *Blue Cross: What Went Wrong?* 7.

7. Law, *Blue Cross: What Went Wrong?*

8. Starr, *The Social Transformation of American Medicine,* 299.

9. Starr, *The Social Transformation of American Medicine,* 299.

10. Karen Davis, Gerard F. Anderson, Diane Rowland, and Earl P. Steinberg, *Health Care Cost Containment* (Baltimore: Johns Hopkins University Press, 1990), 11.

11. National Center for Health Statistics, *Health, United States, 2005* (Hyattsville, MD: NCHS, 2005).

12. Gary Claxton, Jon Gabel, Isadora Gil, Jeremy Pickreign, Heidi Whitmore, Benjamin Finder, Bianca DiJulio, and Samantha Hawkins, "Health Benefits in 2006: Premium Increases Moderate, Enrollment in Consumer-Directed Health Plans Remains Modest," *Health Affairs* 25 (2006): w4-76–w4-85.

13. Ezekiel J. Emanuel and Victor R. Fuchs, "Who Really Pays for Health Care? The Myth of 'Shared Responsibility'." *Journal of the American Medical Association* 299 (2008): 1057–1059.

14. K. N. Lohr, R. H. Brook, C. J. Kamberg, G. A. Goldberg, A. Leibowitz, J. Keesey, D. Reboussin, and J. P. Newhouse, "Use of Medical Care in the RAND Health Insurance Experiment: Diagnosis- and Service-Specific Analyses in a Randomized Controlled Trial," *Medical Care* 24 (1986): September Supplement, S1–S87.

15. Barbara Starfield, *Primary Care: Concept, Evaluation, and Policy* (New York: Oxford University Press, 1992).

16. Gina Kolata, "Co-Payments Soar for Drugs with High Prices," *The New York Times,* April 14, 2008.

17. Henry S. Farber and Helen Levy, "Recent Trends in Employer-Sponsored Health Insurance Coverage: Are Bad Jobs Getting Worse?" *Journal of Health Economics* 19 (2000): 93–119; David M. Cutler, "Employee Costs and the Decline in Health Insurance Coverage," *Frontiers in Health Policy Research* 6 (2003): 27–53.

18. We should note that one way insurers earn money is by investing their premium income, hoping to grow it before it is needed to pay subscribers' medical bills. Their profits may fall if they make bad investment choices or the economy is in a recession.

19. James C. Robinson, "The Commercial Health Insurance Industry in an Era of Eroding Employer Coverage," *Health Affairs* 25 (2006): 1475–1486, p. 1476.

20. James C. Robinson, "Consolidation and the Transformation of Competition in Health Insurance," *Health Affairs* 23 (2004): 11–24; Robinson, "The Commercial Health Insurance Industry in an Era of Eroding Employer Coverage," 1476.

21. Alice Rosenblatt, "The Underwriting Cycle: The Rule of Six," *Health Affairs* 23 (2004): 103–106.

22. Joy M. Grossman and Paul B. Ginsburg, "As the Health Insurance Underwriting Cycle Turns: What Next?" *Health Affairs* 23 (2004): 91–102.

23. Jon Gabel, Roger Formisano, Barbara Lohr, and Steven DiCarlo, "Tracing the Cycle of Health Insurance," *Health Affairs* 10 (1991): 48–61.

24. Grossman and Ginsburg, "As the Health Insurance Underwriting Cycle Turns," 92.

25. Grossman and Ginsburg, "As the Health Insurance Underwriting Cycle Turns," 94–95.

26. Rosenblatt, "The Underwriting Cycle," 103–106.

27. Robinson, "The Commercial Health Insurance Industry in an Era of Eroding Employer Coverage"; Paul Fronstin, *Sources of Health Insurance and Characteristics of the Uninsured: Analysis of the March 2008 Current Population Survey,* Issue Brief No. 321 (Washington, DC: Employee Benefit Research Institute, September 2008).

28. Robinson, "The Commercial Health Insurance Industry in an Era of Eroding Employer Coverage," 1476.

29. Robinson, "The Commercial Health Insurance Industry in an Era of Eroding Employer Coverage," 1477.

30. Robinson, "The Commercial Health Insurance Industry in an Era of Eroding Employer Coverage," 1477.

31. Robinson, "The Commercial Health Insurance Industry in an Era of Eroding Employer Coverage," 1478.

32. Robinson, "The Commercial Health Insurance Industry in an Era of Eroding Employer Coverage," 1478.

33. Robinson, "The Commercial Health Insurance Industry in an Era of Eroding Employer Coverage," 1478.

34. Robinson, "The Commercial Health Insurance Industry in an Era of Eroding Employer Coverage," 1482.

35. Kaiser Family Foundation, *Medicare Advantage Fact Sheet,* September 2008; accessed on September 13, 2008, at www.kff.org/medicare/upload/2052-11.pdf.

36. I am indebted to my colleague Jim Post for this concise formulation of the insurers' options.

37. Joe McFarlane, "Evaluating Managed Care Contracts, In *Efficient Eye Care: Manual of Managed Care Ophthalmology,* Donald S. Fong (ed.), (Boston: Blackwell Science, 2001), 21–38; Keith W. Neely, Robert L. Norton, and Terri A. Schmidt, "State Insurance Commissioner Actions Against Health Maintenance Organizations for Denial of Emergency Care," *Prehospital Emergency Care* 3 (1999): 19–22; Joseph D. Restuccia, "The Effect of Concurrent Feedback in Reducing Inappropriate Hospital Utilization," *Medical Care* 20 (1982): 46–62.

38. Federal Emergency Medical Treatment and Active Labor Act (EMTALA), 1986, 42 USC 1395dd.

39. Julie Salamon, *Hospital: Man, Woman, Birth, Death, Infinity, Plus Red Tape, Bad Behavior, Money, God, and Diversity on Steroids* (New York: Penguin Press, 2008), 87.

40. Paul Fronstin, *Sources of Health Insurance and Characteristics of the Uninsured: Analysis of the March 2007 Current Population Survey,* Issue Brief No. 310 (Washington, DC: Employee Benefit Research Institute, October 2007). See Figures 1 and 18.

41. H. A. Huskamp, P. A. Deverka, A. M. Epstein, R. S. Epstein, K. A. McGuigan, and R. G. Frank. "The Effect of Incentive-Based Formularies on Prescription-Drug Utilization and Spending," *New England Journal of Medicine,* 349 (2003): 2224–2232.

42. Aaron Catlin, Cathy Cowan, Micah Hartman, Stephen Heffler, and the National Health Expenditure Accounts Team, "National Health Spending in 2006: A Year of Change for Prescription Drugs," *Health Affairs* 27 (2008): 14–29.

43. Cindy Parks Thomas, "Incentive-Based Formularies," *New England Journal of Medicine* 349 (2003): 2186–2188.

44. Huskamp, Deverka, Epstein, Epstein, McGuigan, and Frank, "The Effect of Incentive-Based Formularies," 2231.

45. Huskamp, Deverka, Epstein, Epstein, McGuigan, and Frank, "The Effect of Incentive-Based Formularies."

46. A. N. Trivedi, W. Rakowski, and J. Z. Ayanian, "Effect of Cost Sharing on Screening Mammography in Medicare Health Plans," *New England Journal of Medicine* 358 (2008): 375–383.

47. Trivedi, Rakowski, and Ayanian, "Effect of Cost Sharing on Screening Mammography," 375.

48. Trivedi, Rakowski, and Ayanian, "Effect of Cost Sharing on Screening Mammography," 375.

49. Lohr, Brook, Kamberg, Goldberg, Leibowitz, Keesey, Reboussin, and Newhouse," "Use of Medical Care in the RAND Health Insurance Experiment."

50. Lohr, Brook, Kamberg, Goldberg, Leibowitz, Keesey, Reboussin, and Newhouse, "Use of Medical Care in the RAND Health Insurance Experiment."

51. Lohr, Brook, Kamberg, Goldberg, Leibowitz, Keesey, Reboussin, and Newhouse, "Use of Medical Care in the RAND Health Insurance Experiment," S30.

52. Lohr, Brook, Kamberg, Goldberg, Leibowitz, Keesey, Reboussin, and Newhouse, "Use of Medical Care in the RAND Health Insurance Experiment," S30.

53. Lohr, Brook, Kamberg, Goldberg, Leibowitz, Keesey, Reboussin, and Newhouse, "Use of Medical Care in the RAND Health Insurance Experiment," S36.

54. Thomas Rice, "An Alternative Framework for Evaluating Welfare Losses in the Health Care Market," *Journal of Health Economics* 11 (1992): 85–92, at page 87.

55. Rice, "An Alternative Framework," 86.

56. John A. Nyman, "The Economics of Moral Hazard Revisited," *Journal of Health Economics* 18 (1999): 811–824.

57. Rice, "An Alternative Framework," 87.

58. Rice, "An Alternative Framework," 90.

59. Nyman, "The Economics of Moral Hazard Revisited."

60. Milton I. Roemer, "Bed Supply and Hospital Utilization: A Natural Experiment," *Hospitals,* November 1, 1961, 36–42.

61. John Wennberg and Alan Gittelsohn, "Small Area Variations in Health Care Delivery," *Science* 182 (1973): 1102–1108.

62. Mark V. Pauly, "Is Medical Care Different?" in *Competition in the Health Care Sector: Past, Present, and Future,* Warren Greenberg (ed.) (Germantown, MD: Aspen Systems Corporation, 1978), 11–35.

63. Pauly, "Is Medical Care Different?" 13.

64. Jerome Groopman, "Superbugs," *The New Yorker,* August 11 and 18, 2008, pages 46–55.

65. Joint Committee on Taxation, *Tax Expenditures for Health Care,* Report JCX-66-08, July 30, 2008. See page 10.

66. Steffie Woolhandler, Terry Campbell, and David U. Himmelstein, "Costs of Health Care Administration in the United States and Canada," *New England Journal of Medicine* 249 (2003): 768–775.

67. Faced with this situation, some doctors create "concierge" practices in which they charge a monthly fee of, say, $125 for guaranteed access to the physician who has agreed to limit his practice to perhaps six hundred patients. This reduces the

number of available primary care physicians still further, restricts access to people who can afford the monthly fee (which is in addition to their share of insurance premiums), and, not incidentally, adds substantially to the physician's income. (At $125 per month, six hundred patients results in $900,000 in gross income for the physician, from which he deducts the cost of noncovered services to produce his take-home pay.) See Kevin Sack, "Despite Recession, Personalized Health Care Remains in Demand," *The New York Times,* May 11, 2009.

68. John A. Rizzo and Richard J. Zeckhauser, "Reference Incomes, Loss Aversion, and Physician Behavior," *The Review of Economics and Statistics* 85 (2003): 909–922.

69. Rizzo and Zeckhauser, "Reference Incomes, Loss Aversion, and Physician Behavior," 912.

70. H. T. Tu and P. B. Ginsburg, *Losing Ground: Physician Income, 1995–2003,* Tracking Report No. 15 (Washington, DC: Center for the Study of Health System Change, June 2006).

71. J. Reschovsky and J. Hadley, *Physician Financial Incentives: Use of Quality Incentives Inches Up, but Productivity Still Dominates,* Issue Brief No. 108 (Washington, DC: Center for the Study of Health System Change, January 2007).

72. National Center for Health Statistics, *Health: United States, 2007* (Hyattsville, MD: National Center for Health Statistics, 2007), Table 124, pages 378–379.

73. J. Goldsmith, "Hospitals and Physicians: Not A Pretty Picture, *Health Affairs* Web Exclusive, January-February 2007, w72–w75. Available at http://content.health affairs.org.

74. Lawrence P. Casalino, *Physician Self-Referral and Physician-Owned Specialty Facilities* Research Synthesis Report No. 15 (Princeton, NJ: The Robert Wood Johnson Foundation, June 2008).

75. Atul Gawande, "The Cost Conundrum," *The New Yorker,* June 1, 2009.

76. Jon R. Gabel, Cheryl Fahlman, Ray Kang, Gregory Wozniak, Phil Kletke, and Joel W. Hay, "Where Do I Send Thee? Does Physician-Ownership Affect Referral Patterns to Ambulatory Surgery Centers?" *Health Affairs* Web Exclusive, March 18, 2008, w1-65–w1-74, at p. w165. Available at http://content.healthaffairs.org.

77. Leslie Greenwald, Jerry Cromwell, Walter Adamache, Shulamit Bernard, Edward Drozd, Elisabeth Root, and Kelly Devers, "Specialty Versus Community Hospitals: Referrals, Quality, and Community Benefits," *Health Affairs* 25 (2006): 106–118.

78. Casalino, *Physician Self-Referral and Physician-Owned Specialty Facilities.*

79. Reed Abelson, "Some Hospitals Call 911 to Save Their Patients," *The New York Times,* April 2, 2007.

80. R. A. Berenson, P. B. Ginsburg, and J. H. May, "Hospital-Physician Relations: Cooperation, Competition, or Separation?" *Health Affairs* Web Exclusive, December 5, 2006, w31–w43. Available at http://content.healthaffairs.org.

81. Goldsmith, "Hospitals and Physicians," w72.

82. R. A. Berenson, T. Bodenheimer, and H. H. Pham, "Specialty-Service Lines: Salvos in the New Medical Arms Race," *Health Affairs* Web Exclusive, July 25, 2006, w3-37–w3-43. Available at http://content.healthaffairs.org.

83. Salamon, *Hospital.*

84. Kevin Sack, "McCain Plan to Aid States on Health Could Be Costly," *The New York Times,* July 9, 2008.

85. Sack, "McCain Plan."

86. Sack, "McCain Plan."

87. Stephen M. Davidson and Janelle Heineke, "Toward an Effective Strategy for the Diffusion and Use of Clinical Information Systems," *Journal of the American Medical Informatics Association* 14 (2007): 361–367; R. Koppel, J. P. Metlay, A. Cohen, B. Abaluck, A. R. Localio, S. E. Kimmel, and others. "Role of Computerized Physician Order Entry Systems in Facilitation Medication Errors," *Journal of the American Medical Association* 293 (2005): 1197–1203.

Chapter 7

1. C. L. Schultze, *The Public Use of Private Interest* (Washington, DC: The Brookings Institution, 1977). The fiscal crisis that gripped the nation starting in the fall of 2008 was the exception that proved the rule. The problems were so large and pervasive then that liberals and conservatives alike thought massive federal intervention was required.

2. Atul Gawande, "Getting There from Here: How Should Obama Reform Health Care?" *The New Yorker,* January 26, 2009.

3. Alain C. Enthoven, *Health Plan: The Only Practical Solution to the Soaring Cost of Medical Care* (Reading, MA: Addison-Wesley, 1980).

4. Enthoven, *Health Plan,* 119.

5. See, for example, Stuart Butler, "A Tax Reform Strategy to Deal with the Uninsured," *Journal of the American Medical Association* 265 (1991): 2541–2544. Also, Alain Enthoven and Richard Kronick, "Universal Health Insurance Through Incentives Reform," *Journal of the American Medical Association* 265 (1991): 2532–2536.

6. Kaiser Family Foundation, *2008 Presidential Candidate Health Care Proposals: Side-by-Side Summary;* accessed on September 18, 2008, at health08.org.

7. Milton I. Roemer, "Bed Supply and Hospital Utilization: A Natural Experiment," *Hospitals,* November 1, 1961, 36–42.

8. Lawrence D. Brown, *Politics and Health Care Organization: HMOs as Federal Policy* (Washington, DC: The Brookings Institution, 1983).

9. *The Managed Care Backlash,* Special Issue, *Journal of Health Politics, Policy and Law* 24(5) (October 1999).

10. Michael E. Porter and Elizabeth Olmsted Teisberg, *Redefining Health Care: Creating Value-Based Competition on Results* (Boston: Harvard Business School Press, 2006).

11. These points hold even for the many large companies that are self-insured. Although they do not incur all of the costs of private insurers or HMOs, they do incur nontrivial administrative costs. Further, they tend not to have a primary goal of earning a profit on the coverage they provide to their employees.

12. Kenneth E. Thorpe, "Inside the Black Box of Administrative Costs," *Health Affairs* 11 (1992): 41–55, Exhibit 3.

13. Randall D. Cebul, James Rebitzer, Lowell J. Taylor, and Mark Votruba, *Unhealthy Insurance Markets: Search Frictions and the Cost and Quality of Health Insurance,* unpublished manuscript, Case Western University, Cleveland, Ohio, 2008.

14. It is not a problem that insurers like to sell to low-risk groups. In fact, they need large numbers of such people because in health insurance, the healthy subsidize the sick (those who use services). Instead, the problem arises when they act to *discourage* higher-risk people from buying their policies.

15. Cathy Schoen, Sara R. Collins, Jennifer L. Kriss, and Michelle Doty, "How Many Are Underinsured? Trends Among U.S. Adults, 2003 And 2007," *Health Affairs* Web Exclusive, June 10, 2008, w2-98–w3-09. Available at http://content.healthaffairs.org.

16. Atul Gawande, "The Cost Conundrum: What a Small Texas Town Can Teach Us About Health Care," *The New Yorker,* June 1, 2009.

17. U.S. Census Bureau, *Statistical Abstract of the United States: 2008,* 127th edition (Washington, DC: U.S. Census Bureau, 2007). Available at http://www.census.gov/compendia/statab/2008/2008edition.html. See Table 735.

18. Congressional Research Service, *Cost and Effects of Extending Health Insurance Coverage* (Washington, DC: U.S. Government Printing Office, 1989), Table 2.21, page 46; Thorpe, "Inside the Black Box of Administrative Costs."

19. Thorpe, "Inside the Black Box of Administrative Costs," 45–46.

20. Schoen, Collins, Kriss and Doty, "How Many Are Underinsured?"

21. Thorpe, "Inside the Black Box of Administrative Costs."

22. They may be prohibited by ERISA from establishing requirements for self-insured firms since the law has been interpreted as reserving such regulations to the federal government, which to date has not taken advantage of that opportunity.

23. Ezekiel J. Emanuel and Victor R. Fuchs, "Who Really Pays for Health Care? The Myth of 'Shared Responsibility'," *Journal of the American Medical Association* 299 (2008): 1057–1059.

24. Some employers contract with a single insurer, but offer several plans from that carrier. Many large firms self-insure and contract with insurance companies for administrative services only. So while the firm bears the risk itself, an insurer is hired to pay the bills and maintain records based on claims for services used by employees and, if covered, their dependents.

25. Balance billing occurs when the patient is charged not only the cost-sharing specified in the insurance policy (that is, co-payments, co-insurance, or both), but also the balance between what the insurer pays and the provider's charge. Where that occurs, the effect is to raise the out-of-pocket cost of care to the insured patient and, by doing so, increase the financial barrier to utilization that insurance is intended to reduce. In some cases, the provider agrees to accept the insurer's fee schedule as payment in full even if the combination of insurer payment and patient cost-sharing is less than its charges. Among them are participating physicians in Medicare. In Massachusetts, and perhaps other states, balance billing is prohibited.

26. Anne R. Somers, *The Kaiser Permanente Medical Care Program: A Symposium* (New York: The Commonwealth Fund, 1971); John G. Smillie, *Can Physicians Manage the Quality and Costs of Health Care? The Story of the Permanente Medical Group* (New York: McGraw-Hill, 1991).

27. Rational, efficient insurers will not continually cut prices until they reach the minimum (that is, the amount needed to cover costs plus a reasonable profit) because price is only one consideration in their customers' decision making and because it is too risky to depend on their ability to control utilization in order to keep their costs low.

28. Fred Foulkes, *The Honeywell Case* (Boston: Boston University School of Management, n.d.).

29. Jon Gabel, Gary Claxton, Isadora Gil, Jeremy Pickreign, Heidi Whitmore, Erin Holve, Benjamin Finder, Samantha Hawkins, and Diane Rowland, "Health Benefits in 2004: Four Years of Double-Digit Premium Increases Take Their Toll on Coverage," *Health Affairs* 23 (2004): 200–209.

30. Joseph White, "Markets and Medical Care: The United States, 1993–2005," *The Milbank Quarterly* 85 (2007): 395–448.

31. Schoen, Collins, Kriss, and Doty, "How Many Are Underinsured?"

32. Two cogent descriptions of the inadequacies of this competitive system can be found in the writings of Enthoven and Kronick, and in the Clinton Administration's plan for reform. Both propose policies whose aim is to correct the system so that fair incentives can play a significant role in influencing employer and consumer choices. For reasons that should be clear by now, however, their reliance on competition as a device to accomplish that goal is misplaced. See A. Enthoven and R. Kronick, "A Consumer-Choice Health Plan for the 1990s: Universal Health Insurance in a System Designed to Promote Quality and Economy," *New England Journal of Medicine* 320 (1989): 29–37. Also, *The President's Comprehensive Health Reform Program* (Washington, DC: The White House, February 6, 1992), Chapter 3.

33. There may be a political dimension, too, in that it may be more feasible to modify our existing mixed system than to adopt changes that represent a dramatic departure, even if the latter have more promise as solutions to the problems identified at the outset. Consideration of that issue is omitted, however, on the twin assumptions that (1) political feasibility changes with conditions (Harris Wofford's victory in the Pennsylvania Senate Race in the Fall of 1991 put health care reform more firmly on the political agenda than it had been previously) and (2) feasibility can be improved by compelling evidence that specific reforms, even dramatic ones, would produce the desired results.

34. Stephen M. Davidson, *Medicaid Decisions: A Systematic Analysis of the Cost Problem* (Cambridge, MA: Ballinger, 1980).

35. Joint Committee on Taxation, *Tax Expenditures for Health Care,* Report JCX-66-08, July 30, 2008.

36. Enthoven and Kronick's Managed Competition proposal as well as the play-or-pay plans put forth by the Pepper Commission and others recognized this possibility and designed mechanisms to do so. See Enthoven and Kronick, "A Consumer-Choice Health Plan for the 1990s." Also, John D. Rockefeller IV, "A Call for Action: The Pepper Commission's Blueprint for Health Care Reform," *Journal of the American Medical Association* 265 (1991): 2507–2510.

37. Stephen M. Davidson, J. D. Perloff, P. R. Kletke, D. W. Schiff, and J. P. Connelly, "Full and Limited Medicaid Participation Among Pediatricians," *Pediatrics*

72 (1983): 552–559; Stephen M. Davidson, "Physician Participation in Medicaid: Background and Issues," *Journal of Health Policy, Politics, and Law* 6 (1982): 703–717.

38. Julie Connelly, "Doctors Are Opting Out of Medicare," *The New York Times,* April 2, 2009.

39. See the special issue on overhauling the delivery system, including discussions of the medical home and other delivery system innovations: *Health Affairs* 27 (September-October 2008).

40. Julie Salamon, *Hospital: Man, Woman, Birth, Death, Infinity, Plus Red Tape, Bad Behavior, Money, God, and Diversity on Steroids* (New York: Penguin Press, 2008).

41. See the website of the Massachusetts Group Insurance Commission at www.mass.gov/gic/ARFY07.pdf.

42. See the website at www.resolutionhealth.com.

43. Donald M. Berwick, "Continuous Improvement as an Ideal in Health Care," *New England Journal of Medicine* 320 (January 1989).

44. Porter and Olmsted Teisberg, *Redefining Health Care.*

45. Others have reached the same conclusion, though traveling by somewhat different routes. See, for example, Lawrence D. Brown, *Competition and the New Accountability: From Market Incentives to Medical Outcomes,* draft paper, October 1991; and Theodore R. Marmor, *The Pro-Competitve Movement in American Medicine: Overview and Appraisal,* draft paper, March 11, 1992; White, "Markets and Medical Care."

46. Kenneth J. Arrow, "Uncertainty and the Welfare Economics of Medical Care," *The American Economic Review* 53 (1963): 941–973.

47. Arrow, "Uncertainty and the Welfare Economics of Medical Care"; see especially pages 948–954.

48. Arrow, "Uncertainty and the Welfare Economics of Medical Care," 949.

49. Arrow, "Uncertainty and the Welfare Economics of Medical Care," 961.

50. Arrow, "Uncertainty and the Welfare Economics of Medical Care," 961.

51. Arrow, "Uncertainty and the Welfare Economics of Medical Care," 961.

Chapter 8

1. Arnold Relman, *A Second Opinion: Rescuing America's Health Care: A Plan for Universal Coverage Serving Patients Over Profit* (New York: The Century Foundation, 2007).

2. Tom Daschle, *Critical: What We Can Do About the Health-Care Crisis* (New York: St. Martin's Press, 2008).

3. Ezekiel J. Emanuel, *Health Care, Guaranteed: A Simple, Secure Solution for America* (New York: Public Affairs, 2008).

4. Commission for a High Performing Health System, *The Path to a High Performance U.S. Health System: A 2020 Vision and the Policies to Pave the Way* (New York: The Commonwealth Fund, February 2009).

5. Website of the Commonwealth Fund, www.cmwf.org; accessed April 27, 2009.

6. Commission for a High Performing Health System. *The Path to a High Performance U.S. Health System,* 1.

7. Commission for a High Performing Health System. *The Path to a High Performance U.S. Health System,* 15.

8. Emanuel, *Health Care, Guaranteed.*

9. Richard H. Thaler and Cass R. Sunstein, *Nudge: Improving Decisions About Health, Wealth, and Happiness* (New York: Penguin Books, 2009), 33–34.

10. Mary Crowley, "Justice as a Frame for Health Reform," *Hastings Center Report,* January-February 2008, p. 3.

11. Stephen M. Davidson and Janelle Heineke, "Toward an Effective Strategy for the Diffusion and Use of Clinical Information Systems," *Journal of the American Medical Informatics Association* 14 (2007): 361–367.

12. Peter R. Orszag, "Opportunities to Increase Efficiency in Health Care," statement presented at the Health Reform Summit of the Committee on Finance, United States Senate, June 16, 2008, pages 3–4.

13. Victor R. Fuchs, "Economics, Values, and Health Care Reform," *The American Economic Review* 86 (1996): 1–24, page 17.

14. Kenneth Arrow, "Uncertainty and the Welfare Economics of Medical Care," *The American Economic Review,* 53 (1963): 941–973.

15. David M. Cutler, *Your Money or Your Life: Strong Medicine for America's Health Care System* (New York: Oxford University Press, 2004).

16. Theodore R. Marmor, *The Politics of Medicare,* second edition (New York: Aldine De Gruyter, 2000).

17. Michael E. Porter and Elizabeth Olmsted Teisberg, *Redefining Health Care: Creating Value-Based Competition on Results* (Boston: Harvard Business School Press, 2006).

18. Stephen M. Davidson, Joseph D. Restuccia, and the Boston University Health Care Management Program Group, "Competition and Quality Among Managed Care Plans in the USA," *International Journal for Quality in Health Care* 10 (1998): 411–419.

19. It should be noted that physicians and other provider groups and organizations do not acknowledge that they provide services that have no value for their patients in order to earn more income. Yet the evidence is incontrovertible that, for example, patients of physicians who are paid fee-for-service tend to receive more services than patients of physicians paid by salary or capitation. The most benign way to think about this finding is that physicians—and hospitals, etc.—are more likely to tilt in the direction of *providing* a service of uncertain value, especially when the patient has insurance, when paid fee-for-service than when paid by means that are independent of the services used.

20. Relman, *A Second Opinion;* Fuchs, "Economics, Values, and Health Care Reform."

21. Relman, *A Second Opinion;* Anne R. Somers, *The Kaiser Permanente Medical Care Program: A Symposium* (New York: The Commonwealth Fund, 1971); John G. Smillie, *Can Physicians Manage the Quality and Costs of Health Care? The Story of the Permanente Medical Group* (New York: McGraw-Hill, 1991); Stephen M. Davidson, Marion E. McCollom, and Janelle N. Heineke, *The Physician-Manager Alliance: Building the Healthy Health Care Organization* (San Francisco: Jossey-Bass, 1996). Reprinted

as *Building a Health Care Organization: A Challenge for Physicians and Managers* (Washington, DC: Beard Books, 2005).

22. Fuchs, "Economics, Values, and Health Care Reform," 17.

23. Stephen M. Davidson, L. M. Manheim, S. M. Werner, M. Hohlen, G. V. Fleming, and B. Shapiro, *Physician Reimbursement and Continuing Care Under Medicaid: The Children's Medicaid Program,* final report submitted to the Health Care Financing Administration under Grant no. 11-C-98052-04 (Elk Grove, IL: The American Academy of Pediatrics, January 1988); Larry M. Manheim, S. M. Davidson, S. M. Werner, M. Hohlen, and B. Shapiro, "New York: Design and Implementation of a Voluntary Medicaid Case-Management Demonstration," in *Advances in Health Economics and Health Services Research,* Vol. 10, L. Rossiter (ed.) (Greenwich, CT: JAI Press, 1989), 241–264; Mina Hohlen, L. M. Manheim, S. M. Davidson, G. V. Fleming, B. Shapiro, S. M. Werner, and G. Wheatley, "Access to Office-Based Physicians Under Capitation Reimbursement and Medicaid Case Management Findings from the Children's Medicaid Program," *Medical Care* 28 (1990): 59–68; Stephen M. Davidson, Larry M. Manheim, Stephen M. Werner, Mina M. Hohlen, Beth K. Yudkowsky, and Gretchen V. Fleming, "Prepayment with Office-Based Physicians in Publicly Funded Programs: Results from the Children's Medicaid Program," *Pediatrics* 89 (1992): 761–767.

Chapter 9

1. Jonathan Oberlander, "The Politics of Health Reform: Why Do Bad Things Happen to Good Plans?" *Health Affairs* Web Exclusive, August 27, 2003, w3-391–w3-404. Available at http://content.healthaffairs.org.

2. Lawrence Brown, "The Amazing Non-Collapsing U.S. Health Care System—Is Reform Finally at Hand?" *New England Journal of Medicine,* 358 (2008): 325–327.

3. Jill Quadagno, *One Nation Uninsured: Why the U.S. Has No National Health Insurance* (New York: Oxford University Press, 2005), 12.

4. Quadagno, *One Nation Uninsured,* 12–16.

5. David Blumenthal, "Primum Non Nocere—The McCain Plan for Health Insecurity," *New England Journal of Medicine* 359 (2008): 1645–1647.

6. Manya Newton, Carla C. Keirns, Rebecca Cunningham, Rodney A. Hayward, and Rachel Stanley, "Uninsured Adults Presenting to U.S. Emergency Departments: Assumptions vs. Data," *Journal of the American Medical Association* 300 (2008): 1914–1924; Cathy Schoen, Robin Osborn, Sabrina K. H. How, Michelle M. Doty, and Jordon Peugh, "In Chronic Condition: Experiences of Patients with Complex Health Care Needs, in Eight Countries, 2008," *Health Affairs* Web Exclusive, November 13, 2008, w1–w16. Available at http://content.healthaffairs.org.

7. David Blumenthal and James Morone, *At the Heart of Power: The Health Care Presidency from Franklin Roosevelt to George W. Bush* (Berkeley: University of California Press, 2009).

8. Haynes Johnson and David S. Broder. *The System: The American Way of Politics at the Breaking Point* (Boston: Little, Brown, 1996, 1997), 93.

9. Johnson and Broder, *The System,* 92.

10. Johnson and Broder, *The System,* 93.

11. Johnson and Broder, *The System,* 92.

12. This result may be likely, but is not a foregone conclusion. The reason is that the new utilization under universal, comprehensive insurance coverage would have two parts: more people would use primary care services, which are relatively inexpensive; at the same time, fewer people would need to use costly emergency departments either for routine services or for a serious illness that might have remained relatively minor if they had had early access to appropriate care. The elimination of a single, typical ER visit would pay for the routine visits of at least several patients to community-based primary care physicians. What is not clear is what the relative distribution of the two types of visits will be in the proposed new system—that is, will the savings from reduced ER use pay for the increased use of routine office-based primary care and specialist services?

13. This section is based primarily on two books: Richard Harris, *A Sacred Trust* (Baltimore: Penguin Books, 1966 and 1969); and Theodore R. Marmor, *The Politics of Medicare,* second edition (Hawthorne, NY: Aldine de Gruyter, 2000).

14. Marc A. Rodwin, *Medicine, Money, and Morals: Physicians' Conflicts of Interest* (New York: Oxford University Press, 1993); American Medical Association, "Principles of Medical Ethics; accessed on September 28, 2009, at http://www.ama-assn.org/ama/pub/physician resources/medical-ethics/code-medical-ethics/principles-medical-ethics.shtml.

15. Harris, *A Sacred Trust,* 25.

16. Marmor, *The Politics of Medicare,* 10–11.

17. Marmor, *The Politics of Medicare,* 15.

18. Marmor, *The Politics of Medicare,* 27.

19. Marmor, *The Politics of Medicare,* 29.

20. Doris Kearns Goodwin, *Lyndon Johnson and the American Dream* (New York: St. Martin's Press, 1976, 1991).

21. David Blumenthal and James Morone, "The Lessons of Success—Revisiting the Medicare Story," *New England Journal of Medicine* 359 (2008): 2384–2389.

22. Blumenthal and Morone, "The Lessons of Success," 2386.

23. Indeed, for more than forty years this has been the accepted narrative of the passage of Medicare. Blumenthal and Morone have recently discovered, however, that staff at the Department of Health Education and Welfare, under the leadership of Wilbur Cohen, had been working on a three-part plan and were ready when Mills turned to Cohen at a dramatic point in a hearing and asked him to prepare legislative language incorporating all three parts. Blumenthal and Morone, *At the Heart of Power.*

24. Blumenthal and Morone, "The Lessons of Success," 2385.

25. Blumenthal and Morone, "The Lessons of Success," 2387.

26. Lawrence D. Brown, "The Politics of Medicare and Health Reform, Then and Now," *Health Care Financing Review* 18 (1996): 163–168, p. 164.

27. Brown, "The Politics of Medicare and Health Reform, Then and Now," 164–165.

28. Thomas R. Oliver, Philip R. Lee, and Helene L. Lipton, "A Political History of Medicare and Prescription Drug Coverage," *The Milbank Quarterly,* 82 (2004): 283–354.

29. Jacob S. Hacker, *The Road to Nowhere: The Genesis of President Clinton's Plan for Health Security* (Princeton, NJ: Princeton University Press, 1997), at 117.

30. Theda Skocpol, *Boomerang: Clinton's Health Security Effort and the Turn Against Government in U.S. Politics* (New York: W. W. Norton, 1996), xii.

31. Skocpol, *Boomerang,* 38.

32. Skocpol, *Boomerang,* 14.

33. Hacker, *The Road to Nowhere,* 123.

34. Daschle, *Critical,* 83.

35. Hacker, *The Road to Nowhere,* 129.

36. Hacker, *The Road to Nowhere,* 131.

37. Skocpol, *Boomerang,* 103.

38. Skocpol, *Boomerang,* 60.

39. Daschle, *Critical,* 88.

40. Darrell M. West, Diane Heith, and Chris Goodwin, "Harry and Louise Go to Washington: Political Advertising and Health Care Reform," *Journal of Health Policy, Politics, and Law* 21 (1996): 35–68, page 40.

41. Daschle, *Critical,* 94.

42. West, Heith, and Goodwin, "Harry and Louise Go to Washington," 40.

43. Skocpol, *Boomerang,* 145.

44. Skocpol, *Boomerang,* 146.

45. Skocpol, *Boomerang,* 158ff.

46. Hacker, *The Road to Nowhere,* 138–139.

47. West, Heith, and Goodwin, "Harry and Louise Go to Washington," 42, 43.

48. West, Heith, and Goodwin, "Harry and Louise Go to Washington," 44.

49. West, Heith, and Goodwin, "Harry and Louise Go to Washington," 38.

50. West, Heith, and Goodwin, "Harry and Louise Go to Washington," 46.

51. Daschle, *Critical,* 92.

52. West, Heith, and Goodwin, "Harry and Louise Go to Washington," 39, 41.

53. West, Heith, and Goodwin, "Harry and Louise Go to Washington," 42.

54. Hacker, *The Road to Nowhere,* 141.

55. West, Heith, and Goodwin, "Harry and Louise Go to Washington," 52.

56. Daschle, *Critical,* 90.

57. West, Heith, and Goodwin, "Harry and Louise Go to Washington," 55.

58. West, Heith, and Goodwin, "Harry and Louise Go to Washington," 58.

59. West, Heith, and Goodwin, "Harry and Louise Go to Washington," 59.

60. Daschle, *Critical,* 92.

61. West, Heith, and Goodwin, "Harry and Louise Go to Washington," 49.

62. Lisa Disch, "Publicity-Stunt Participation and Sound Bite Polemics: The Health Care Debate 1993–1994," *Journal of Health Policy, Politics, and Law* 21 (1996): 3–33.

63. Disch, "Publicity-Stunt Participation and Sound Bite Polemics," 19.

64. Disch, "Publicity-Stunt Participation and Sound Bite Polemics," 20.

65. Disch, "Publicity-Stunt Participation and Sound Bite Polemics," 20.

66. Disch, "Publicity-Stunt Participation and Sound Bite Polemics," 21.

67. Disch, "Publicity-Stunt Participation and Sound Bite Polemics," 18.

68. Disch, "Publicity-Stunt Participation and Sound Bite Polemics," 24.

69. Skocpol, *Boomerang.*

70. Disch, "Publicity-Stunt Participation and Sound Bite Polemics," 24–25.

71. Oliver, Lee, and Lipton, "A Political History of Medicare and Prescription Drug Coverage," 324.

72. Oliver, Lee, and Lipton, "A Political History of Medicare and Prescription Drug Coverage."

73. Oliver, Lee, and Lipton, "A Political History of Medicare and Prescription Drug Coverage," 326–327.

74. Oliver, Lee, and Lipton, "A Political History of Medicare and Prescription Drug Coverage," 326.

75. John W. Kingdon, Agendas, Alternatives, and Public Policies (New York: HarperCollins, 1984).

76. Oliver, Lee, and Lipton, "A Political History of Medicare and Prescription Drug Coverage," 327.

77. Oliver, Lee, and Lipton, "A Political History of Medicare and Prescription Drug Coverage," 328.

78. Oliver, Lee, and Lipton, "A Political History of Medicare and Prescription Drug Coverage," 329.

79. Jonathan Oberlander, "Through the Looking Glass: The Politics of the Medicare Prescription Drug, Improvement, and Modernization Act," *Journal of Health Politics, Policy and Law* 32 (2007): 187–219, page 188.

80. Oberlander, "Through the Looking Glass," 188.

81. Oberlander, "Through the Looking Glass," 190.

82. Oberlander, "Through the Looking Glass," 190.

83. Oberlander, "Through the Looking Glass," 190.

84. Oberlander, "Through the Looking Glass," 191.

85. Oberlander, "Through the Looking Glass," 195.

86. Blumenthal and Morone, *At the Heart of Power.*

87. Hacker, *The Road to Nowhere,* 153.

88. Brown, "The Amazing Non-Collapsing U.S. Health Care System.

Chapter 10

1. Alexander Hamilton, James Madison, and John Jay, *The Federalist Papers* (New York: Bantam Classic, 1982 and 2003).

2. Niccolo Machiavelli, *The Prince* (Chicago: University of Chicago Press, 1985).

3. Jill Quadagno, *One Nation Uninsured: Why the U.S. Has No National Health Insurance* (New York: Oxford University Press, 2005).

4. Lawrence R. Jacobs, "Talking Heads and Sleeping Citizens: Health Policy Making in a Democracy," *Journal of Health Policy, Politics, and Law* 21(1) (Spring 1996), 129–135, at page 129.

5. Lawrence R. Jacobs, "Manipulators and Manipulation: Public Opinion in a Representative Democracy," *Journal of Health Policy, Politics, and Law* 26 (2001): 1361–1374, page 1362.

6. Jacobs, "Manipulators and Manipulation."

7. Darrell M. West, Diane Heith, and Chris Goodwin, "Harry and Louise Go to Washington: Political Advertising and Health Care Reform," *Journal of Health Policy, Politics, and Law* 21 (1996): 35–68, page 37.

8. Mark Leibovich, "The Man Between Obama and the Press," *The New York Times Magazine,* December 21, 2008, 33–37.

9. West, Heith, and Goodwin, "Harry and Louise Go to Washington," 38.

10. West, Heith, and Goodwin, "Harry and Louise Go to Washington."

11. Jacob S. Hacker, *The Road to Nowhere: The Genesis of President Clinton's Plan for Health Security* (Princeton, NJ: Princeton University Press, 1997), 141.

12. William A. Gamson and Andre Modigliani, "Media Discourse and Public Opinion on Nuclear Power: A Constructionist Approach," *The American Journal of Sociology* 95 (1989): 1–37, page 2.

13. Gamson and Modigliani, "Media Discourse and Public Opinion on Nuclear Power," 3.

14. Gamson and Modigliani, "Media Discourse and Public Opinion on Nuclear Power," 3 (italics in the original).

15. Todd Gitlin, quoted in Gamson and Modigliani, "Media Discourse and Public Opinion on Nuclear Power," 3.

16. Gamson and Modigliani, "Media Discourse and Public Opinion on Nuclear Power," 3.

17. James N. Druckman, "On the Limits of Framing Effects: Who Can Frame?" *The Journal of Politics* 63 (2001): 1041–1066, at page 1042, citing Matthew Rabin, "Psychology and Economics," *Journal of Economic Literature* 36(1) (1998), p. 36 italics in the original).

18. Richard H. Thaler and Cass R. Sunstein, *Nudge: Improving Decisions About Health, Wealth, and Happiness* (New York: Penguin Books, 2009), 36.

19. Druckman, "On the Limits of Framing Effects," 1042.

20. Druckman, "On the Limits of Framing Effects," 1043.

21. Druckman, "On the Limits of Framing Effects," 1043.

22. Druckman, "On the Limits of Framing Effects," 1044.

23. Druckman, "On the Limits of Framing Effects," 1044.

24. Druckman, "On the Limits of Framing Effects," 1044.

25. Druckman, "On the Limits of Framing Effects," 1045.

26. Druckman, "On the Limits of Framing Effects," 1041.

27. Druckman, "On the Limits of Framing Effects," 1042.

28. James A. Morone, "Morality, Politics, and Health Policy, in *Policy Challenges in Modern Health Care,* David Mechanic, Lynn B. Rogut, David C. Colby, and James R. Knickman (eds.) (Piscataway, NJ: Rutgers University Press, 2005), 13.

29. Morone, "Morality, Politics, and Health Policy," 13.

30. Morone, "Morality, Politics, and Health Policy," 15.

31. Morone, "Morality, Politics, and Health Policy," 13.

32. Morone, "Morality, Politics, and Health Policy," 13–14.

33. Morone, "Morality, Politics, and Health Policy," 15.

34. Morone, "Morality, Politics, and Health Policy," 15.

35. Morone, "Morality, Politics, and Health Policy," 17.

36. Morone, "Morality, Politics, and Health Policy," 18.

37. Morone, "Morality, Politics, and Health Policy," 18.

38. Morone, "Morality, Politics, and Health Policy," 24.

39. Theodore Lowi, *The End of Liberalism* (New York: W. W. Norton, 1969).

40. Theda Skocpol, *Boomerang: Clinton's Health Security Effort and the Turn against Government in U. S. Politics* (New York: W. W. Norton, 1996), 115.

41. Malcolm Gladwell, "Getting There from Here," *The New Yorker,* January 26, 2009; Skocpol, *Boomerang,* 122.

42. John Iglehart and Chris Fleming, "Oberlander: Health Reform Likely to Depend on (Budget) Reconciliation," *Health Affairs* Blog, March 30, 2009; accessed June 14, 2009, at http://healthaffairs.org/blog/2009/03/30/oberlander-health-reform-likely-to-depend-on-budget-reconciliation.

43. David Blumenthal and James Morone, *At the Heart of Power: The Health Care Presidency from Franklin Roosevelt to George W. Bush* (Berkeley: University of California Press, 2009).

44. Blumenthal and Morone, *At the Heart of Power.*

45. Skocpol, *Boomerang,* 93.

46. Skocpol, *Boomerang.*

47. Reed Abelson, "Follow the Money," *The New York Times,* June 14, 2009, Week in Review section, pages 1, 4.

48. I refer to these considerations in partisan terms because the history of health care reform efforts tells us that the proponents of reform are likely to be Democrats and, further, that proposals for comprehensive reform are likely to receive serious consideration when Democrats are in the majority in the Congress and especially when a Democrat is in the White House.

49. Skocpol, *Boomerang.*

50. Skocpol, *Boomerang,* 113.

51. Skocpol, *Boomerang,* 145.

52. Skocpol, *Boomerang,* 111.

53. Skocpol, *Boomerang,* 91.

54. Skocpol, *Boomerang,* 98.

55. Skocpol, *Boomerang,* 99.

56. Hacker, *The Road to Nowhere.*

Chapter 11

1. Tom Daschle, *Critical: What We Can Do About the Health-Care Crisis* (New York: St. Martin's Press, 2008), 205.

2. James Morone, "One Side to Every Story, *The New York Times,* op-ed page, February 17, 2009.

3. James Morone, Interview, *The News Hour.* Broadcast on public television, February 17, 2009.

4. Morone, "One Side to Every Story."

5. Atul Gawande, "Getting There from Here: How Should Obama Reform Health Care?" *The New Yorker,* January 26, 2009.

6. The requirement that individuals have insurance without tying their coverage to work or requiring employers to offer insurance to employees focuses the effort on the right level. After all, the goal is for individuals to have coverage. It also accomplishes an important political purpose: an employer mandate would surely generate unwelcome and unnecessary opposition from employer groups. Setting the requirement on individuals avoids that problem.

7. Karen Pollitz, Eliza Bangit, Jennifer Libster, Stephanie Lewis, and Nicole Johnston, *Coverage When It Counts: How Much Protection Does Health Insurance Offer and How Can Consumers Know?* (Washington, DC: Center for American Progress Action Fund, May 2009).

8. See *Health Affairs* Web Exclusive, September 14, 2005, for a series of articles about the Massachusetts plan. Available at http://content.healthaffairs.org.

9. Sharon K. Long and Paul B. Masi, "Access and Affordability: An Update on Health Reform in Massachusetts, Fall 2008," *Health Affairs* Web Exclusive, May 28, 2009, w5-78–w5-87. Available at http://content.healthaffairs.org.

10. Pollitz, Bangit, Libster, Lewis, and Johnston, *Coverage When It Counts*, 5.

11. Pollitz, Bangit, Libster, Lewis, and Johnston, *Coverage When It Counts*, 10.

12. Ezekiel J. Emanuel, *Health Care, Guaranteed: A Simple, Secure Solution for America* (New York: Public Affairs, 2008), Chapter 6.

13. Jacob S. Hacker, *The Case for Public Plan Choice in National Health Reform: Key to Cost Control and Quality Coverage* (Berkeley, CA: University of California, Center on Health, Economic, and Family Security, Spring 2009).

14. Hacker, *The Case for Public Plan Choice*, 1.

15. Hacker, *The Case for Public Plan Choice*, 2.

16. John Iglehart and Chris Fleming, "The Public-Plan Option: Highlights of a Roundtable," *Health Affairs* Blog, April 30, 2009; accessed on September 28, 2009, at http://healthaffairs.org/blog/2009/04/30/the-public-plan-option-highlights-of-a-roundtable/; Jeff Goldsmith, "The Public Plan: Not Worth The Risks," *Health Affairs Blog,* May 15, 2009; accessed on September 28, 2009, at http://healthaffairs.org/blog/2009/05/15/the-public-plan-not-worth-the-risks/?source=promo.

17. Emanuel, *Health Care, Guaranteed.*

18. Alain Enthoven, "Health Care with a Few Bucks Left Over," *The New York Times,* op-ed page, December 28, 2008.

19. Enthoven, "Health Care with a Few Bucks Left Over."

20. We must also recall that policies that appear "actuarially equivalent" may result in widely different out-of-pocket expenditures for sick patients. Under those conditions, it is likely that some patients would go without needed services because they could not pay the cost-sharing amounts.

21. Enthoven, "Health Care with a Few Bucks Left Over."

22. Emanuel, *Health Care, Guaranteed.*

23. Emanuel, *Health Care, Guaranteed,* 107–108.

24. Enthoven, "Health Care with a Few Bucks Left Over."

25. Emanuel, *Health Care, Guaranteed.*

26. Enthoven, "Health Care with a Few Bucks Left Over."

27. Daschle, *Critical;* Emanuel, *Health Care, Guaranteed.*

28. Daschle, *Critical.*

29. Emanuel, *Health Care, Guaranteed.*

30. Emanuel, *Health Care, Guaranteed,* 90–91.

31. Daschle, *Critical,* 170ff.

32. Ted Sorensen, *Counselor: A Life at the Edge of History* (New York: HarperCollins, 2008).